THE RISE OF
ROMANTIC OPERA

THE RISE OF
ROMANTIC OPERA

EDWARD J. DENT

Edited by Winton Dean

CAMBRIDGE UNIVERSITY PRESS

Cambridge

London • *New York* • *New Rochelle*
Melbourne • *Sydney*

Published by the Press Syndicate of the University of Cambridge
The Pitt Building, Trumpington Street Cambridge CB2 1RP
32 East 57th Street, New York, NY 10022, USA
296 Beaconsfield Parade, Middle Park, Melbourne 3206, Australia

© Cambridge University Press 1976

First published 1976
First paperback edition 1979
Reprinted 1979

Printed in the United States of America
Typeset at the University Press, Cambridge
Printed by Vail-Ballou Press, Inc., Binghamton, New York

Library of Congress Cataloguing in Publicaiton Data
Dent, Edward Joseph, 1876—1957.
The rise of romantic opera.
Lectures originally delivered at Cornell University,
1937 – 8.
1. Opera—Addresses, essays, lectures. I. Title.
ML1704.D46   782.1'094   76-14029
ISBN 0 521 21337 1 hard covers
ISBN 0 521 29659 5 paperback

CONTENTS

v

PREFACE

These lectures, the typescript of which is preserved in the Rowe Music Library at King's College, Cambridge, were delivered at Cornell University (the Messenger Lectures) in the winter of 1937–8. Although Dent lived for another twenty years, he made no attempt to publish them. During this final period of his life he often spoke of a substantial work he was contemplating on Romantic Opera, with specific reference to Weber; and it seems probable that he withheld the lectures with a view to expanding the material into a broader and fuller treatment of the subject. Ill-health and other work prevented the fulfilment of this plan.

Dent would not have printed the lectures as they stand. He drew a firm distinction between a course of lectures and a book. 'The function of lectures is not to convey information, which we can now obtain far better from books, but to stimulate interest in a subject.' He does in fact convey a great deal of information, much of it recondite; but his principal aim was to serve as a kind of *agent provocateur* to goad his listeners into thinking for themselves. He was capable, in lectures as in private teaching and conversation, of making outrageous pronouncements and deliberately overstating a case to this end. I remember him girding at Beethoven and even his beloved Mozart when he thought that Haydn was underestimated, and irritating the fashionable worshippers of J. S. Bach by maintaining the superior merits of Handel.

This propensity accounts for a number of generalized statements that may strike the reader as rash or even perverse: for example his claim that the melodies of Cherubini's *Démophoon* have much more charm and grace than Gluck's, his relative estimate of Weber and Schubert as opera composers, his dismissal of all Rossini's serious operas except *Guillaume Tell* and a single scene of *Otello*, and his remark that E.T.A. Hoffmann's musical technique was not far short of Weber's. Something must be

vii

allowed too for his chronic itch to take a shy at certain favourite *bêtes noires*, notably the church and the Germans; this was part of his rebellion against the conventions of the society in which he grew up.

Many such passages might have been modified, at least in emphasis, had Dent prepared the lectures for the press. He would unquestionably have filled a number of gaps, pursued to their conclusion many stimulating ideas thrown off as casual asides, and enriched his discussion of the music with printed examples, especially from the operas whose plots he analyses in detail. He might have softened his rather harsh treatment of Weber and Rossini, and would scarcely have ignored the use of *Leitmotiv* in *Euryanthe* (which he censures for formlessness) and *Fierrabras*, or in discussing Spohr have omitted all reference to his chromatic harmony.

The reader must also bear in mind the date at which Dent was writing. After nearly forty years a few – surprisingly few – of his utterances have lost their force. The operas of Berlioz, Rossini (other than *Il barbiere di Siviglia*) and Bellini are no longer strangers to the theatre, though the French operas of the Revolution decade to which he rightly ascribes such significance are still (apart from Cherubini's *Médée*) as unfamiliar as ever. It is difficult to imagine Dent finding nothing to admire in *Le Comte Ory*, which he does not mention; and he might have been less censorious of the inability of modern singers to do justice to Rossini and Bellini.

Despite these reservations there seem to me three potent reasons for publishing the lectures now, in the centenary year of Dent's birth. In the first place, they explore an important turning-point in musical history that has still not received full or even adequate study in print. Comparatively little of Dent's work, based on a detailed examination of scores and librettos and a wide knowledge of cultural history, has been overtaken by later research. Only in very recent years have musicologists extended their concentration on earlier periods to take in the nineteenth century. Dent reached conclusions that may still startle musicians and others brought up on accepted traditions: that the true initiators of Romantic Opera were the French, that it derived not from serious but from comic opera, and that it was the principal source of the nineteenth-century German symphonic and in-

PREFACE

strumental style. If a detail here and there is exaggerated, I believe the main conclusions to be sound.

Secondly, the lectures are full of characteristically sharp perception, clearly and often entertainingly expressed, on composers familiar and unfamiliar and on the relationships between them. Readers of Dent's other books, and students who had the good fortune to be taught by him or to hear him speak, will recognize many examples of that provocative wit, compounded of penetration and paradox, with which he forced them to confront the music of the past. Those who never knew him may discover, if they have not done so already, why he enjoyed a reputation as one of the world's foremost musicologists and the man who raised British musical scholarship to an international level.

Thirdly, by their demonstration, implicit and explicit, of the methods of a great scholar and a great teacher, the lectures convey an important message to critics and historians of music. For Dent the primary value of research lay in 'a training of the imagination', and he was always urging that 'we must sharpen our critical faculties'. The chief obstacle to this exercise he considered to be the cult of 'the classics', which he mentions in the second paragraph of Lecture 9 and to which he returns at the end of Lecture 12. It was not that he himself thought little of the classics; but he distrusted the uncritical acceptance of traditional standards. 'Our minds are rendered sluggish by the constant habit of veneration'; this was the attitude he was concerned to shake. He urges his listeners to put their imaginations into training, 'to cultivate imaginative experience for the enrichment of memory and life, and at the same time to develop a habit of perpetual scepticism and criticism as regards all so-called acknowledged masterpieces. If you have ever allowed yourselves to reverence the great masters, I hope you will abandon that attitude, which is merely a polite mask for lazy-mindedness.' Only thus, Dent was convinced, can we clear our ears of the lumber of the past and 'have mental space as well as freedom of judgment to welcome and enjoy the art of today and tomorrow'.

The editing of the lectures has presented certain difficulties. They were composed straight on to the typewriter and only lightly revised. The revision generally took the form of marginalia hastily scribbled in pencil, sometimes modifying and sometimes supplementing the text, and occasionally marking a point for reconsideration. I have incorporated this material in the text where it involved little disturbance, and elsewhere placed it in footnotes indicated by Dent's initials. Other footnotes are my own. In delivering the lectures Dent used live illustrations performed by students, and sometimes played and sang examples himself. With one or two exceptions, neither their placing nor their content can be identified, and I have made no attempt to supply the deficiency. The two brief musical examples on pages 12 and 22 were notated in Dent's hand.

Dent was a fastidious writer of English. The lectures contain occasional solecisms of syntax, awkward sentences and repetitions of words and phrases that he might have tolerated in speech or not bothered to alter, but would never have admitted to print. Following a number of his own amendments, I have slightly modified such passages, and shortened a few others where he repeats a point in almost identical terms. I have regularized titles of operas and names of characters, corrected a few slips and wrong dates, and omitted or adapted an occasional sentence where Dent bases a statement on premises now known to be erroneous. Provided his argument remains unaffected, a pedantic insistence on the letter would have done no service to his memory. I have not however interfered with generalizations which some scholars might wish to qualify, and only annotated them when they seemed to me likely to mislead. The lectures should not be regarded as a complete statement of Dent's views; the script probably served to some extent as a basis for improvisation and spontaneous elaboration. But while the style never received a final polish, its tone of urbanity seasoned with wit and a touch of *malizia* is unmistakeable, and will surely be relished by all admirers of its erudite and idiosyncratic author.

My thanks are due to Dr David Charlton and Mr John Warrack for many helpful suggestions, and to my son Stephen for subjecting the material to a testing scrutiny that would have elicited Dent's amused approval.

WINTON DEAN

February, 1976

1

INTRODUCTION

The historical phenomenon known as the Romantic Movement is one which it is very difficult to define. Even if we were to limit its scope to literature alone, we should find no clear understanding of when it began or when it ended, and when we come to consider its relation to drama, music and the plastic arts, to say nothing of religion and morals, the study of it in detail is obviously beyond the comprehension of any one historian.

Let us try to make a start by considering what are the ordinary educated person's general conceptions of the Romantic Movement. Here we are at once faced by the question of that ordinary educated person's nationality. If he is English, he will probably pick out Wordsworth as the representative Romantic; in an earlier generation he would have named Byron. But in any case his first associations with Romanticism will be literary: Romanticism for him means first of all poetry – Wordsworth, Coleridge, Byron, Shelley, Keats – and then perhaps the Romantic novelists. Scott will be the first name that he mentions, and then, if he is something of a literary connoisseur, Mrs Radcliffe and Horace Walpole. A Frenchman, on the other hand, will say at once that the Romantic Movement began with Victor Hugo's plays; but he will probably maintain that the Romantic Movement in France was pictorial rather than literary. Painting means more to him than it does to the average Englishman; he might even go so far as to mention a musician – Hector Berlioz. Ask a German: he can hardly ignore his Romantic poets, but he will probably feel that even Schiller is less of a Romantic than Weber. The Romantic art of Germany is music, and it is almost safe to say that the characteristic of Romantic literature in Germany is its close association with music, its interpretation of music and its attempt to produce the effects of music with words.

Many writers have said that music is the essentially Romantic art. Susceptibility to music is eminently characteristic of Romantic

I

poets, even such as were from a musician's point of view almost unmusical. Byron, Keats and Shelley seem to have known practically nothing about music, but their poems show that they at least enjoyed listening to it and were capable of being moved by it in some sort of way. The other extreme of devotion to music is to be found in the German poets and writers, such as Wackenroder, E. T. A. Hoffmann and Grillparzer. The French poets may have had less technical knowledge of the art, but there can be no doubt about their appreciation of it.

It ought surely to be obvious then that no study of Romanticism can be complete without an understanding of its musical aspects. Unfortunately historians of literature are very seldom musical enough to realize the importance of this musical side of Romanticism. They at least remember the dictum of Beaumarchais, 'ce qui est trop sot pour être dit, on le chante', and it is generally an axiom with them that any words which have been set to music or have been written to be set to music must be beneath contempt. Historians of drama wash their hands completely of opera and all allied forms of it,[1] with the result that they sometimes arrive at altogether erroneous conclusions.

Let us leave the men of letters for a moment and ask some questions of the musicians. As the literary historians seized on Byron as the representative Romantic poet, so it has been customary to select Weber as the typical Romantic musician. Along with Weber we shall find associated Berlioz, Schumann, Chopin and Liszt. Whether Beethoven is to be regarded as a Romantic is as difficult a problem as that of Goethe. It will be observed that the names which I have mentioned are not those of operatic composers, with the exception of Weber. Beethoven wrote one opera, and so did Schumann, but we are accustomed to think of these operas as almost negligible compared with the rest of those composers' output. Berlioz wrote three operas – one might almost count them as four – but performances of them are so exceedingly rare that most musical people, including most professional musicians, have practically no knowledge of them.[2]

The selection of names which I have put forward as typical for modern audiences – typical certainly for England, and I think for

---

[1] This is no longer true: see for instance Heinz Kindermann, *Theatergeschichte Europas*, 9 vols (Salzburg, 1959–70).

[2] Dent himself was largely responsible for invalidating this statement.

2

Germany too – is due to the fact that opera, at any rate in Germany and England, is for some reason regarded as a rather inferior branch of music. The neglect of opera in England is notorious; one cannot say that it is neglected in Germany and Austria, where the number of theatres is very large and the standard of performances still astonishingly high. Why then should opera, at any rate in Germany, be regarded as not quite on a level with concert music? It would be outside the scope of these lectures to pursue this question in serious detail, but I am obliged to mention it, because one of the fundamental principles on which this course of lectures is based is that opera, at any rate for the Romantic period, is by far the most important of all musical forms. The German attitude towards opera is not difficult to explain. As we shall see in the course of these lectures, Germany was a long way behind Italy and France in the development of opera. Throughout the eighteenth century opera in Germany – whether at Hamburg or Vienna – meant French or Italian opera, either in the original languages, or translated into German;[3] the number of original German operas produced before 1800 is simply negligible compared with the enormous quantities composed in Italy and France. The nineteenth century was the great age of German opera, at any rate as we foreigners see the history of that century; but inside Germany French and Italian opera were and are still dangerous competitors. No German theatre of to-day can afford to ignore Verdi and Puccini, Gounod and Ambroise Thomas, and to the ordinary German music-lover opera is still very largely a luxury imported from abroad. Symphonies, on the other hand, are an almost exclusively German product. Moreover, during the latter half of the nineteenth century there grew up in Germany, as also in England, a sort of religious attitude to music; music has now come to be regarded by many people almost as a substitute for religion – at any rate, people who go to concerts are expected to behave as reverently as they would in church.

In the early days of Romanticism there were fewer concerts,

---

[3]   This is not true of Hamburg in the early years of the century. German operas were produced there between 1678 and 1738, and the leading composer, Reinhard Keiser, enjoyed a European reputation. See H. C. Wolff, *Die Barockoper in Hamburg* (Wolfenbüttel, 1957) and Basil Deane, 'Reinhard Keiser: An Interim Assessment', *Soundings iv* (1974), 30–41.

3

and such as there were were of a less solemn type.[4] We must remember too that most concerts were given in theatres; the building of large concert-halls was the achievement of much later generations.[5] Nowadays, serious-minded musicians are inclined to be almost shocked if they are asked to go to a concert in a theatre; it makes them as uncomfortable as it would to attend a church service in a theatre. The history of music is determined to a very large extent by the conditions under which music has been performed. In the Middle Ages we find church music on a vast scale, because churches were the only buildings available in which a large audience could be assembled to listen to music constructed on a large scale. There was nothing that could be called chamber music in the modern sense of the word, until people began to live in conditions of suitable comfort; there could be no chamber music before a large class of people inhabited houses that were reasonably warmed and lighted, with living-rooms set apart for indoor pleasures.

Even in the Middle Ages, music was divided into the two categories of church and chamber, it being assumed that music was an appanage of great princes. Martin Luther said that it was the positive duty of princes to maintain 'chapels' – that is to say, bodies of singers and players, performing music both sacred and secular – in order that ordinary people might enjoy the benefit of hearing them. Evidently at that date, the ordinary citizen had no chance of hearing music unless he and a few friends made music in their own houses, or went to worship at some royal chapel.

It was in the seventeenth century that opera came into being; and the whole of seventeenth-century music is dominated by it. During the course of that century opera became firmly established, first at Venice, then in Paris, Vienna, Naples and other centres. An attempt was made to develop a national school of opera in England in the days of Purcell, but his untimely death brought it to an end, and from the beginning of the eighteenth

[4] This is not wholly true of Paris, where the Concerts du Conservatoire, started in 1800, included new as well as traditional music played by the students; Beethoven's first three symphonies were performed in 1807–11. Habeneck, who championed Beethoven and other Romantic composers in France, and in 1828 founded the Société des Concerts du Conservatoire, cut his teeth as a conductor there.

[5] The concert-hall at the Paris Conservatoire, opened in 1811, had 966 seats as well as standing room.

century opera – that 'exotic and irrational entertainment', as Dr Johnson defined it[6] – was for London mainly Italian.

Throughout the seventeenth and eighteenth centuries, and most of the nineteenth, opera is historically the most important kind of music there was. The opera-house was the place where all the arts met: not only music, but poetry, painting, architecture and the dance. The opera is the source of all real musical expression. If we attempt to study in detail the history of musical form, the shapes of musical movements, we may have to pursue that study among symphonies and sonatas. Historians are easily tempted to believe that instrumental music is a thing apart, and that there is something peculiarly sacrosanct about the great instrumental forms. But it is an indisputable historical fact that these forms originated in the theatre; what is called sonata form may be traced in operatic arias long before its appearance in harpsichord music, and the symphony for orchestra is well known to be nothing more than what we should nowadays call the 'overture' to an Italian opera.

People often talk of musical form as if it meant formalism: a set of rules constructed by academic pedantry, which it is the first duty of genius to shatter. This is complete nonsense; the people who say that sort of thing simply do not know what form is. Musical form is in itself expression; so far from being destructive of true expression, it is nothing more nor less than the device by which human expression is made artistic, that is, made to convey the maximum of expression with the minimum of effort. Every piece of music, like every poem, however short it be and however simple, must contain somewhere an emotional climax; what we call form is merely the arrangement by which this climax is put in the most effective place.

The musical drama naturally requires emotion to be expressed in the intensest as well as in the subtlest possible manner, and it is for that reason that opera has always been the workshop in which methods of human expression in music have been created. After they have made their first appearance in opera they are utilized for concert music, or it may be for church music too. We often hear it said that certain types of church music are too operatic, and the criticism is occasionally made about concert

<hr/>

[6] Johnson's definition, in his life of John Hughes, was confined to Italian opera in London.

music also; but what this criticism really means is that the so-called operatic phrases or passages are reminiscent of phrases which have already become stale and purely conventional in the opera-house itself. Musical critics sometimes express opinions on questions of this kind which the serious historical student of music can only find ridiculous.

In recent years the Catholic church music of the eighteenth century has been severely condemned for its secularity and its theatrical style. Theatrical it certainly is, in so far as it makes use of emotional effects learned first by musicians in the theatre. The historian can only say that in its own day it met with the approval of ecclesiastical authority. But there are exceptions to this general condemnation, and among the few sacred works of that operatic century to escape censure is Pergolesi's *Stabat Mater*, which is always spoken of in terms of devout respect. It is interesting to note that Padre Martini, who lived only half a century after Pergolesi, and who was also himself a Catholic priest, a man of devout life and at the same time a musician of enormous learning, said plainly that Pergolesi's *Stabat Mater* was written in the style of a comic opera. Anyone who studies the comic operas of Pergolesi himself and his contemporaries can see at once that Padre Martini was perfectly right; the style is unmistakeable.

If we go back to the sixteenth century – that century in which (as I have heard it said) church music reached its perfection of devotional expression, a century which some people will maintain to have been completely dominated by the ideals of the Church – we shall come across a number of motets to sacred words which make a powerful appeal to modern audiences by the intensity of their verbal expression. Much has been written about their mystical inspiration and so forth; modern research has shown clearly that this so-called mystical expression is simply an imitation of the style employed by the composers of secular madrigals, especially in the expression of erotic emotions.

Religious emotion, if it is not imitated directly from the erotic emotion of the theatre – I need hardly say that I speak only of musical expression and make no attempt to analyse the actual emotions themselves – is generally conveyed in music by a suggestion of antiquity. A modern composer who wishes to create a religious atmosphere in an opera or in any kind of music, secular or sacred, can easily do so by introducing a succession of chords such as he might find in the works of Palestrina. He will find the same chords in some madrigal of Marenzio, but his audience will know nothing about that; it sounds old, and therefore it sounds sacred.[7] This method of producing a religious atmosphere has been practised for many generations; it was practised even in that wickedly theatrical eighteenth century, by such composers as Haydn and Mozart. I need hardly point out that it can be observed plentifully in the nineteenth, in Beethoven, Liszt, Meyerbeer and Wagner. I draw your attention to this well-worn dodge of faking religious emotion, because it is a very useful piece of stage scenery for opera, and we shall find it eminently characteristic of the type of opera that we call Romantic.

The purpose of these lectures is to study Romantic opera. The composers whom I select as typical Romantics are Weber and Bellini. You might expect me to talk to you about Donizetti, Wagner, Verdi and perhaps Berlioz; but I may tell you at once that I do not intend to discuss any of these directly at all. I invite you rather to pursue with me an inquiry into how the Romantic style of these early Romantics – Weber and Bellini – originated: whether we cannot perhaps find traces of Romanticism in much earlier composers. It will be generally agreed, I think, that Weber and Bellini are Romantic; but what constitutes their Romanticism? The stories of their operas are Romantic, of course; but in what sense is their music Romantic?

I began once to try to think out this problem, but I soon came to the conclusion that it was hopeless to attack it in so direct a way. It is easy enough, as we listen to an opera in the theatre, or play it through on the pianoforte at home, to pick out some one phrase which seems to be the very essence of Romantic expression; but when we try to analyse the whole opera cold-bloodedly, and ask ourselves on every page, bar by bar, 'is this Romantic or not?', the task becomes impossible, and even if we could answer the question by mere instinctive feeling, we should have no sound basis for a scientific judgment.

I came to the conclusion therefore that the best way to study the problem was to begin some hundred years earlier, and follow the gradual development of opera in different countries, keeping

[7] Play 'Matona mia cara' (E.J.D.). The reference is presumably to the opening bars of Lassus's *villanella.*

an eye carefully open for anything in the earlier operas which seems in any way to foreshadow effects and methods generally considered characteristic of the acknowledged Romantics. I must tell you frankly that I mean to talk to you about a number of composers whose works you are never likely to see on the stage. As I studied their scores, many of which have now become museum rarities, I always asked myself whether I could possibly endeavour to get them put on the stage again; and I confess that in practically all cases I came to the conclusion that a revival would be out of the question. But I hope you will have at any rate an opportunity of hearing a few extracts from some of these forgotten operas, and I present these specimens to you, not as masterpieces, but as experiments and studies in the technique of emotional expression. I present them to you also as exercises for yourselves, exercises of the imagination, asking you to call up before you the vision of a stage, with its appropriate scenery, its singers, and the dramatic situations which the music is intended to illustrate.

The more closely I studied these old operas, the more difficult I found it to decide in my own mind what was to be considered 'Romantic' in style – that is, in purely musical style. Even as regards the literary subjects and the pictorial accessories I found it difficult to come to any conclusion. When I read Le Sueur's opera *La Caverne* (1793), with a delightful picture on the title-page representing the cavern, in which a band of brigands has imprisoned a noble lady, while her distressed husband wanders about in a forest planted on the roof of the cavern; when I found that the husband entered the cavern disguised as an old blind minstrel and that after his followers had fought a battle with the brigands (in which they destroyed most of the cavern itself) it was discovered that the brigand chief was the lady's long-lost brother – then I thought that here surely was typical Romanticism. But I reflected that the whole opera might have been set to music by Handel, with words in Italian instead of French, and with slight changes of names and situations. Prisons, ruins, robbers, repentant villains, are common enough in the operas of Handel's day; the only difference is that the scene is set in ancient Greece or mediaeval Antioch instead of seventeenth-century Calabria. We are told that Gluck reformed the opera by getting rid of the long formal arias of Handel's time; but what was the good of that if

8

he only led the way for Cherubini to burden his operas with still longer and more formal trios and quartets? Can we not reasonably say that Handel's operas are no less Romantic than those of the early nineteenth century? Schumann wrote an opera on the story of patient Griselda, and the story of Weber's *Euryanthe* is very much the same; how truly Romantic, say the critics, because the story of Griselda is taken from a mediaeval romance. But they forget, or perhaps they do not know, that Griselda was the heroine of an opera by the elder Scarlatti in 1721 – an opera, too, in which there are some startling dramatic effects. If Schumann is Romantic and Scarlatti is Classical when they both treat the same story, then there must be some essential difference of musical style, apart from the obvious difference between two composers who lived more than a hundred years apart.

We are faced at once with deeper psychological problems. It is generally acknowledged that Shakespeare is in many ways Romantic; some of his contemporaries, such as Webster, are even more conspicuously Romantic. But once we acknowledge Romanticism in the early seventeenth century we can begin looking for it at any period. Monsieur Hazard of Paris, lecturing last year at Harvard, showed us a Romantic of 1730 – the Abbé Prévost – a hundred years before the official Romantic, Victor Hugo. There are romanticists and classicists in all periods of history; it is not a question of epoch but of personal temperament. Admit this, and we at once quote the well-known line of Goethe about the two souls in our own breast; we are all of us Classical and Romantic by turns.[8] It is the Nietzschean doctrine of Apollo and Dionysus.

I have suggested this line of thought to you merely in order to show how futile it is as a guide to the study of our own subject. But we must not dismiss the whole idea without further consideration. It has been suggested by certain writers that *all* music is Romantic. The other arts may be Classical or Romantic at different times or in different places, but music, even when it is officially called Classical, is of its innermost essence invariably a Romantic art. Music deals with pure feeling and nothing else; the other arts deal with facts, even if they falsify them.

This view of music has been held, I believe, by composers; but

---

[8] Faust's 'Zwei Seelen leben, ach, in meiner Brust' is however not a reference to Classicism and Romanticism.

9

it seems to me to be a literary man's interpretation of music and not a musician's. There are many historic observations on the subject of music, by Gòethe, Carlyle, Walter Pater and other eminent men of letters; but the important question for us is, how much did these learned men know about music itself? When Carlyle says that 'music is well said to be the speech of angels' we may reply that Herrick said so some two centuries earlier and said it much more prettily. Walter Pater's famous dictum that 'all art constantly aspires towards the condition of music' seems to imply more recognition of the intellectual aspects of music; however much or little he may have known about the art, he at any rate envisages it as a Classical art, an art in which form is predominant. But here again we are faced by the problem of individual temperament; those who agree with Pater will be Classically minded, those who disagree, Romantic.

Once more I seem to have led you to an example of pure futility; but this question of individual temperament is worth taking into account. Alfred Einstein, in his *Short History of Music*, has some very illuminating remarks on the beginnings of the Romantic Movement. 'The essence of romanticism', he says, 'lies in the incessant absorption of fresh material from musical or outside sources and the moulding of all this into new unities.' 'There had been romanticism in music long before there were romantic composers – long, even, before the word "romantic", a literary term to begin with, was coined...What now happened was not so much a discovery as the choice of a new angle of vision. The spirit of the age regarded the things of art exclusively in a romantic light, and saw in them all only the dazzling enchantment of sympathetic colours.'

'Thus almost the whole of Beethoven came to be hailed as romantic. The prodigious power of his symphonic works seemed a fulfilment of the oracular saying of the eighteenth-century poet Wackenroder to the effect that instrumental music was the one true art, a heaven that was to be gained by the renunciation of reality.'

Einstein, for all his determination to be internationally-minded and to write of everybody with the strictest justice, cannot escape from the normal German habit of seeing the history of music, and especially the history of Romantic music, as an exclusively German affair. From Wackenroder he passes to the *Knaben*

Wunderhorn, to Schubert, Weber and E. T. A. Hoffmann, as a matter of course. None the less, his remark about the new angle of vision gives us the clue to the whole situation, at any rate as far as it affected Germany during the days of Beethoven and after. It was not that people wanted a new kind of music altogether, but that they began to put a new interpretation on the old. They saw Beethoven as a Romantic because they wanted to make him into a Romantic, to make him into one of themselves. They were in fact rather like Hoffmann as he appears in Offenbach's opera, wearing the magic spectacles which make the most ordinary things seem wonderful.

Hoffmann – I shall have occasion to talk about him more in detail in a later lecture – is, for that Beethoven–Weber period, the most Romantic of all Romantics, and intensely conscious of his own Romanticism. But let us inquire what Hoffmann's own taste in music was: what was the music that so profoundly thrilled him? Mozart, and the old Italians, such as Leo and Durante – composers who to us seem typical of the coldest Classicism! We may call this Romantic receptivity; it is not creative Romanticism.[9] But we must remember that Leo and Durante were not so very remote from Hoffmann in date; they were in fact rather nearer to him than Mendelssohn and Schumann are to us. They would represent for his day merely a conservative taste, whereas to us their interest is definitely antiquarian. It was quite reasonable that he should respond to them emotionally; it ought to be our business to learn to respond emotionally to composers who to us seem typical of the coldest Classicism! That sort of response is the product of scholarship, not of instinctive feeling.

If we try to sum up the Romantic interpretation of older music in one word, that word must be 'exaggeration' – unkind and disrespectful as it may sound. If we want to find a more charitable name for it, let us call it 'intensification'. We can play many of the works of Johann Sebastian Bach on an instrument such as a harpsichord which gives no variety of colour and no gradation of loud and soft, but merely one even tone-quality; the music will still be beautiful and even expressive. Try the experiment with

---

[9] Hoffmann was a composer before he became a critic or man of letters; his enthusiasm for the music of the past was only one ingredient in his Romantic outlook.

the first prelude of the '48', playing it as far as possible without the slightest 'expression' or variation of tone-quality; it will make its own expression by the beauty of its form. Play it with Gounod's violin melody, or with a voice singing it, and you have Bach romanticized; the expression is intensified to an almost unbearable extent. But if you try the experiment of playing a piece of Weber without any expression or changes of dynamics, the result will merely be dull and lifeless; Weber, the typical Romantic, depends for his very existence upon intensification or exaggeration.[10]

If we of the present day consider in turn the operas of Mozart, Beethoven and Weber as we are in the habit of doing, a habit induced by the reading of musical history as written under German influences, we shall inevitably wonder how it ever became possible for the style of Mozart to evolve naturally into that of the two later composers; the difference between all three of them is too striking. The explanation lies in the fact that the various operas by lesser composers which filled the gaps have now been forgotten; if we search for these and study them, we shall soon see how much both Beethoven and Weber learned from the French and Italian composers. The development will then present a continuous line. We shall find, too, that the study of the forgotten operas will often throw valuable light on details of the well-known ones, sometimes from a musical, sometimes from a dramatic or theatrical point of view. It was a common custom in the days of Beethoven for one libretto to be set to music by several different composers, often in different languages. There are for instance three different settings of the *Fidelio* story before Beethoven's, and it is pretty certain that Beethoven was acquainted with two of them. In this case I cannot suggest that any of Beethoven's predecessors attained to his level of sublimity, but a study of them will give us the background of Beethoven's audiences, and also an idea of what musical conventions were common property at the time and in no way peculiar to Beethoven himself.

I propose then in this course of lectures to trace the history

---

[10]   The quotation appears to be a telescoped reminiscence of the opening bars of Weber's Grande Polonaise for piano (op. 21).

of opera throughout the eighteenth century, considering methods and tendencies rather than individual composers. I shall speak only in a summary fashion of the earlier half of the century, as it is not necessary to consider the earlier operas in detail; all that is needed is to give you some fairly clear conception of the difference between *opera seria* – serious opera, grand opera, as people would call it nowadays – and *opera buffa*, the Italian type of comic opera or musical comedy.

In the first half of the century these two types run side by side in Italy, and are exported from Italy to foreign countries: to Vienna, to London, later on to Copenhagen, Stockholm and St Petersburg, as well as to the minor German courts. They were exported to Spain and Portugal too; the whole of Europe except France was subject to the domination of Italian opera. France had its own style, the opera created first by Lully, an Italian by birth, and continued by Campra and Rameau. In the middle of the eighteenth century Paris was invaded by a company of Italian comic singers; the invasion is well known to musicians under the name of the Querelle des Bouffons, the war of the comic opera. Like most of these musical wars, it was a war of journalists and amateurs rather than a war of musicians; and the Querelle des Bouffons derived its fame chiefly from the fact that Jean-Jacques Rousseau played an important part in it. As a result of the war more Italian composers came to France and in a very short time established a new sort of comic opera that eventually became distinctively French in style.

By the middle of the century, or at any rate about 1760, serious opera was in a bad way, both in Italy and in France. There was no French composer worthy to succeed Rameau, and it may be doubted whether the Parisians really wanted one.[11] Comic opera became so popular during the latter half of the century that the serious form was almost completely eclipsed. But this later type of comic opera was not quite the same sort of thing as the first comic operas produced at Naples in the days of Scarlatti. As the century progressed comic opera, which at first had been light-hearted and satirical, tended to become more and more sentimental. The first performers of comic opera had made no pretensions to be singers; they called themselves actors, and

---

[11] Rameau composed actively until his death in 1764, but most of his late works are ballets and pastorals.

one notable characteristic was that there were no artificial sopranos among them. But as comic opera became more and more popular, not only at Naples, but at Venice and outside the frontiers of Italy, there grew up a regular class of comic opera singers, with whom serious opera singers were often associated. When the 'bouffons' came to Paris in 1752 the reason why they at once fascinated the audiences of that city was because their little pieces were sketches from real life, instead of the mythological pomposities of classical grand opera exemplified in the works of Rameau.[12]

The next step was the invitation to an Italian composer, Egidio Romoaldo Duni, to settle in Paris and produce comic operas in French. A French school of comic opera arose very quickly, headed by Monsigny and Dalayrac;[13] they learned their technique from the Italians, but soon began to substitute French for Italian themes in the airs which were intended to suggest popular folksong. Just about the same time there began the vogue for sentimental plays – *comédie larmoyante*. It was a taste which naturally affected the comic operas, and still more naturally found its ideal expression in music. Although the French school and the Italian school, generally speaking, went their separate ways, there was nevertheless a certain interchange of ideas and even of operas.[14] Italian operas were translated into French, and French literary ideas were always carefully studied in Italy. At the same time it was the firm conviction of all Italians that the French were a completely unmusical race, and the English agreed with them in describing a French opera performance as something too excruciating for words.

A very important moment in the history of opera is reached when Vienna became a great international operatic centre, just about the time of Mozart. Mozart himself had practically nothing to do with it. He composed Italian operas which to us of to-day are the only operas of that period which still hold the stage; but in his own time he was neglected in favour of a number of minor

[12] They were also, by common consent, superior to the French as singers and actors.

[13] Grétry, Belgian by birth but trained in Italy, was the most successful composer of this school.

[14] Haydn's *La vera costanza* (1779) was produced in Paris as *Laurette* in 1791; the libretto of his *L'incontro improviso* (1775) was translated and adapted from that of Gluck's *La Rencontre imprévue* (1764).

Italians and a few French as well. Both French opera and Italian opera came to Vienna and spread over the whole of Germany; for several years the German opera-houses were almost entirely dependent on a foreign repertory. It took the Germans several generations before they learned to compose music for the stage, at least to words in their own language. Two Germans, Hasse and Mozart, achieved real greatness in opera; but it was in Italian opera, not German. Hasse, as far as I know, never wrote German operas at all; Mozart's two, *Die Entführung* and *Die Zauberflöte*, achieved greatness only in the face of serious obstacles. The main reason why the early German operas are unsatisfactory is because their librettos are so badly made. The musicians were accomplished enough; it was the poets or dramatists who did not understand their trade.

It is at the end of the eighteenth century that we begin to be aware of a new kind of opera which we can now regard as Romantic in intention, and what I want to impress upon you from the outset is that Romantic Opera was derived from comic opera and not from *opera seria*. Opera became Romantic, one may say, because audiences wanted to hear trivial music sung by first-rate singers. That has always been the desire of audiences, and it is the desire of popular audiences to this day. Romanticism in opera is marked by the gradual infiltration of all kinds of popular, I might say of trivial, music into serious opera; or rather, I should say that the mixture of comic opera with all kinds of heterogeneous elements became serious again, and led to a revival of serious opera, for the curious reason that audiences, even cultivated audiences, are inclined to take *all* music seriously. They will take it seriously even when the music itself is painfully trivial and vulgar, provided that this music is presented to their ear with a sufficient intensity and amplitude of physical sound. The songs that are sung on patriotic or political occasions are for the most part contemptible from an artistic point of view; but they impress the multitude with a sense of seriousness when they are sung by several hundred people at once. We find just the same thing in some of Beethoven's symphonies; Spohr has been censured by the devout for calling the famous tune of the Ninth Symphony a 'Gassenhauer', but it is really a just criticism; like the themes of the last movement of the C minor, it achieves dignity only by the massiveness with which it is treated. Even one massive voice, as those old enough to remember the great contraltos of Victorian and Edwardian days will confirm, is enough to confer authority on the paltriest of melodies. One of the most curious aspects of Romanticism is its glorification of the trivial. Looking back on these old operas, as we do now after more than a hundred years, we can perhaps see the triviality more easily than the romance, especially if we only hear fragmentary examples played on the pianoforte, instead of witnessing the operas as complete wholes, with all the appropriate action and scenery. I invite you to seize these opportunities of exercising your imagination, and also of analysing your own emotional reactions. The history of Romantic Opera may in itself be of no very vital importance; what is important is that you should train up your own imaginative sensibilities, and that you should perpetually ask yourselves what it is that you receive from the experience of music.

2

THE CONVENTIONS OF OPERA

Historians of music have never wearied of repeating that old list of operatic conventions quoted by George Hogarth in his *Memoirs of the Opera* – *aria di bravura, aria d'agilità, aria di portamento* and so forth – as if every opera during the first half of the eighteenth century really conformed to these requirements in detail. The fact is that every age has had its theatrical conventions, and has had too the kind of commercially-minded people who delight in classifying them and maintaining them, to the destruction of all individuality. Theatrical rôles have always been conventionally classified in all countries, just as voices are classified into soprano, mezzo-soprano, contralto, etc. A singer will no doubt begin by admitting that she is, let us say, a contralto, but if it is a question of engaging her, she will very soon make it clear that she is not just like any other contralto in compass and in style. It was the same thing with the early operas of the eighteenth century; singing-masters may have classified the arias into categories, and second-rate composers may have turned them out like machines; but the great men wrote what they pleased, even if they conformed to the general style of their period.

It must however be admitted from the outset that Italian opera during the first half of the century was very strictly conventional. There had been far more variety during the latter half of the seventeenth century, at any rate as regards the dramatic framework of opera, ranging from the extravagant absurdities of some of the Venetian operas, with their elaborate changes of scene, their sumptuous pageantries and their irresponsible comic episodes, to the neat little comedies, based generally on Spanish plays, requiring few characters and little elaboration of scenery, that were characteristic of the early years of Scarlatti.

It was Scarlatti, more than anyone else, who brought about the first stage of operatic conventionalization. In his early operas he writes songs in a variety of forms, but from about 1700 onwards he restricts himself entirely to the well-known ternary or 'da capo' form. He covers a wide range of emotions, his music has beauty and often a marvellous intensity of emotional expression, but the form is invariably the same. And, at the same time, the poet Apostolo Zeno was conventionalizing the operatic drama. It was invariably in three acts;[1] the comic characters were conventionalized into two, generally soubrette and basso buffo, and their appearances were strictly regularized; they were allowed occasional comic remarks in the course of the *recitativo secco*, but no arias until the end of each act, when they had a scene to themselves. In the third act, this comic scene had to come in just before the end, so that the real end might be taken up with the *dénouement* – the untying of the knots and the conventional short choral finale, sung not by a chorus, but by the principal characters in harmony. In the older operas the comic characters had sometimes been interchanged as regards sex: a soprano page, sung by a woman, and a comic old woman, sung by a tenor. The more elegant taste of the new century seems to have disapproved of the old woman, though in later generations she has reappeared on the musical stage.

Apostolo Zeno was followed by Metastasio, who between 1724 and 1750 produced some two dozen dramas written to be set to music, in addition to librettos for oratorios and other entertainments. The importance of Metastasio lies in the fact that he was a real poet, who is still recognized as such by all authorities on Italian literature. Metastasio was much influenced by Racine, and he succeeded in simplifying and systematizing the scheme of the operatic libretto with so much skill that his librettos were set to music over and over again. Even as late as 1830 there were almost a dozen operas written every year to books by him, and at the height of his fame, in the middle of the eighteenth century, there would have been far more than a dozen. Some of his dramas, such as *Adriano in Siria*, were set to music by over forty different composers.[2] It is no wonder that serious Italian opera became a stereotyped convention and that the public eventually tired of it altogether. Metastasio's dramas have great beauty of sentiment

---

[1] Some librettos written by Girolamo Frigimelica-Roberti for Venice early in the century had five acts.

[2] The *Enciclopedia dello Spettacolo* lists 60 settings of *Adriano in Siria* and even more of other Metastasio librettos.

and elegance of language, but they are all too much alike. It does not much matter what the subject is; there are always the same situations and the same emotions: the same lady or gentleman in disguise whose true identity is revealed only at the end, the same rages and griefs, jealousies and remorses, the same heroism and the same chivalrous self-sacrifices – and invariably[3] the same happy end. The comic characters were abolished altogether. Metastasio's operas thus became standardized arrangements of standardized emotions. The musical public must soon have known all his dramas by heart; the only novelty to be enjoyed would be that of the songs (for the recitatives were inevitably much the same, whoever set them) and that of the singers. The fatal thing about Metastasian opera was that it inevitably encouraged the false spirit of connoisseurship, a spirit which we know only too well at the present day, when every amateur thinks himself a final arbiter of good singing and a pontifical judge of good taste.

Comic opera, as an independent type of musical drama, began at Naples in 1709, and for a long time it was definitely Neapolitan in character. We must distinguish carefully between real comic opera and the so-called *intermezzi*, of which the classic example is *La serva padrona* of Pergolesi (1733). This very attractive work is often held up as the typical comic opera, and it is suggested that in those days comic and serious opera were performed in alternate acts – as if acts of *The School for Scandal* were to be played in the intervals between the acts of *Hamlet*. The comparison is perfectly absurd. In the old Venetian operas of the seventeenth century the comic characters came on the stage at any time, joined in serious conversations making ludicrous remarks, and sang their comic airs and duets whenever the author thought fit. In Zeno's librettos the comic characters were confined to the conventional scenes (with alternate songs and a duet to finish) at the ends of the acts; Metastasio abolished the comic scenes altogether as integral parts of the drama. But this simply meant – at any rate in Naples – that the same conventional comic scenes were played just the same, only between the acts instead of as part of them.[4] They were sometimes by the same composer, sometimes not; and

---

[3] *Didone abbandonata* and *Catone in Utica* are exceptions.
[4] The difference is very slight when we remember that the curtain did not fall at the end of an act. (E.J.D.)

as they were no longer integral to the main opera, the *intermezzi*, as they were called, could be played with any serious opera. *La serva padrona* became immensely popular when it was played in Paris in 1752, nineteen years after its first production; and for the Paris performance it was lengthened by additional songs. All this time there had existed since 1709 a regular series of comic operas in three acts which occupied a whole evening's performance, being just as long as the serious operas. They too had *secco* recitative, and *da capo* arias, and in some cases special comic characters as well, with what were practically *intermezzi*, as in the serious operas, although the whole opera was light in character. They began by being satirical and very local, with several characters who talked the dialect of Naples, but in a very short time, even by the time of Pergolesi, they began to grow sentimental in character.

The comic operas never employed *castrati*. The first singers of comic opera were not even professional singers, but only actors who could sing; no doubt a definite school of comic singers was very soon developed. But so fixed in the minds of opera-goers was the notion that all heroes must sing soprano that the heroes of the comic operas had to be sopranos too, and these parts were sung by women.

It is interesting to note in this connexion that in England, in the seventeenth century, long before any Italian *castrato* had been heard on the stage, women took male parts in Thomas Duffett's parodies of the English operas, and the chief female part was taken by a male comedian. And later on, when Italian operas were introduced to London at the beginning of the eighteenth century, the soprano heroes' parts were often sung by women, because at that time it was impossible to persuade the *castrati* to risk the journey to London, where they were sure that their voices would be ruined by the climate.[5]

It is important to remember this appearance of women, and this absence of *castrati*, in the comic operas, because obviously one of the first signs of the Romantic Movement will be the emergence of the tenor hero instead of the soprano. We shall see, later on, that the tenor hero makes his first appearance in operas of the

---

[5] There appears to be little evidence for this. *Castrati* were easily attracted to London by high fees; and many women specialised in male roles, in Italy as well as in England.

comic type, while the *castrato* retains his throne right on into the nineteenth century.

There are various other features of the Neapolitan comic opera which must be noticed. The best-known characteristic is the so-called 'concerted finale'. It is not true that ensemble movements were absolutely excluded from serious opera, but they were rare, and in no case were they finales in any way resembling the familiar finales of Mozart. Scarlatti is the inventor of what I call the 'ensemble of perplexity', sung by four characters at some moment in the action when an embarrassing situation has arisen and nobody knows what to do. He employs it first in his one comic opera *Il trionfo dell' onore*, giving it to four serious characters in one act, and then parodying his own invention by making the four comic characters sing a similar ensemble in the next, in which they all abuse each other as violently as they can. But in both cases, and in most cases of such ensembles in the works of Handel,[6] the ensemble of perplexity conforms to the scheme of the *da capo* aria. Scarlatti calls it an *aria a quattro*, a song for four people, and it is nothing more or less than an ordinary *da capo* aria with the phrases split up between the four voices, though they sometimes sing in harmony as well.

The ensemble of perplexity is therefore common to both types of opera, whereas the finale belongs to comic opera alone. It arose out of the comic duets in the early serious operas, because the comic characters were the only people who could do anything so undignified as to sing short and lively phrases, generally abusive, at each other and work up to a spirited climax. The elaborate finale was not achieved by Scarlatti; it is generally credited to Logroscino, but was certainly employed long before by Leonardo Leo. Later on it was further elaborated by Galuppi and Piccinni.

Another characteristic of comic opera was the employment of sharply syncopated rhythms which are not unlike those of modern jazz. These no doubt originated from Neapolitan folk music, and also from the natural vehemence of Neapolitan speech. As comic opera spread to other centres this syncopated rhythm became more common, and from the Italian comic operas it passed into the symphonic music of the classical symphonists.

[6] Only three such ensembles in Handel's operas and dramatic oratorios are in *da capo* form.

THE CONVENTIONS OF OPERA

Lastly, I would mention as a conspicuous feature of the comic operas the so-called *canzonetta* – the unmistakeable Neapolitan folksong.[7] It begins by being Neapolitan, but as comic opera moves to other regions, it takes on local characteristics. From Italy it passes to Fràance, and when we come to study French opera we shall find the folksong just as indispensable as at Naples: the only difference is that it has become French and calls itself a *romance*. This folksong type is peculiar to comic opera; there was no possible place for it in *opera seria*. Its presence anywhere is proof, if any is needed, that the opera is comic; and we shall find a very conspicuous example in the famous serenade of *Don Giovanni*, accompanied by the mandoline. Another example from Mozart is Pedrillo's 'Moorish' ballad in *Die Entführung*.

Comic opera has a continuous history at Naples right on into the nineteenth century, and it is curious to see how constant the tradition remained, in spite of the inevitable changes of purely musical style. Scarlatti was one of the first composers to write rapid patter-songs for the basso buffo, and this type of patter-song remains substantially the same down to the days of Bellini. It survives even to-day in the English operettas of Sullivan, which are obviously imitated from Rossini.

French comic opera begins with the French imitators of the Italians. In some of the early operas the style is still so Italian that one can hardly see anything definitely French in it; but from the first the French abandoned *secco* recitative, and substituted spoken dialogue. They admitted accompanied recitative, for they had always had it in the operas of Lully and Rameau; but it must be remembered that the recitative of the older French operas was always in formal verse of a type unsuited to comic opera. The French had nothing that corresponded to the natural rapid parlando, in irregular verse, of the Italian operas, and it was easier to substitute spoken dialogue in plain prose. In operas of a serious cast, however, verse was still used, and was also spoken, even in the very last years of the century, after the musical elements of the opera had in France been enormously expanded.

---

[7] Play 'Amaje na mpesa e bà' of Leo. (E.J.D.). Dent is again quoting from memory. He prints Leo's canzona in full, in 12/8 time, in his article 'Leonardo Leo', *SIMG* viii (1906–7), 560ff.

From a purely musical standpoint the French composers soon developed a style of their own. The French were never great singers, and the Italians always had the greatest contempt for their vocal achievements. But whereas the Italians always pursued the ideal of attractive melody above all others, the French seemed more interested in the words than in the music. French melody is curiously bleak and unattractive, though at certain moments it achieves a tender simplicity which has a unique charm of its own. But it is evident that the French composers appealed to their public much more by energy of declamation, even in their songs.[8] We often find indications in the printed scores such as 'avec concentration', and the general style and shape of the airs, as well as their instrumental accompaniments, point to a more sharply accentuated style of playing and singing than the Italian scores demand. The harmony is bare and commonplace, but determinedly logical, and this gives the French composers the power to build up much longer and more complex movements than we find in the Italian operas. It was probably from a consciousness of their own vocal shortcomings that the French soon began to concentrate on concerted numbers. They wrote immensely long duets, trios and quartets, formal in shape, but very energetic in character. They had indeed too much energy, for they run to enormous length, and the voices are often very cruelly treated, at least according to modern ideas.

Beethoven is notorious for ill-treating the voices, which have to continue shrieking on their top notes against a large orchestra for several pages without interruption. This bad habit has sometimes been ascribed to Beethoven's deafness; but it is simply an imitation of Cherubini, whose opera Médée is probably one of the most exhausting works ever written for the stage. Cherubini himself was merely following the normal French practice.[9] One can only imagine that French singers were accustomed to this sort of labour, and their audiences too. One result of this French habit of writing long ensembles is that very little happens in the course of an act,[10] although sometimes the action progresses a little in the course of an ensemble.

[8] See Grétry's memoirs and the musical illustrations to them. (E.J.D.)
[9] Cherubini's vocal style was not typical of French opéra-comique before the Revolution.
[10] Except during the spoken dialogue.

THE CONVENTIONS OF OPERA

One very conspicuous difference between French and Italian opera, and a difference which is of the greatest importance for the development of Romantic Opera, is that the Italians never had any sense of background music, music intended to describe natural happenings such as storms. The old Italian operas are full of the most elaborate changes of scenery, and the scenes themselves are wildly Romantic in character, if I may be allowed to use the word in connexion with the theatre of the seventeenth century. Ruins, floods, conflagrations and so forth are frequent items, and when we look at the pictures that have come down to us, we wonder why the musicians did not make the slightest attempt to provide music descriptive of all these horrors, such as Wagner gives us in the *Ring*.

Probably it was impracticable to synchronize stage transformations with the music of the orchestra; but the more important reason almost certainly was one of fundamental principle: the composers were concerned only with the human characters on the stage and their personal emotions. In the French operas, on the other hand, there is always a good deal of descriptive music; it is rather primitive in the operas of Lully, but Rameau provides remarkably picturesque orchestral descriptions of storms and other scenic effects. We shall see later on how this descriptive music reaches Germany through Cherubini, while Mozart almost entirely ignores it. There is a fine storm in *Idomeneo*, but what Mozart is really painting is not the visible storm. He leaves that to the designer of the scenery; the music is concerned with the effect of the storm on the emotions of the people on the stage. The same situation arises in that scene in *Idomeneo* where the monster rises from the sea. Wagner, one imagines, would have described the monster musically, as he does the dragon in *Siegfried*; Mozart is only concerned with the terror it inspires in the chorus. In *Die Zauberflöte* Wagner would have given us wonderful descriptive music for the fire and water scenes: we have only to remember the *Ring* to see how completely at home he was in those elements. Mozart takes no notice whatever of the fire and the water; he creates an astonishing atmosphere of tense concentration by the sound of the magic flute itself. The minds of the spectators are by this means fixed firmly on the two human beings who are going through these symbolic dangers.

The dramas of Metastasio offered no occasion for descriptive orchestral music. They were concerned only with human emotions. They demanded elaborate scenery, but it was always the scenery of a long established convention, and it was merely a convention that the scene should be changed as often as is indicated. The operas were composed for performance at court theatres where money was lavishly spent; we have to thank the extravagance of the German princes for the fact that engravings were often made as souvenirs of the magnificent productions. Fabris,[11] a scene-painter who worked for Handel in London and afterwards went to Copenhagen, left a treatise on scene-painting with a series of designs for scenes that would be necessary in any opera – there are various palace scenes, and others such as a prison, a scene of ruins, and an amphitheatre. We are accustomed to class the horrible and the macabre as typically Romantic; if so, why are not these scenes Romantic?

The question is worth asking. If it is replied that such scenes are Classical because they are conventional, and recur over and over again in every opera, we may reply that the Romantic designs of the early nineteenth century are equally conventional in their style, and that they were repeated over and over again for some fifty years or more. It might perhaps be argued that the scenery of Handel's day, and of the seventeenth century too, is Classical in spirit because of the symmetry with which it was designed – the rows of columns or rocks ranged on each side of the stage. But that is a merely technical matter; scenery was designed in parallel wings because it was the most convenient type of mechanism; all designs had to conform to it, because every theatre was built on those lines. And we might also point out that Romantic scenery of the nineteenth century, or of the Italian opera stage at the present day, which still carries on the realistic traditions of long past generations, is equally conventional in its structure, though the conventions of scene-building have changed in the course of a hundred years.

[11] Jakob (Giacopo) Fabris (c. 1689–1761), born in Venice of German parents, practised at Karlsruhe (1719–21), Hamburg (1724–30) and Berlin (1740–7), before settling at Copenhagen in 1747. His *Instruction in der teatralischen Architectur und Mechanique* (ed. Torben Krogh) was published in four volumes in 1930 from the manuscript in the Royal Library, Copenhagen. He is not known to have worked for Handel in London, but he designed the sets for the production of Handel's *Giulio Cesare* at Hamburg in 1725; one of them appears as frontispiece to the printed libretto.

THE CONVENTIONS OF OPERA

It would be easy enough to write the history of Romantic Opera if we were willing to accept the doctrine, often maintained, that all musical manifestations of the world's cultural movements take place several years after the corresponding manifestations in literature and the other arts. For generations it has been stated that the Renaissance, which for the art of painting we are accustomed to date from about 1480, did not begin to have any effect on the art of music until 1600, more than a whole century later. Modern research has shown that this doctrine is quite inconsistent with historical fact, and indeed modern German historians consider the new music of 1600 to be the starting point of what they call the Baroque period, a period which goes down to about 1750. But it is the natural tendency of all German writers on music to suppose that the history of music is mainly the history of German music, and that whatever is not German is comparatively negligible. The Romantic Movement is often treated as if it were exclusively German, and this is hardly surprising, considering how important a part Germany undoubtedly played in most of its aspects. Accepting the common doctrine of the retarded musical expression of ideas already long current in literature, it is easy to begin Romantic music with Weber, a good half century later than the beginnings of Romanticism in German literature, as represented for instance by Schiller's play *Die Räuber* and his story *Der Geisterseher*. Cultural history is naturally written in the first instance by men of letters, who see life from the literary angle, and often regard music as a thing not worth taking into consideration at all.

The poet Thomas Gray makes an interesting comment on the situation in a letter which he wrote in 1763 to Count Francesco Algarotti, who in 1755 had published his *Saggio sopra l'opera in musica* in which he set forth the ideal of an opera which should re-unite, as Gray observes, 'the congenial arts of poetry, music and the dance, which with the assistance of painting and architecture, regulated by taste, and supported by magnificence and power, might form the noblest scene, and bestow the sublimest pleasure, that the imagination can conceive. But who shall realize these delightful visions?' he asks. Not even Frederick the Great, the patron of Algarotti himself, 'could govern an Italian *virtuosa*, destroy her caprice and impertinence, without hurting her talents, or command those unmeaning graces and tricks of voice to be silent, that have gained her the adoration of her own country'.

'One cause, that so long has hindered, and (I fear) will hinder that happy union, which you propose, seems to be this: that poetry (which, as you allow, must lead the way, and direct the operation of the subordinate arts) implies at least a liberal education, a degree of literature, and various knowledge, whereas the others (with a few exceptions) are in the hands of slaves and mercenaries, I mean, of people without education, who, though neither destitute of genius, nor insensible to fame, must yet make gain their principal end, and subject themselves to the prevailing taste of those, whose fortune only distinguishes them from the multitude.'

Gray is evidently of the opinion that musicians were all ignorant and uncultured people who were interested in nothing but making money. It is one of the notable characteristics of the Romantic Movement in its later phases that it brought the art of music more closely into contact with the world of letters. Hoffmann, composer and novelist, is the most striking example of this new outlook on music, and Hoffmann was followed by Weber, Schumann, Liszt and Berlioz, all of whom were men of letters as well as musicians. But the literary outlook on music begins long before Hoffmann, and the country in which it really began was France. From Rousseau onwards there is a succession of French musicians who kept closely in contact with the literary world and often made their own contributions to letters. Grétry's memoirs are not merely his autobiography, but a series of discussions on the relations of the State towards music and musical education. Le Sueur, the teacher of Berlioz, was a student of ancient music, and the author of a remarkable essay expounding his ideas on the subject of church music and the application of contemporary musical technique to ecclesiastical ceremony.[12] On the Italian side there was Giuseppe Sarti, who was not only a distinguished composer but also a mathematician and an acoustical investigator.

[12] *Essai de musique sacrée...pour la Fête de Noël* (Paris, 1787), expanded later in the same year as *Exposé détaillé d'une musique une, imitative, et particulière à chaque solemnité*. For Le Sueur's relationship to French musical thought of the period, see Ora Frishberg Saloman, 'La Cépède's La poétique de la musique and Le Sueur', *Acta Musicologica*, xlvii (1975), 144–54; also Donald H. Foster, 'The Oratorio in Paris in the 18th Century', *ibid.*, 114ff.

Algarotti's book has often been referred to as a forerunner of the writings of Wagner, and his ideal theatre seems indeed to forecast Bayreuth. It is likely that he and Gluck, whom he may well have influenced, and whose *Orfeo* appeared in 1762, were reflecting ideas generally current at the time, discussed, no doubt, by word of mouth in many musical circles, and only formulated some years later. It is obvious from Gray's letter, for instance, that he was just as tired of the conventional *opera seria* as Algarotti was; and its continuation throws a further light on current opinion. Gray goes on to say that some ten years before he had seen a company of Italian comic-opera singers at one of the minor London theatres, where there was a very rough sort of audience, with every prejudice against foreigners; and he relates how he and the whole house had been captivated by the acting and singing of Nicolina Giordani in Cocchi's *Amanti gelosi,* the success of which is noted also by Burney. It shows how comic opera had begun to divert opera-goers away from the serious opera, in London as in Paris, because of its greater truth to nature.

I do not propose in these lectures to speak about the operas of Gluck; so much has been written about him already that I can add nothing new, and I should only be wasting your time if I repeated what must be perfectly familiar to you. But we must at least consider the position of Gluck as regards the Romantic Movement, and that we shall find curiously difficult to estimate. There can be no doubt that Romantic music, and especially Romantic Opera, derive many of their methods from Gluck, but it is difficult to regard Gluck himself as a Romantic. We need not pay much attention to the writings of Richard Wagner, who naturally was glad enough to make use of the name of that great master in order to present himself as his natural successor. Modern criticism has reacted violently against the Wagnerian interpretation of Gluck, and has sought rather to accentuate his eighteenth-century characteristics. We have already seen that Wagner's ideas of a *Gesamtkunstwerk* had been completely and entirely anticipated by Algarotti; and Algarotti himself was saying practically nothing that had not already been said by Emilio dei Cavalieri and the other originators of opera about 1600.

The school of the French Revolution, about which I shall have much to say in a later lecture, is sometimes called the school of Gluck; I need hardly add that this name has been given to it by

German writers, who lose no opportunity of claiming all great musicians for their own country. It would be far truer to say that Gluck's own style, and especially the style which he adopted in Paris, was based largely on French models.[13] Handel, who lived for the greater part of his life in England, and certainly managed to impose his own style on the serious music of the English composers who directly followed him, never dominated the music of the lighter English composers. They were eclectic, and imitated the Italians and the French too, but they kept a certain tradition of their own, especially in their vocal music and in their comic operas. If this was the case in England, how much stronger was the native tradition in France, where music had for a whole century enjoyed a far more distinguished history than we have any right to claim for England.

The inter-relation of French and Italian music is of peculiar interest at this moment. In the previous century, at the time when Italian opera was first introduced to Paris, we might say that the Italians were Romantic as compared to the French. The French did not at first take at all kindly to Italian music; it offended their taste because it was so violent in its expression. There is an amusing little dialogue in one of Lully's ballets, between La Musique Française and La Musique Italienne, in which the style of each is hit off with great skill and humour. The French lady is shocked at the vehemence and energy of the Italian lady, who replies

Io di te canto più forte, perchè amo più di te
(I sing louder than you do, because my passions are stronger)

– to which the French singer answers that the more she loves, the more gently she sighs.

If that was the case, it was not promising for the start of French opera; and, as we know, French opera had to be started by an Italian, Lully.[14] But by the middle of the next century we may wonder whether French music was not becoming more passionate than Italian. It does not look so, at first sight; the impression that one receives from the study of French scores is that they are all incredibly dry and devoid of emotional expression. Yet their lighter music has undeniable grace and charm, and their

[13] On this question see Julian Rushton, 'From Vienna to Paris: Gluck and the French Opera', *Chigiana* xxix–xxx (1972–3), 283–98.

[14] More strictly by Cambert's *Pomone* (1671).

serious music rises to great heights of grandeur and dignity, bare and cold as it may seem in comparison with the Italian. The invariable tendency of the French composers in this period – a period lasting from about the middle of the eighteenth century or a little later down to the end of the Napoleonic Empire – is to make greater use of conventional melodic formulae. Phrases are repeated over and over again which to our ears seem disastrously stale and barren – plain scale passages, arpeggios up and down a common chord, reiterations of tonic and dominant. Yet with these they build up huge movements; the trios and quartets in their operas, to say nothing of their finales, might be whole movements out of a symphony, and indeed they are built up with a symphonic technique. The only way in which we of to-day can try to realize their emotional effect – and we can have no doubt that a considerable emotional effect was intended, from the dramatic situations in which these movements occur – is by playing them, or imagining them played, with a much more intense and fervid style of execution than we are accustomed to think suitable for the music of the eighteenth century. In the days of my youth, when the music of Mendelssohn was beginning to lose that devout adoration which had been paid to it in early Victorian times, I used to hear it said – I think it was actually said by Stanford – that the faster you played Mendelssohn the better it sounded. It was an amusing criticism, for in those early Victorian times Mendelssohn himself had always been accused of taking things too fast when he conducted. It was certainly a characteristic of Romantic music, and especially of Weber, that it demanded, and indeed in its own notation indicated, a notable exaggeration of accent, a rhetorical manner of playing and singing, a deliberate intention, in fact, of putting more 'expression' into the music than the music itself actually contained.

How far back does this practice of over-accentuation go? That is a question which it is extremely difficult to answer, because each one of us, if he takes the trouble to think seriously about it, will respond according to his own personal temperament. I think that modern audiences would be gravely offended if anyone applied this Romantic exaggeration to the works of Mozart. Gluck might bear it better; it would be utterly inappropriate to the music of Handel. And yet Handel is a dramatic composer; the moment we put Handel on the stage, we have to find a dramatic way of singing him. Consider Rameau: the rhetorical style will be not so very inappropriate in his case. And go back still further, to Purcell and to Lully. It has been pointed out by Romain Rolland that Lully's declamation is grossly exaggerated as compared with the accurate modern French declamation of Debussy. On the subject of Purcell we can form our own judgment, as he sets our own language; and it is quite clear that Purcell was constantly aiming at the greatest possible intensity of rhetorical expression. As we follow the seventeenth century further and further back we become more and more conscious of this vehemently accentuated style; it is very noticeable in the works of Matthew Locke, we can observe it in the cantatas of Luigi Rossi, such as La Gelosia (it was *his* music, in fact, which so shocked the old-fashioned French connoisseurs), and we reach the climax in the madrigals and the operas of Monteverdi. Monteverdi is no isolated example; even some of the English madrigalists, like Tomkins, call for the sharply accentuated style of performance. There can be no doubt that the change which came over music about 1600 was essentially a change of rhythmical outlook, a growing tendency to accentuate sharply what we should call the first beat of a bar. It is in fact the moment when bar-lines first began to be written or printed in music. And we may also notice that it is the period of Shakespeare and Webster. Shakespeare and Webster are often called Romantics: are we to call Monteverdi and his contemporaries Romantics too?

All that we can do in studying the music of the past is to analyse and classify its technical characteristics.[15] Feeling and emotion are certainly not to be denied or repudiated; but our difficulty is, not that they cannot be analysed, but that they cannot command any safe measure of agreement. Our interpretation of them is too individual and personal. I might possibly succeed in persuading you to agree with my own interpretation of a piece of music – I mean as regards its emotional aspect – but I have no means of convincing you by argument. I draw your attention to this difference, because in musical criticism as it is generally practised we are so much accustomed to the method of persuasion, or even to that of dogmatic assertion, that few people are

---

[15] Dent noted in the margin: 'Sing illustrations Pergolesi and Perez. Methods of Perez influenced by comic opera.' It is not quite clear how he related this to the text.

really ready to give their minds to an argument based on technical and ascertainable facts. The persuasive method is to most people the more attractive; and it is especially in the case of Romantic music that it has been elaborated with every literary artifice. There are many interpretations of music in words which take high rank in the company of *belles-lettres*; but, all the same, they are unscientific and fundamentally dishonest.

3

THE HERITAGE OF GLUCK

Metastasio died at Vienna in April 1782, and among the aspirants to the vacant post of court poet were two fellow countrymen of his, both closely connected with the operatic stage – the Abbé Giambattista Casti from Montefiascone, and the Abbé Lorenzo Da Ponte from Ceneda. The Emperor Joseph II seemed to be in no hurry to appoint a new poet, and indeed he never appointed one at all; but in 1784 Casti and Da Ponte were both in Vienna, each endeavouring by every possible intrigue to secure the coveted post. Da Ponte was definitely in favour with the Emperor, and if his memoirs are to be believed, the Emperor was firmly determined that nothing should induce him to appoint Casti, who was a man of somewhat unsavoury life and the author of a series of tales in verse which were notorious for their very doubtful morality.

Both poets came before the Viennese public with opera librettos in this year 1784 – Da Ponte provided *Il ricco d'un giorno* for Salieri, and Casti *Il re Teodoro in Venezia* for Paisiello. Casti's poem was a landmark in the history of opera, for it introduced an entirely new type of comic libretto; Da Ponte's, clever as it was, did no more than continue the traditional style. Of the two composers neither is much remembered at the present day, but at that moment they were at the height of their fame.

Salieri has often been mentioned in connexion with Mozart; he was alleged to have caused his death by poisoning him. This story is now completely discredited, but it seems true that Salieri's relations with Mozart were never very friendly, at any rate until shortly before Mozart's death, when he went with Mozart to a performance of *Die Zauberflöte* and expressed the greatest admiration and delight.

It has sometimes been said that Mozart was the heir to the traditions of Gluck, but the only opera of Mozart which shows affinity to Gluck is *Idomeneo*; whereas Salieri, who was actually

33

the most intimate pupil of Gluck, absorbed so much of his master's style that he seems to have hardly any of his own. It was in this very year 1784 that Salieri became famous in Paris as the composer of *Les Danaides*. Gluck himself had accepted a contract to write this opera for Paris, but owing to ill-health he was unable to fulfil it. The opera was announced in Paris as the joint composition of Gluck and Salieri; it was supposed that the master had himself composed a good part of it, and that Salieri had merely completed it under his direction. But as soon as it was known that the opera was a definite success, Gluck confessed publicly that the whole work was Salieri's – Gluck having done no more than give Salieri advice and criticism.

Les Danaides is a thoroughly Classical opera on a classical subject; if it has not the genius of Gluck, it has at least a certain Italian elegance of outline which is Salieri's, as well as being a wonderfully accomplished imitation of Gluck's general manner. It is admirably laid out for the stage and has moments of immense dramatic effect and power, though I cannot feel that it ever shows any signs of Romanticism. I may mention one striking effect which is of particular interest at the present day. Those who know Alban Berg's opera *Wozzeck* will recall the moment where the single note B is held by the whole orchestra beginning *pianissimo* and gradually increasing to a *fortissimo* which is almost unbearable. In *Les Danaides*, Act IV, at the moment when 49 out of the 50 daughters of Danaus carry out their father's command to slay their newly married husbands on their wedding-night, exactly the same device is employed by Salieri, though on a smaller scale. The note is B flat, and it is held for three bars only, but with a crescendo from *pp* to *ff*; the intention at least is the same.

This opera is a good example of the French grand opera of its period and the principles on which it is laid out. The French planned their *tragédies lyriques* so as to secure the maximum of musical emotion in the sung numbers and the maximum of spectacle in the instrumental. The actual story progresses very slowly, and no single act contains more than one definite situation and main action. A great deal of time is taken up with ballets, and in Gluck's operas modern audiences find the ballets the most attractive part of the entertainment. The vocal numbers, in spite of Gluck's determination to do away with long introductory symphonies, *da capos*, and superfluous ornamentation, are always very extended, and quite as long, I should imagine, as any of the conventional arias of the earlier Italians. They avoid the *da capo* form, but as a matter of fact it was being given up everywhere about this date; and the hearer is just as conscious of repetitions because the extended sonata form makes them extremely prominent, if in a slightly different arrangement.[1] Moreover, the dropping of the *da capo* form was little more than a pretence, for the *da capo* came back in the shape of the new-fashioned rondo, very characteristic of the French and of Mozart too; it had the additional advantage that the repeated rondo-theme was always short, simple and definitely attractive in character, which naturally secured it all popularity.

Salieri had made a success in Paris, but he was not quite so sure of success in Vienna. His next opera, *Il ricco d'un giorno*, is a fairly amusing comic opera, but has no outstanding merit beyond that of some elaborately built-up ensembles. The long ensemble is quite a typical feature of all Salieri's operas, comic or serious.

Salieri's immediate rival Paisiello (we can never regard Mozart as a very serious rival) was a Neapolitan, one of those typical Neapolitans who may have genius, as the poet Gray suggests in the letter I quoted in my last lecture, but regard music merely as a trade. His music is always pleasing, and often singularly vapid; indeed he seems to have created a fashion for little songs of rather self-conscious innocence. Some of them will be familiar to you all, though you may never have seen an opera of Paisiello on the stage; Beethoven and others wrote variations on them, and most of us have had to learn them as pianoforte pieces in our childhood. Paisiello was fluent and accomplished, with a certain sense of humour too – that is, he could write the usual effective patter songs for the bass buffo. But he was not on the same intellectual level as his librettist Casti, who, whatever his morals may have been, was certainly a man of real wit and originality. Casti is the creator of an entirely new type of comic opera – the *dramma eroicomico*.[2] The essential idea of this heroic-comic drama was to take some historic character of universal fame, and present him as completely laughable. Casti in fact bears

[1] These extended forms, common in Italy, are not typical of Gluck's French operas.
[2] This is an example of the 'absorption of new material' cited by Einstein as characteristic of Romanticism: see p. 10.

considerable resemblance to W. S. Gilbert, and he ought to have found composers of the type of Offenbach.

His first heroic comedy, *Il re Teodoro in Venezia*, has an actual historic personage for its hero – Theodore Baron Neuhoff, who in 1736 was made King of Corsica. He came of a noble German family and was born at Metz in 1696; his parents were much reduced in circumstances, but he was eventually sent as a page to the French Court, and after that had a very adventurous life. Corsica at that time belonged to the republic of Genoa, but the inhabitants revolted against the Genoese, and Theodore got himself elected their King. He managed to carry on this situation for some time by obtaining war-supplies on credit from various foreign governments, but eventually he was obliged to fly to England, where he soon got into debt and was imprisoned.[3] Casti makes no pretence of historical accuracy in his libretto, but invents what episodes he likes. He shows us Theodore staying at an inn in Venice, in strict incognito under the name of Count Alberto, accompanied by his faithful prime minister Gafforio, who is also a historical character. Another visitor to Venice, also incognito, is the deposed Sultan of Turkey, Achmet, and the misfortunes of these two needy adventurers are extremely amusing.

In the following year Casti wrote a libretto for Salieri, *La grotta di Trofonio*. This is in the same sort of literary style, although Trophonius, the central figure, is a purely imaginary character.[4] The play is like a play for marionettes; Casti makes no pretence of treating his characters like real people – they are simply absurd caricatures. Trophonius is a magician, who lives in a cave or grotto infested with spirits. The cave has a magical effect on all who enter and pass through it, for it has two entrances or exits; the effect of this passage is to change the entire temperament and character of the person in question, but he can be restored to

[3] He obtained his release by mortgaging his kingdom. He died in a Soho lodging-house and was buried in St Anne's churchyard off Shaftesbury Avenue, where he has a memorial tablet with a neatly-turned epitaph by Horace Walpole. In Spain he married (and soon deserted) the daughter of an Irish earl who was lady-in-waiting to the Queen; his son by her shot himself in Westminster Abbey in 1797. Theodore's birth is variously dated between 1686 and 1696.

[4] In Greek legend Trophonius, one of the architects of the temple of Apollo at Delphi, after his death operated an oracle in a cave near Lebadia in Boeotia.

his original character by going through the cave again in the reverse direction. The cave is visited by a father with two daughters; one girl is worldly and frivolous, the other is what used to be called a bluestocking. Each young lady has a suitor of corresponding character; it can be imagined what complications arise when a visit to the cave changes the characters of the young ladies, and eventually those of the young gentlemen too. But it is not this chain of misunderstandings which makes the opera interesting for us now: all that belongs to the spirit of old-fashioned *opera buffa*. There is however something new about the character of Trophonius, although he is obviously descended from Rousseau's *Devin du village*. Rousseau's village sorcerer makes great play with his magic words and gestures, but no spirits appear at his command. Trophonius, on the other hand, is no less genuine a wizard than Mr John Wellington Wells in Gilbert's operetta *The Sorcerer*; he invokes the spirits, and the spirits actually reply and sing a chorus. Here, I think we may say, is a beginning of real Romanticism. The old Classical opera had often shown scenes of magical incantations; Medea, Armida and Alcina were well-known operatic figures long before even Handel. And the old Italian composers equally saw how amusing it was to make a comic character go through a parody of the incantation scene. But in the older operas the scenes of magic belonged naturally to the world in which the drama took place, if they were serious; and when they were comic, nothing happened as the result of all the mock incantations. In Casti's play, however, magic is mixed up with everyday occurrences, as it is in the tales of Hoffmann, and in a great many fairly modern English stories, such as Dickens' *Christmas Carol*, or some of F. Anstey's novels. When we consider Salieri's music to this scene, it is difficult to say whether the music is Romantic or not. Its actual technique is much the same as Gluck's; I am inclined to think that its apparent Romanticism comes from its position, in contrast to the frankly comic scenes of the ordinary human characters. We cannot call *La grotta di Trofonio* a Romantic opera, but it has at any rate this Romantic moment.

It is curious to note that in this same year 1785 another opera with the same title was produced at Naples. The music was by Casti's former friend and collaborator Paisiello; but on this occasion he availed himself of a different librettist, presumably

37

a Neapolitan, G. Palomba. Palomba admitted that he borrowed one or two numbers from Casti, but on the whole the opera is a different work, though based on the same plot. Paisiello has not the least feeling for romance or mystery, and he gives us nothing at all to correspond with the invocation of the spirits. The whole score is in fact a very dull and stupid affair.

The next year, 1786, was the year of Mozart's *Le nozze di Figaro.* Salieri was in Paris, where his new opera *Les Horaces* was a hopeless failure, in spite of the efforts of Marie Antoinette herself to secure its success. It was followed in 1787 by *Tarare*, for which the libretto had been written by Beaumarchais. It would be interesting to know whether Beaumarchais was acquainted with Casti's *Re Teodoro* at the time when he wrote *Tarare.* According to Mosel's life of Salieri, published within a few years of his death, both these French librettos, *Les Horaces* and *Tarare*, were given to Salieri by the management of the Opéra after the production of *Les Danaides*, before he left for Vienna. It is further stated that Beaumarchais offered *Tarare* first to Gluck, and that Gluck declined it on account of his failing health. If so, perhaps Salieri was instructed to offer the libretto to Gluck when he took it home with him. In any case, there is evidence that Salieri corresponded with Beaumarchais from Vienna about it, and suggested alterations, which Beaumarchais accepted with great willingness. It is possible that Salieri may have told Beaumarchais something about Casti's *Teodoro* in these letters, but the text of them is not extant.

Beaumarchais himself gives a very interesting explanation of how he came to choose the subject of *Tarare.* An opera, he says in his introduction, is neither a tragedy nor a comedy, but something of both. The style of tragedy, he thinks, is too severe; comedy offers too little scope for the passions, and its musical expression would often be wanting in *noblesse.* He is of the opinion that historical subjects would be less successful than purely imaginary ones; but he is suspicious of *sujets de pure féerie*, in which the marvellous is always impossible. He classes them with mythological subjects, in which the dénouement is brought about by the wave of a wand or by a *deus ex machina*; all these things leave him too cold. He therefore looks for an environment which is somewhere between the historical and the fantastic, and finds it in the East, where despotism and slavery are intermingled, where passion can be ferocious, and the general disorder can stimulate the poet's imagination; 'il imprime un trouble à l'esprit qui dispose aux *étrangetés* (selon l'expression de Montaigne)'. Here, certainly, we have a beginning of Romanticism: the words *désordre* and *étrangeté* are evidence enough. The real subject of this opera, he says, is *the dignity of man*. The scene is laid at Ormuz, near the Persian Gulf, where Atar, a man of thoroughly abominable character, rules as absolute despot. In contrast to him we have Tarare, the real hero, a simple soldier, virtuous and brave, adored by the people, in spite of a name which Beaumarchais says he chose on purpose, because it has ridiculous associations for the audience.

The rest of the characters help us to see more and more clearly how Romantic is the whole intention. There is a heroine, of course, Astasie, the wife of Tarare, virtuous and beautiful, snatched away by command of the tyrant to adorn his own harem. There is also the High Priest Arthenée, proud and ambitious of power. It is curious to note how in almost all operas the High Priest, if there is one, is always a most unpleasant character.[5] And as comic characters are essential to Romantic operas and plays, the tyrant Atar has a chief eunuch, Calpigi, who is expressly described as a European slave, a singer from some Italian church, a man of feeling and a cheerful soul. Calpigi is a delightful character; he is always amusing, and is a devoted friend to Tarare, who saved his life when he was first taken prisoner by the Persians. His name is obviously derived from the Greek.[6]

The most extraordinary part of this opera is the Prologue, in which a storm introduces the appearance of Nature and the Genius of Fire; they summon unborn souls from the void, and question them before they are sent to earth as human beings. They see the souls of Atar and Tarare: in this state they are utterly colourless, without any sort of feeling or desire. The printed version of the play, in the collected works of Beaumarchais (1821), is a little different from that in the engraved score; for in this the shade of Astasie is summoned up, and she at any rate admits to having a desire to be loved. All this Prologue is

---

[5] Sarastro is an obvious exception; and the priest in Berton's *Montano et Stéphanie* (1799) was too sympathetic for the authorities, who promptly censored the text.

[6] Presumably from καλλίπυγος, 'with beautiful buttocks'; but the etymology seems dubious.

very mysterious, and Salieri has brought out the atmosphere of mystery very effectively, although his introductory storm is not very terrifying. Salieri, like many other composers of his day, Gluck included, has very little idea of inventing descriptive figures; whenever he wants to paint a storm or any form of violent motion, he can seldom think of anything except scales running up and down in semiquavers.

Another European character in this opera is the soubrette, who is called Spinetta; she is a singer from Naples, and the wife of Calpigi, whom she persistently ill-treats. All these characters seem familiar to us; they remind us of Constanze and Blonde, Belmonte and Pedrillo in *Die Entführung*, or Reiza and Fatima, Huon and Sherasmin in Weber's *Oberon*. Beaumarchais was by no means the first librettist to hit on an oriental subject. There is however this peculiarity about *Tarare*, that its chief characters all belong to the East: there is no making the hero and heroine European, as in *Oberon* and *Die Entführung*. But we discover casually in the course of the play that Tarare himself is a Christian, though how he and his followers come to be so is never explained, and he never alludes to the matter himself: it is only mentioned disparagingly by Arthenée. The High Priest reveals himself as actually more bloodthirsty in principle than the tyrant Atar: in fact he instructs Atar on principles of government, and there are a few lines curiously appropriate to the conditions in certain countries to-day:

> Tant qu'ils s'accordent bien ensemble,
> Que l'esclave ainsi garrotté,
> Souffre, obéit, et croit, et tremble,
> Le pouvoir est en sûreté.

(*Ils* in line 1 refers to Brama and Soudan, the gods.)

One thing that we notice at once on reading this play is the drastic simplification of character. If one were to see the opera performed with Salieri's music on the stage, one might easily forget this; the music would control our feelings and probably divert our thoughts. Besides, the work is an opera, and if we have seen a great many operas, we accept this simplification of character as one of the ordinary conditions. We expect opera to be what we call *melodramatic*, forgetting, perhaps, that *melodramma* is the old-established classical Italian name for 'opera' and that the plays of the nineteenth century which were called melodramas derived their name from the fact that they began as something very like operas. They took over, in fact, the operatic psychology. It was not necessary to draw characters in detail in the book of words, because that would only get in the way of the composer; and it was the composer's business to give them subtlety of expression.

Tarare met with an enormous success in Paris, and Salieri, on returning to Vienna, commissioned Lorenzo Da Ponte to translate it into Italian for performance at the Imperial Opera. Da Ponte soon found that to translate it was impossible. How interesting it would be if we could know exactly what passed between poet and composer during the reconstruction of *Tarare*, in the way that we can follow the mentalities of Hofmannsthal and Richard Strauss in their published correspondence! The opera was not translated: it was entirely reconstructed. In the first place the mystical Prologue was done away with altogether: one can well imagine that the Viennese censorship would have regarded it with suspicion. The Revolution had not yet broken out in France, but things had already gone far enough for Vienna to be extremely nervous. Da Ponte's words are fairly harmless; and if the opera turned on the overthrow of a tyrant, it at any rate ended with a triumph for Christian forces, though the religious element is kept very much in the background. Probably Da Ponte was much more concerned to remodel the opera according to more Italian traditions. For one thing, it was reduced to four acts, like Mozart's *Figaro*; both the French originals having been in five, according to French custom. The details of the plot were changed too, although its main outline is the same.

The story begins, in the Italian version, with a short duet for Atar[7] and his wife Aspasia, interrupted by the outbreak of a fire, with a shrieking chorus that anticipates that of Mozart's *La clemenza di Tito*. In the confusion Aspasia is lost and Atar is left in despair. In the second act we are introduced to the tyrannical king Axur, and his chief eunuch Biscroma, who sing a comic duet. Axur has any number of wives, whereas Atar has only one; but polygamy apparently does not make for happiness, and Axur covets Aspasia, and for this reason has ordered Atar's house to be set on fire and his wife carried off. She is brought in at this moment, with a chorus of slaves; she is naturally much

[7] Note the change of names: Atar, formerly the tyrant, is now the hero. (E.J.D.)

embarrassed, and all Axur can do is to send her in to his harem. Atar now arrives, to claim reparation for the fire and the loss of his wife, whom he supposes to have been carried off by pirates. Axur pretends to be sympathetic and offers him wives in plenty, but he declines them; Axur also mentions that he has just acquired a new lady who at present resists his passion – her name is Irza, which Beaumarchais tells us means the flower of all flowers. Finally Axur agrees to fit out Atar with a naval expedition to find and rescue Aspasia; he informs the audience aside that Atar will certainly never come back again.

In Act III Axur receives the High Priest Arteneo, who informs him that a dangerous war is in prospect. Axur suggests that Altamor, the son of the priest, should be commander-in-chief; Arteneo, rather surprised, asks why he does not name Atar, the popular hero. 'Atar is dead' says the King; Arteneo warns him that he may lose his crown and his life too, if the people find out that he has had Atar assassinated. Next comes a scene in which Biscroma tells Atar that Aspasia has not been captured by pirates, but is a prisoner in the harem under the name of Irza. Atar sings an aria, marked 'con forza concentrata' – this is significant, as it shows that Salieri was aiming at a more French intensity of style than the Italians generally cared for. The scene changes to a temple, where Arteneo instructs a boy who is to be inspired by the god and pronounce the name of the chosen general; he hints to him that Altamor would be an appropriate name. A very Romantic march opens the ceremony; the boy, when he has to speak, blurts out the name of Atar, which the chorus instantly take up with immense energy. This is a most dramatic moment. The High Priest does his best to protest and suggest obstacles, but the people become more and more insistent, and finally Atar is acclaimed with a march tune that seems to look forward to the marches of *Norma* and *Aida*.

Act IV takes place in the seraglio, illuminated for an entertainment. There is an amusing instrumental prelude for strings, rather suggesting Monostatos when he is approaching Pamina asleep. Axur and Biscroma have another comic duet, quite in the manner of Cimarosa. The French version of the opera had a great ballet at this point; the Italian version substitutes a comic terzetto in Venetian dialect for Smeraldina, Arlecchino and Brighella; this irruption of the Venetian masks into the East reminds us of the fairy plays of Carlo Gozzi. Biscroma then sings a ballad to the guitar, telling the story of his own life, and how he was rescued by Atar – Atar! the very sound of his name makes Axur furious and Aspasia gives a piercing shriek on a high note. There is a scene of confusion, with a long instrumental episode, dying down to a *pianissimo*, very like the music of Don Giovanni's disappearance. Atar has invaded the harem by a ladder, in disguise. He is left alone on the stage with Biscroma, who hastily disguises him as a negro. Axur is furious because Aspasia still refuses his advances, and orders the negro to be dressed up in royal robes and sent to ravish Aspasia by force. Atar at this point has what I believe is the earliest example of the operatic *preghiera* which was so frequent a feature of later operas – a prayer, definitely addressed to the Christian Divinity. This is a notable step towards the Romantic style.

Aspasia is in great distress, but agrees that Fiametta, her maid, shall change clothes with her and receive the negro in her place. Atar enters, and betrays himself; at that moment soldiers come in to carry out a new order of the capricious Axur – they are to kill the supposed negro. Atar reveals himself, and the officer decides that they cannot take the risk of killing him, now that they know who he is. The opera ends with a popular rising, which leads Axur to commit suicide; Atar and Aspasia are called to the throne by popular vote.

Da Ponte, at the time when he was adapting this opera for Salieri, was working for two other composers. He was writing *L'arbore di Diana* (which he considered his best libretto) for Vicente Martín y Soler, and *Don Giovanni* for Mozart. That was probably the reason why he took so much of *Don Giovanni* from an older libretto by Bertati; but it must be remembered that in those days there was no protection of librettos by copyright, and every librettist was just as unscrupulous in adaptation. *Don Giovanni* came out at Prague in the autumn of 1787; perhaps it was in order to destroy the impression of that work that Salieri produced *Axur* at Prague in 1788. *Axur* had plenty of success and was given at Vienna and Pressburg as well. It also went to Germany and to London; there are several German translations of it.

In this same year, 1788, Salieri composed another opera, which was never performed at all – a most unusual thing for a composer who had just reached the height of a very successful career. This opera was called *Cublai*, and was another of the heroico-comical operas of Casti – on the subject of Kubla Khan. There can be little doubt that it was written in deliberate imitation of *Axur*, and Casti probably wanted to show that he could be more amusing than Da Ponte and more satirical than Beaumarchais. Unfortunately the libretto was too satirical for the Viennese authorities, and the opera was forbidden altogether. One can imagine their feelings when Posega, the High Priest and the tutor of Kubla's idiot son Lipi, admits that he has purposely educated him to imbecility in order to establish a theocracy. Kubla intends to marry this son of his to Alzima, an Indian princess, who is in love with Timur. Hence the fury of the High Priest:

Shall it be in vain that I have cultivated in this idiot boy foolishness, laziness, ignorance, veneration for the gods and for the priests, in order that he may remain celibate, and thus, when he ascends the throne, allow the Mogol Empire to become subject to the supreme sacerdotal authority? His marriage might destroy these vast ideas.

As in Beaumarchais's play, there are two Europeans in the cast: Memma, an Italian woman of easy morals, a favourite of Kubla, and her husband Bozzone, who supplies him secretly with wine, which he consumes incognito at Bozzone's house. He tells Timur frankly that Posega, the priest, is an impostor.

Much fun is made of the oriental desire to be European; and all the ridiculous side of European court life is in this way satirized. Memma persuades the Khan that he must have a master of ceremonies, but the unfortunate Orcano, who is given this post, finds that it merely makes him the laughing-stock of everybody, Kubla included. Memma also arranges a 'gala di corte' in the European manner, which gives the author a good opportunity for caricaturing the ceremonial etiquette of the court of Vienna.[8]

There is one more of Salieri's numerous operas which deserves mention here, and that is his *Falstaff*, performed at Vienna in 1799. It is not the first operatic treatment of Shakespeare, or the first opera on the subject of Falstaff; there had been earlier French operas based on *The Merry Wives of Windsor*.[9] It is curious

[8] Compare Gilbert in *Utopia Limited*. (E.J.D.)
[9] Papavoine's *Le Vieux Coquet, ou les deux amies* (Paris, 1761) and Philidor's *Herne le chasseur* (composed 1773); also P. Ritter's *Die lustigen Weiber* (Mannheim, 1794) and Dittersdorf's *Die lustigen Weiber von Windsor und der dicke Hans* (Öls, 1796).

to note that it bears many resemblances to Boito's more famous libretto, written for Verdi. Boito was a man of wide reading and great learning, and it is quite possible that he studied this libretto of De Franceschi when planning his own version. Salieri's opera is in no way Romantic, though very amusing. The first scene begins with a dance in the house of Slender, who is substituted for the husband of Mistress Page. The idea is obviously imitated from *Don Giovanni*: Salieri explains in his own manuscript notes that when the curtain rises a dance is just over, and refreshments are being handed round. This is exactly the situation at the beginning of the ballroom scene in Mozart's opera. But Salieri, carrying another idea of Mozart's still further, makes his whole overture into a succession of *contre-danses*, which are very attractive and cheerful, providing an admirably spirited introduction to the opera.

It is only at rare moments that Salieri can be considered Romantic, but he is a composer of considerable importance in the history of opera, because he links together the French and Italian tendencies of his age, together with a certain amount of Viennese instrumental influence. That instrumental style of Vienna, which is often claimed as German, is really a mixture of Italian popular music with Slavonic instrumental virtuosity. Practically all the great instrumentalists of the time, and many of the symphonic composers, were Slavs, either from Bohemia or from Croatia. Even in the previous generations the instrumental music played in Germany had been mainly French (school of Lully), and to a slight degree English too.

In considering the history of Romantic music we must not expect to see a definite Romantic style emerging all at once; we can only watch the various tributary streams from different countries which eventually combined to form the Romantic Opera. Italy supplied the vocal element: the charm of melody, the expressive and emotional values of pure singing. Italy, too – Naples, in fact – was the home of the buffo and the soubrette: the comic bass and the light and frivolous soprano. It is one of the most persistent characteristics of Romanticism that the comic element always came into its plays, even its tragedies. Shakespeare may have been the ancestor whom the historians of literature prefer to claim for the comic element, but the musician knows quite well that this was present, in the form of the Comedy of Masks, in the older Italian theatre, and that from this source it found its way into seventeenth-century Venetian opera, and from there into the Neapolitan opera of the eighteenth. There exists still, or existed until recently, a type of Italian tragi-comedian, almost invariably Neapolitan, popular in Italy, and I believe in the United States also, who is Romantic and melodramatic, but at the same time fundamentally comic in the broad old-fashioned way. He is a relic of the old Italian opera.

France supplied a more literary element. Romantic ideas came originally from England, and were part of the French Anglomania of the later eighteenth century. The desire for energy of declamation comes from the French side, and this energy of spoken declamation found musical expression too, not so much in recitative as in the declamatory song, and most of all in the declamatory and rhetorical treatment of choral and orchestral music.

A characteristic feature of music at this time – the third quarter of the eighteenth century – is the increasing interest in the orchestra, and in the orchestral treatment of music generally.[10] Orchestral music derived most of its impulse from the Slav violinists; but in all countries, even in Italy, we can note a growing tendency to the construction of long movements, mostly in vertical harmony, with the greatest possible emphasis on the alternation of tonic and dominant. We are apt to think of this style – a style well illustrated in the symphonies of Mozart – as essentially formal and classical, the very antithesis of all that is Romantic. The Romantics had eventually to get rid of it; but they could not get rid of it entirely, and they could never have achieved their own Romantic technique without it.

[10] For important aspects of this development see David Charlton, 'Orchestra and Image in the later Eighteenth Century', *PRMA* cii (1975/6), in the press.

4

THE SCHOOL OF PARIS – I

We must turn our attention now to the works of the French school during the Revolution and the Napoleonic period. Three composers stand out as pre-eminent – Cherubini, Méhul and Le Sueur. It might seem obvious that a separate lecture should be devoted to each of these three, but their joint output as a whole is so remarkably unified in style and tendency that I have thought it better to treat of them all together, taking their most important operas more or less in chronological order.

The first of these three musicians was not a Frenchman, but an Italian, with an Italian training. Cherubini is remembered at the present day mainly as a dry pedant who wrote a treatise (which he did not write) on counterpoint and fugue. He was in reality one of the most extraordinary personalities in the history of music – extraordinary in two ways: first, that it is difficult to understand how he arrived at his very individual style and his astonishing technical skill, secondly, because the music of his maturity, although now almost totally forgotten, had the most powerful formative influence on Beethoven, Schubert, Weber and Mendelssohn.

Born at Florence in 1760, he became a pupil of Giuseppe Sarti. Sarti is remembered now only by the air from one of his comic operas which is quoted by Mozart in the supper scene of *Don Giovanni*. Yet Sarti had an international reputation: he visited Paris, London, Copenhagen, and St Petersburg, and he died in Berlin. Wherever he went he had been honoured and admired. He was not only a successful composer of operas, but a musician of learning as well, and it was this learned outlook on music that he communicated to his devoted pupil Cherubini. Sarti was a student of Palestrina, and insisted on Cherubini learning to compose church music in the style of the strictest counterpoint. This was not unusual in those days for composers who wished to devote themselves to the church; but young musicians in the eighteenth century seem generally to have had much the same aversion as those of to-day for contrapuntal studies, and most of them wanted to lose no time in becoming known as composers of opera.[1]

Cherubini's early operas were regarded as unduly serious in style; we are reminded of the youthful Handel, who when he first arrived in Hamburg was laughed at for his old-fashioned cantatas and his ignorance of the modern operatic manner. When Cherubini was twenty-four he went to London, with an engagement secured for him by Sarti; but his career there was only moderately distinguished.[2] He became known in society, and he wrote a great many arias for insertion in other people's operas, as was the custom of the time; but he produced nothing of permanent importance. From London he went in July 1786 to Paris, which from that moment became his home.[3] It was there that he heard a symphony of Haydn for the first time, and he immediately began to study Haydn's symphonies with care. If this is true, it is a very interesting piece of information. To what extent music circulated internationally in those days it is difficult to say; certain works were printed and must have been fairly easily accessible, at any rate in large centres, but others – all the Italian operas, for instance – remained in manuscript, and were jealously guarded, as there was no regular copyright to protect them.[4] Cherubini about the age of 27 made his first acquaintance with Haydn's symphonies, and it seems extremely probable that he knew even less of the works of Mozart. Haydn is one of the few composers who became, as one might say, a classic in his own life-time, as it used to be said of Saint-Saëns; but Mozart and Beethoven certainly were not classics until after they were dead.

[1] Play march of Sarti. (E.J.D.) Perhaps from *Giulio Sabino* (III. 5), quoted by Ernst Bücken, *Der heroische Stil in der Oper* (Leipzig, 1924), 56–7.

[2] For Cherubini's London career, see anon., 'Cherubini in England', *MT*, xlix (1908), 159–62, and Margery S. Selden, 'Cherubini and England', *MQ*, lx (1974), 421–34.

[3] He was employed as an assistant to Viotti at the Théâtre de Monsieur (later Feydeau), opened in January 1789, where he directed Italian operas and composed additional music for those of others. See G. Confalonieri, *Prigionia di un artista: il romanzo di Luigi Cherubini* (Milan, 1948), I, 109ff.

[4] For the dissemination of music, manuscript and printed, at this period, see Barry Brook, 'Piracy and Panacea in Music-Printing of the Eighteenth Century', *PRMA* cii (1975/6), in press. Many French and some German operas were printed, as well as a great deal of instrumental music. Cherubini, who was welcomed in Paris society, must have had access to ample material.

And yet in the following year, 1788, Cherubini produced a French opera, *Démophoon*, which in its technical accomplishment is as masterly as anything of Mozart's. If any work ever deserved the epithet 'classical', it is *Démophoon*. It met with no success, although its classicality was in the manner of the period. Sacchini's famous *Oedipe à Colone* is much the same sort of thing – descended from the French operas of Gluck but with a more Italian style of melody. Sacchini had charm and tenderness, but little dramatic force. Cherubini, one might say, had more force, but less charm; on the other hand, *Démophoon* must be allowed to have an extraordinary sense of beauty and dignity.

To a modern reader – and one is obliged to form one's judgments on Cherubini by reading him, for there is no chance of hearing any of his operas on the stage,[5] except for a rare performance of *Les Deux Journées* – there is nearly always something cold-blooded about Cherubini's music. I feel convinced that this judgment must be a false one, for it cannot have won the enthusiastic admiration of Beethoven and Weber unless it had genuinely vital qualities. *Démophoon*, like Mozart's *Idomeneo*, is technically far more accomplished than anything of Gluck's, and its melodies have much more charm and grace. If it seems cold-blooded to us, it may be just because every movement of it is so exquisitely finished. The music is formal, because the drama (adapted from an older libretto by Metastasio) is formal;[6] it belongs to a convention very remote from our own conceptions of drama. There certainly is not one bar in it that could be regarded as Romantic. For this reason it ought not to come within the scope of these lectures; but I mention it, and describe it, because it is the starting-point of Cherubini's career in Paris, and because it makes his later Romanticism all the more startling by contrast.

If we compare *Démophoon* with one of the serious operas of Sarti, such as *Giulio Sabino*, we notice generally a much more symphonic treatment of the orchestra, and a far greater employment of the chorus. In the older Italian operas, serious or comic,

---

5 This is no longer true. Several of Cherubini's operas have been staged in more than one country since the 1939–45 war.
6 But the librettist, J. F. Marmontel, introduced developments that would be unthinkable in Metastasio; the lover-victims defy an oracle and use physical force to gain their ends. See G. Knepler, 'Die Technik der sinfonischen Durchführung in der französischen Revolutionsoper', *BMw* i (1959), 4–22.

the choruses are as a rule negligible. Audiences probably did not want them, and managers did not want to have to pay for them. Chorus-singers in those days, especially in Italy, never learned their parts from notes; even in France there were few who could read at sight, and they were expected to acquire their music by ear. This naturally made elaborate choruses impossible. But in France there had been a tradition of choral singing in opera ever since the days of Lully, and we shall find that in all French operas, comic as well as serious, the chorus plays a considerable part.

While we are on the subject of Cherubini and Classical opera, we may take the opportunity of considering the problem of musical form in opera. According to Fétis, the analysis of musical forms, which is so indispensable a feature of modern composition-teaching, was not practised at all in the eighteenth century; Fétis was probably stating the truth, for as far as my knowledge of the older treatises goes, no explanation was ever given of such things as concerto and sonata form and so forth. What was important in those days was fugue; this was because in the previous century fugue, or as we should now probably say, *fugato,* was the normal method of composing *any* serious piece of music. The teaching of fugue therefore survived, as teaching methods in many subjects do, long after it had ceased to be of practical utility. When Cherubini was a student, fugue had come to be regarded mainly as a form for sacred music, and Albrechtsberger's method of teaching shows that it was a severely practical method of composing orthodox church music; the first necessity about a fugue for church purposes being that it should *not be too long.* Rameau, like Handel, frequently used fugal methods in his choruses, but by the time of Cherubini fugal imitations were not much in fashion. Arias, from the first, had been written in an elementary kind of binary form, even *da capo* arias – for the first part, the part which is repeated, is in itself binary. Choruses, on the other hand, were almost always in dance forms, because in the operas of Lully and Rameau the chorus was always closely associated with the ballet – in fact the ballet very often danced to the music of the choruses. All dance-forms are binary too, but on more primitive lines. The dance inevitably requires regular periods of eight bars. In the operas of Rameau and Gluck both the vocal parts and the dance music are on a certain level of dignity which gives the whole opera a classical unity of style. We shall soon see how in the

Romantic operas, or in any which show the beginnings of Romanticism, the dances and choruses stand out from the arias by a sharp contrast of style, a contrast due to differences of form and rhythm. Local colour of various kinds begins to play an important part,[7] and we shall find that local colour is to a large extent applied in terms of the ballet, which means that it is applied also to the chorus. The solo portions of the opera have to deal almost exclusively with the expression of emotions, so that all that the Romantics can do with these is to exaggerate them; their fundamental style remains the same. We may expect to find then that in Romantic operas the solo parts will be more developed and more intense in expression than they were in Classical operas, but on the other hand the choruses will tend to lose in dignity, and to become more definitely picturesque – that is, more like ballet-dances of sailors, gipsies, etc, than expressions of communal feeling, as for instance in the choruses of Mozart's *Idomeneo*.

This analysis of form may seem dry and academic, but it has a distinct bearing on emotional expression in opera. Cherubini and the French composers had certainly learned the general outline of extended binary form, but music in general was reaching a period when this was becoming a tyranny. It was in his treatment of form that Mozart invariably showed his marvellous technical mastery of the ingenuities of expression. Any ensemble movement of Mozart, any trio or quartet in the operas, will be in some sort of binary form, first subject in the tonic, second subject in the dominant, stop, first subject starting in the dominant and made to lead back to the second subject in the tonic. Mozart never writes in this form without making the third quarter of the piece (where the first subject starts from the dominant) the most emotional and dramatic part, nor without taking care that the second subject, when it returns in the tonic, shall be more dramatic and more vocally effective than it was on its first appearance in the dominant. Cherubini in *Démophoon* manages this very skilfully; but he has not the conciseness of Mozart. Mozart is often supposed to be very formal, and we laugh to-day at his eighteenth-century mannerisms; but we have only to

[7] Gluck, and Grétry in his Académie operas, had introduced local colour in the form of 'characteristic' and national dances, for example those of the Scythians in *Iphigénie en Tauride*.

compare him with Cimarosa (who is about the best of his rivals in comic opera) to see how very thinly Cimarosa's inspiration is spread. One cannot help being reminded (and often with Cherubini too) of an economical person who is buttering bread and determined to make the smallest amount of butter go the furthest possible way. Modern audiences delight in Mozart and are bored with Cimarosa; but in their own day the verdict was reversed. It is quite certain that audiences of about 1790 liked their music spread thin.

We cannot just leave the matter at that. We must, as historical investigators, try to think ourselves into the feeling of those times, and discover why Cherubini's audiences were so much thrilled by music which leaves us so cold.[8] One cause must have been the mere sonority of it all, the masses of vocal and instrumental sound. The taste for ensemble movements and for long choruses was definitely French. The Italians held out against it as long as they could, as some of them held out too for the soprano hero, but there was a certain group of Italians who surrendered to the French and apparently acquired popularity by doing so.

The Revolution made a serious break in Cherubini's activities, and nearly cost him his life, for he was known to be friendly with members of the aristocracy. He was enrolled in the National Guard, which entailed the custody of prisoners and the escorting of them to the scaffold. How long this continued is not certain; he was, at any rate until 1792, held to his contract at the Théâtre Feydeau, for which he had undertaken to write two operas. The first of these, *Lodoiska*, on a libretto by C. F. Fillette Loraux, came out in 1791.

Lodoiska shows at once the change of mood caused by the Revolution. Technically it is a French *opéra-comique*; it had spoken dialogue instead of recitative, except in certain highly emotionalized moments. The French, when they started comic operas earlier in the century, had never admitted the characteristic Italian *recitativo secco*. Their idea of comic opera was what they called it for some generations – *comédie mêlée d'ariettes*, comedy mixed with little songs; it was in this way much nearer in spirit to the English ballad opera. But in the course of time the *ariettes* had grown longer and more important. Another

---

[8] Cherubini's popularity in France, never sensational, was confined to the last decade of the century; his operas after 1800 were all failures.

noticeable feature of the *opéra-comique* is its ever increasing tendency to employ ensembles in the course of the work. There was a fundamental difference on this point between the French outlook and the Italian. The Italian theory was that all arias were static in their emotion;[9] the dramatic conflict, whatever it might be, was carried on in the recitative, and the aria merely expressed the emotional result. The singer informed the audience that he was like a ship on a stormy sea without a rudder, and then left the stage. A duet was only possible when the two singers were more or less in agreement. In the ensembles of perplexity, the Scarlattian *arie a quattro*, the four characters might be in four quite different situations as far as their private affairs went, but they were at least agreed on one point – that they were in despair and did not know what to do. It will be seen that, if this theory is accepted, there can be no great objection to the formal *da capo* aria; the second section does not contradict or even develop the emotion expressed in the first; it merely explains it, so that a return to the first part (which is always more definitely lyrical and purely musical) was the most satisfactory way of ending the song. The proof that this was felt to be the case lies in the fact that when the later composers – Mozart, for example – decided to abandon the old *da capo*, they found that it was not enough, as a rule, just to keep the first section, even when its binary form became considerably lengthened and extended; they felt it necessary to add some sort of a coda. This coda takes various forms; sometimes it is simply an ordinary coda, part of the same movement, repeating very probably the well-known cadence that we generally call the 'Rossini' cadence. Italian composers often added one coda after another – this is typical of Verdi in his earlier period. But another way of making up for the lost *da capo* was to add a coda movement in a quicker tempo. This ultimately developed into the convention known as cavatina–cabaletta – the cavatina being on the slow and quiet side, the cabaletta quick and brilliant. In later generations the form underwent many modifications; we find cases where the cabaletta becomes the main movement, and the cavatina is hardly more than a slow introduction. The reason why the brilliant cabaletta

---

[9] This does not apply to comic opera after about 1760. Even in *opera seria* there are exceptions to some of the generalizations in this paragraph, notably in Handel.

was found necessary was because in the old days the singer always sang the *da capo* with new variations, so as to make the most brilliant possible finish before his exit.

The French took no notice of these Italian rules. They introduced duets, trios and ensembles wherever they liked, and they were quite capable of giving a character a song after which he did not leave the stage but remained for further conversation and another song, or it might be a duet. But about the period which we are considering a difficulty arose. The musical numbers became longer and longer. No sense of proportion seems ever to have been maintained between the length of the musical numbers and the length of spoken dialogue in between, which was sometimes in prose and sometimes in verse. Moreover, the composers complicated matters by becoming more definitely dramatic in their duets and ensembles. The poets provided words in which the drama was carried a step further; information was given, opinions were exchanged on the stage. That in a certain way was a great step in advance; but the composers none the less felt themselves obliged to maintain something like the conventional sonata form, so that in the completed movement a great deal of this dramatic conversation has to be sung twice over. And the longer all this business becomes, the more urgent is the musical need for a symphonic coda. Mozart's little formalities are a mere nothing compared to the interminable codas of the French, in which tonic and dominant harmony alternate for pages and pages, with the characters repeating some unimportant words, all together in block harmony, so as to end with a grand *fortissimo*.[10]

At the end of an entire opera, or even at the end of an act, this is not so unreasonable. Mozart does it always. It is a necessary piece of operatic business, in order to stimulate the applause of the audience. As far as I can ascertain, those noisy symphonic codas of reiterated tonic and dominant chords, which are the characteristic feature of all 'classical' music, whether symphonies or operas, made their first appearance in the Italian opera overtures, called *sinfonia*, which by being played separately at concerts led to the adoption of the form and the name as a regular type of pure concert music. It was a convenient way of

[10] This impression is strengthened by the higher ratio of ensembles to solos in French *opéra-comique* of this period.

employing the orchestral players to fulfil the duties of a *claque*. It is a device which is not to be found, at least not in any very noticeable degree, in the music of the Bach–Handel period, still less in that of the seventeenth century. As long as music, and opera too, was mainly in the hands of princes and aristocratic patrons, a *claque* was quite unnecessary; it is only when opera becomes a thoroughly commercial business that popular applause is a definite factor in the commercial valuation of a singer or a composer.

If we take the trouble to measure the length of some of these movements in *Lodoiska* and compare them with a few in *Don Giovanni*, we shall find that the actual number of bars in each is not very different. The real fact of the matter is that Cherubini's melodic inspiration is thin as compared with Mozart's. Every now and then we come across phrases so Mozartian that we are almost compelled to imagine that Cherubini was acquainted with the score of *Don Giovanni*. The illusion is heightened if we read *Lodoiska* in the convenient form of the vocal score published by Peters with German words, for the translator has obviously noticed the resemblance between the situation in Act I and the beginning of *Die Zauberflöte*, and his translation is full of reminiscences of Tamino and Papageno.

The scene of the opera is laid in Poland, presumably in some remoter century. The third partition of Poland was yet to come, but the country was full of mystery and romance for Western audiences. The stage, in the first act, represents a forest. At the back there is an ancient castle, with a moat and a draw-bridge; the castle has a high tower which stands out towards the front of the stage. At the top of the tower there is a small window, protected by an iron grating. On the right and left are trees and rocks. That forest and castle had, as a matter of fact, been utilized before; they had no doubt served for Dalayrac's opera *Camille*, performed on March 19, 1791. Cherubini's *Lodoiska* came out on July 18, and another *Lodoiska*, by Rodolphe Kreutzer, the Kreutzer of the Kreutzer Sonata, followed on August 1. The same scenery and the same costumes served for both:[11] that was the regular custom of the stage in Paris. *Camille* is an opera to which I shall have occasion to return later.

[11] But *Camille* and Kreutzer's *Lodoiska* were produced at a different theatre, the Favart.

To continue the description of *Lodoiska*: when the curtain rises, it is night. Titzikan, a Tartar chief, is seen stealthily advancing, followed by a horde of Tartars. After an introductory number sung by Titzikan and the male chorus, during which they reconnoitre the situation, the chief explains, in spoken prose dialogue, that this is the castle of Baron Dourlinski. 'Cet homme, né féroce, fut de tout temps inutile à sa patrie, mais, vous le savez, funeste à nos contrées.' The Tartars are bent on obtaining vengeance for the crimes of Dourlinski, and Titzikan orders them to surround the castle and take prisoner anyone whom they may meet in the forest. But he warns them strictly that they are to respect the lives of casual travellers – 'the innocent must not suffer for the guilty, and you must never forget, my brave men, that one must on no account pursue one's own interests at the expense of justice and humanity!' Those noble words would no doubt have provoked thunders of applause from a French audience in 1791. But the worthy Tartar has no idea whatever, as he admits to his confidential friend, what form his vengeance is to take. The Tartar confidant suggests that they should catch the Baron when he goes out with only a small escort, especially as the escort might be bribed to turn against him; Titzikan is indignant at such an outrageous proposal, and at once sings an aria to the words

> Trionfons avec noblesse, devons tout à la valeur,
> La ruse est une faiblesse, elle flétrit le vengeur.

Titzikan is in fact Rousseau's noble savage, at his most noble. At this point he observes strangers approaching and discreetly retires. The two strangers are Count Floreski and his servant Varbel, who is carrying a small valise. Their horses have already been taken from them by Tartars, and they do not know what to do. Floreski is in search of his lady-love, Lodoiska. For political reasons, Lodoiska's father has refused to allow her to marry him, and has had her conveyed to some secret place. He has since died, and the secret of her captivity has died with him, so that Floreski has no idea where she is shut up. Varbel is the faithful and devoted servant, rather like Papageno in *Die Zauberflöte*; very much bored with all these adventures, but determined to stick to his master through thick and thin, and at times showing an ingenious and resourceful mind. The couple may be compared to Don Quixote and Sancho Panza; but for our purposes Varbel is recognizable at once as the typical Italian bass-buffo, and as soon as he begins to sing, Cherubini gives himself away as a former composer of Italian comic operas.

Titzikan re-enters with his faithful Tartar, and calls upon the two Poles to lay down their arms. Floreski is rather bad-tempered about it and refuses, challenging Titzikan to fight; after singing a quartet, they do so. Varbel drives the Tartar brigand into the wings, and Floreski disarms Titzikan, but spares his life, on which, as might be expected, they swear eternal friendship and sing another quartet, assisted by the chorus. The Tartars leave the stage, but Titzikan cannot depart without a final speech in prose, in which he incidentally mentions that the castle belongs to Dourlinski. Otherwise the speech is a mass of noble sentiments, so much so that even Floreski, after Titzikan has left the stage, remarks 'Quel étonnant langage!' By this time it is daylight, and as there is nothing else to do, Floreski and Varbel sit down to eat some breakfast, which they have brought with them. Varbel sings a sort of polonaise, quite in Papageno's manner, about the pleasures of eating, drinking and making love; Floreski follows it with a rather dull sentimental ditty about love alone. They then sing their two songs simultaneously and find that they combine in counterpoint, which perhaps accounts for the slight dullness of Floreski's air. We see here the beginning of a device which later on was much practised by Berlioz.[12]

The result of this duet is that somebody drops stones on them from the tower, and on one of the stones Floreski finds a few words written by Lodoiska, who has recognized him and begs him to deliver her, but at the same time to be prudent. Her voice is heard; she appears at the window in the tower, and at first she seems to be a very long way off. But as the trio goes on, she becomes more confidential in style, and warns them that it is no use their trying to storm the tower. Finally, in a more lively movement, she suggests that if Floreski will write her a letter, she can at midnight let down a string and draw it up. Varbel now has the happy idea that, as Lodoiska's father has died, they can pretend to be two persons sent by her mother to inform her of the sad news and ask for her return. They ring the bell of the castle; Altamoras, the captain of Dourlinski's guards, comes out and eventually consents to receive them. The act ends with a march

[12] Compare also César Franck's *Les Béatitudes* and Spohr's *Die Weihe der Töne*. (E.J.D.)

during which they are escorted by the guards into the castle, and the orchestra dies away in a *pianissimo* as the curtain falls.

The scene of the second act is a gallery in the castle with doors and arcades leading on the left to the guardroom and on the right to the fortress. In the middle is an equestrian statue, decorated with reliefs representing the tyranny of the Baron. Lodoiska is discovered in conversation with her old nurse, Lysinka. Altamoras explains that Lodoiska might be set free if she would consent to yield to the passion of Dourlinski. She refuses indignantly, with a very fine and expressive air. Enter the Baron, who presses his suit; Lodoiska from the first answers him with no attempt at courtesy. Since she says that she prefers imprisonment to the Baron's embraces, he orders her to be locked up in the most secret part of the tower, and to be deprived of the company of her nurse. This gives occasion for an ensemble, in which the nurse protests vigorously and struggles to follow Lodoiska but is dragged away by the guards. Dourlinski is the conventional stage tyrant, and his music, in this septet, is curiously like that of Pizarro in Beethoven's *Fidelio*. Beethoven has often been severely criticized for his failure to make Pizarro into a credible human being; we can now see plainly the character who served him as a model.

Dourlinski prepares to receive the mysterious strangers, who pass themselves off as two brothers, sent by Lodoiska's mother. Floreski makes rather a poor pretence, and Dourlinski is at once suspicious, and very reasonably so, because they have brought nothing in the shape of written credentials. However, on the advice of Altamoras (this is all a trio) he agrees to allow them to sleep the night in the castle. Varbel has been sent out of the room during this interview; he now comes back and warns Floreski that he has overheard Altamoras arranging that the two strangers are to be given a sleeping-draught in their wine at supper. He has no sooner made this communication than supper is brought in by three 'emissaries', as they are called in the score – just like the three genii in *Die Zauberflöte*. Mozart's opera was only just in process of being composed, hardly more than begun, at the time when Cherubini's was put on the stage, so that it is quite impossible that Cherubini could have known it. But I draw your attention to these amusing resemblances in order to point out how much, in the history of the musical theatre, is drawn from

common stage tradition. Writers of librettos never give themselves more trouble than is necessary. Floreski at once suggests
Florestan,[13] and Lodoiska Leonora; when Bouilly invented those
names for the opera that eventually became *Fidelio*, he must have
remembered this opera of Cherubini. The name of Altamoras,
too, reminds us of Altamor, the captain of the guard, or something like it, in Salieri's *Tarare*.

What exactly happens during the scene which now follows I
am unable to tell you, as the stage directions are not printed in
the score. The three emissaries – or, as the German version calls
them, officers – have brought a bottle of drugged wine, which
they place conspicuously in the middle of the table. They offer
Floreski a drink, which he refuses, on the grounds that he has
just had a meal outside. He is trying to gain time, and for this
purpose says he wants to write a letter; he writes it after Varbel
has provided pen and paper, and Varbel eventually tears it up.
Varbel, again like Papageno, seems desirous of starting on the
drink, which makes Floreski very nervous. The three villains do
not want him to drink by himself: it is part of their plan that the
two Poles shall both drink together, so as not to run the risk of
one discovering the plot by the collapse of the other. At this point
there is a longish stretch of instrumental music; Floreski appears
to be writing during this, and by some means or other Varbel
manages to change the bottles, so that the honest wine is poured
out for himself and Floreski, while the soporific is consumed by
the three villains.

The music of this quintet is unusually bright and amusing for
Cherubini; there can be no doubt that the whole scene was
intended to be extremely comic. It ends with the three villains
becoming more and more intoxicated – their condition is very
amusingly suggested by syncopated triplets in the orchestra, and
by syncopated phrases which they themselves sing; finally they
collapse into complete unconsciousness. Floreski and Varbel have
a short agitated duet, but do not know how best to use their
opportunity. At this moment the Baron comes in; he grasps the
situation at once, and Floreski openly admits who he is. The
Baron summons his vassals and Floreski and Varbel are committed to prison. This ends Act II.

Act III begins with the same scene, and Dourlinski in triumph;

[13] Compare Florindo, a favourite name for young lovers in Goldoni. (E.J.D.)

he thinks he can make sure of Lodoiska now, by threatening her with the death of her lover. In a very beautiful and expressive air she pleads for his life and says that she is quite willing to sacrifice her life for his. The following conversation then takes place (spoken):

DOUR. Soyez mon épouse et Floreski est libre.
LOD. Seigneur, donnez-moi du moins quelque temps...
DOUR. Non. Il faut prononcer à l'instant.
LOD. Sans mon père, seigneur, je ne peux pas disposer de moi.
DOUR. Ne comptez plus sur votre père, il a terminé ses jours.
LOD. Grands dieux! Je me meurs! (Elle s'évanouit.)

At this moment Floreski is brought in: he sees his beloved unconscious and rushes to her assistance. Here there is a quartet, Altamoras supplying the fourth voice; it is a very impassioned piece of music, and beautiful as well, but as completely formal as anything in Mozart's *Idomeneo*. After the quartet comes the final *dénouement*. The firing of cannon is heard and a soldier rushes in to say that the castle is being attacked on all sides. Dourlinski sends Lodoiska back to her cell, and goes off to take command of the situation. Floreski is left alone, and there follows a 'symphonie guerrière', in the intervals of which he makes a few remarks. The symphony begins almost in the style of Purcell or Handel; it is incredibly old-fashioned and academic, but it goes on for a long time and develops into a considerable piece of music, which if it is always formal is at least noisy enough to accompany the startling events that happen on the stage.

The gallery in which Floreski is standing collapses at the back and shows the whole stage full of Poles and Tartars fighting. The castle is on fire and falling into ruins. Titzikan enters, meets Floreski, takes a sabre from a Tartar and hands it to him; they rush off into the battle. Lodoiska is seen at the top of her tower in imminent danger of being cut off by the flames. Floreski runs across a narrow bridge to rescue her; as soon as he has done so the bridge collapses. The lovers leap from the tower into the arms of the Tartars; Varbel jumps out of another window and helps Titzikan and the Tartars carry the fainting Lodoiska to the front of the stage. Dourlinski appears below and rushes at Floreski with a dagger; Titzikan springs to his rescue and disarms Dourlinski. The fire all this time becomes more and more furious. It is now time to sing the general finale, in which Dourlinski asks how much

Titzikan wants for a ransom, and Titzikan replies that he never thinks about money and only means to condemn the Baron to lifelong captivity. The other characters utter equally proper sentiments, and apparently the Tartars destroy everything, for the orchestra settles down to a diminuendo and the curtain falls.

I have described the opera in detail, because there can be no doubt about the full-bloodedly Romantic character of the play and the spectacle. Nothing could be further from the antique stateliness of *Démophoon*. The question now arises, how far can Cherubini's music be considered Romantic? If the operas of Weber are present to our minds as a standard of what Romantic music ought to be, then our first impression of *Lodoiska* is that there is nothing conspicuously Romantic about the music. It is something between Mozart and Beethoven, roughly speaking; this is a good general description of Cherubini altogether. A minuter analysis will show us more anticipations of the Romantic style.

One noticeable characteristic of Cherubini, which is certainly not characteristic of either Mozart or Beethoven, is his skill in making a little go a long way. We notice this conspicuously in his overtures, and especially in their introductions, where the conventional preparatory phrases seem to us to be very long drawn out. This is a criticism of to-day; it would not have been said fifty years ago, and we may be quite certain it would have been considered outrageous in Cherubini's lifetime. The remarks of contemporary musicians such as Weber and Mendelssohn do not suggest at all that they were bored by these short phrases and long rests in between. Cherubini may have created something which we find tedious, but it was a novelty when he created it. He seems to have had an appreciation of orchestral colour that was rare in his day, and in this he is the precursor of Berlioz. Mozart's treatment of the orchestra is always delightful in sound, and nobody would ever wish to retouch it at the present day, whereas many people have felt impelled to reorchestrate Beethoven. Cherubini however seems to take a more conscious delight than Mozart in the isolated sounds of the instruments, not only in their special colour or timbre, but in the kind of phrases they can be made to play. No classical composer ever wrote so many conspicuous solos for single instruments of the orchestra; Cherubini ought to be the favourite composer of those conductors who aim at bringing the virtuosity of their individual players to absolute perfection. Mozart may give the flute two bars to play; Cherubini will give him eight or ten, as if he were performing a miniature concerto. Another instrument which interests him is the horn; he writes quite conventionally for it, but he makes it stand out, often with a certain virtuosity, as if it gave him an almost sensuous delight. The horn is often supposed to be the German Romantic instrument *par excellence*; there are innumerable examples in Weber of its Romantic appeal; but this style of writing had been developed by the French during the last ten years of the eighteenth century. Beethoven's famous passage in the slow movement of the Ninth Symphony may go further than anyone had gone before in horn difficulties, but the men of the French Revolution had set the example and had shown Beethoven effects that he could never have learned from Mozart or Haydn.

Another favourite Romantic instrument is the clarinet. Haydn had practically no understanding of it, Mozart only in his later life. For Mozart it was almost exclusively a solo instrument for a virtuoso, as we see it in the Clarinet Quintet. Beethoven uses it in a more modern way, but he does not offer it the conspicuous opportunities for sentiment that we find in Weber and Mendelssohn. The beginnings of this kind of expression are to be found in Cherubini. There are little instrumental interludes running all through the trio in the second act of *Lodoiska* (after Floreski has asked for hospitality), when the three characters, Floreski, Dourlinski and Altamoras, express their suspicious feelings in subdued tones; in all these little interludes it is the clarinet which has wonderfully expressive phrases.

The single airs are often conventional; Cherubini has not been able to cast off the older Italian traditions, and we are too painfully conscious of the old-fashioned *allegro moderato* in common time, in which the voice sings long sustained notes against a rapidly moving accompaniment which is supposed to give the impression of excitement. Perhaps it did excite people in those days; to our ears it is intolerably conventional. And the real reason why these airs sound so dull is because they have no coloratura. Here Cherubini is conforming to French taste, and the result is the skeleton of an Italian aria, just the dry bones, set for a tenor too, instead of the brilliant Italian soprano with all his flourishes and divisions. The ensembles are more French, and more expressive. There is some sort of conversation, and what the French liked, the natural intonations of the speaking voice. Here Cherubini's skill with the instruments stands him in good stead; he utilizes little figures to keep the movement going, and makes his voices enter quickly one upon the other. They have so little to say that they have no great chance of musical expression; Cherubini has to provide this by unexpected modulations. Here again is the beginning of Beethoven's dramatic effects, and still more those of Schubert and Weber.

5

THE SCHOOL OF PARIS – II

One of the strangest figures in the history of the French Revolution and its music is Jean François Le Sueur, remembered now
only as the teacher of Berlioz. If Cherubini was academic, Le
Sueur was still more so, and that in his whole nature. At an early
stage of his career he was in charge of the music at Notre-Dame,
where he endeavoured to develop orchestral music at four of the
principal church festivals. This is not the occasion on which to
discuss Le Sueur's ideas of church music, which he set forth in
a book of considerable size.[1] Another interest of his was ancient
Greek music. At the time of the Revolution the neo-classical
movement dominated French taste, the poems of André Chénier
being the most notable result of this in the artistic realm.[2] Opera
had for generations kept up the tradition of classical subjects, and
although one would not have expected them to appeal much to
revolutionary audiences, still, there was a popular notion that the
Republicans were the embodiment of the ancient Roman virtues,
and a fashion arose for operas on classical subjects with a contemporary reference.

One of Le Sueur's first attempts at opera was on a Greek
subject – *Télémaque*. The opera was not brought out until 1796,
but I treat of it here because it was composed some years earlier;
in fact it was begun in 1788, the year of Cherubini's *Démophoon*.[3]
The engraved full score is a curious document, for it is full of
information about the Greek modes and rhythms in which Le
Sueur thought he was composing. Every single number of the
opera has its mode and its *nomos*; but the general result is
nothing more than a very adequate imitation of Gluck, with some
admixture of what one might call the style of Cherubini.

[1] See note on p. 27 and the article by Foster there cited.
[2] The paintings of Jacques Louis David are perhaps a more conspicuous
example.
[3] *Télémaque* is said to have been began under the guidance of Sacchini, who
died in 1786, but few sketches of the first version survive, and the published
score probably dates from the 1790s.

64

It is not necessary to analyse this opera in detail, but it is worth noting that Le Sueur had some interesting ideas of musical drama which find expression in his marginal notes. The opera, like *Lodoiska*, has spoken dialogue, but in this case the dialogue is in very formal verse, as befitted a mythological subject. It also contains a good deal of ballet music, very much after the manner of Gluck; and the composer generally calls these movements *air* or *symphonie hypocritique*; the epithet is to be understood in its original Greek sense, as meaning simply dramatic. On practically every occasion he gives minute directions how the actions of the dancers are to be fitted to the notes, and he explains very carefully that they must not appear to be doing their actions to music; he wants them to look absolutely spontaneous, and to produce the illusion that the music is created by their movements. This direction is given not once but several times; Le Sueur evidently regarded it as a very important matter of principle. It is possible that he may have derived it from Noverre, the famous ballet-master and creator of ballet-pantomime; but in any case it is even now a fundamental artistic principle which ought to be more carefully observed than it generally is. The dancers possibly carry it out, but in post-Wagnerian days, when every character has his *Leitmotiv*, it is urgently necessary for the singing actors to bear Le Sueur's teaching in mind. The usual practice is that the singer waits for the orchestra to play his motive and then remembers to make the appropriate gesture; he ought on the other hand to make his gesture in such a way that the audience can imagine it to be the cause, and not the effect, of the motive played by the orchestra.

Another point of interest about the directions in *Télémaque* is the frequent occurrence of 'voix concentrée' or 'très-concentré'. Le Sueur, in fact, is one of those composers who feel a great deal more than they know how to express. He was a man of most lofty conceptions, but it must be admitted that he was not always successful in carrying them out. The chief interest of his works is that they are the forerunners of all that we find most typical in Berlioz; a study of Le Sueur is most illuminating with regard to his great pupil, and we can see how enormously Berlioz was indebted to the inspiration of his master.

Le Sueur gained his first noticeable success in 1793 with the Romantic opera *La Caverne*. There is a story that he had great trouble with the orchestra at the rehearsals, as the players treated him very disrespectfully, and he was much too gentle to respond with severity. Cherubini came to a rehearsal, and from that moment took rehearsals and performances in hand himself, with very successful result; is is further said that he also got the opera performed at Rouen.[4]

La Caverne is supposed to have been inspired by Schiller's play *Die Räuber*; its Romantic plot is clearly indicated by the picture on the title-page of the score. The scene, which remains the same for all three acts. represents a rocky cavern inhabited by a band of robbers; it is a spacious apartment illuminated by a lamp hung from the roof. Above the natural roof we see the surface of the ground, which is the floor of a forest, and is practicable, so that actors can be seen walking about on it. The entrances and exits to the cavern are mysterious and do not lead directly to the ground above.

The overture at once suggests Berlioz, with its long and elaborate horn solo, followed by a very passionate *allegro* in C minor. One sees at once that all that Berlioz style which his critics have called 'bad Beethoven' comes really from Le Sueur. And here it may be said that many of Berlioz's strangest effects of harmony come from Le Sueur too. Berlioz has often been severely censured for his 'schoolboy blunders' in the matter of harmony; it can only be said that Le Sueur does much the same thing, and in his case 'schoolboy blunders' are out of the question, for he was academically as learned as Cherubini. The probable reason for these curious harmonies is that Le Sueur wrote them of deliberate purpose because he believed them to be Greek.

The story of *La Caverne* follows the usual formula of the 'rescue opera'. Seraphita has been captured by robbers, and believes her husband Alphonse to be dead. She is attended by the usual comic servant, Gilblas, who appears to have joined the robber band in the hopes of rescuing her. Gilblas goes away early in the first act, and we do not see him again until near the end, so he does not contribute much to the comic part of the opera. There is however an old woman, Leonarda, who acts as housekeeper to the robbers, and is kind and friendly to Seraphita. The robbers come

---

[4] This statement is not confirmed in Loewenberg's *Annals of Opera*; but *La Caverne* was produced in many countries, including Russia, in the next twelve years.

back to the cave after an excursion, headed by Roustan, a man of terrifying appearance with enormous moustaches and a very violent manner; but he is not the real captain of the band. This is Rolando, who is in reality a man of noble birth and corresponding manners; he has taken to the robber life on account of youthful indiscretions, but we are assured that he has noble instincts, and he may be expected to make use of them when the time comes. At present he is wildly in love with Seraphita, who naturally refuses his advances, all the more so as she faintly hears the voice of Alphonse singing in the forest above, where the audience can see him wandering about and looking for his wife.

In Act II Alphonse manages to enter the cave disguised as a blind minstrel with a hurdy-gurdy. Seraphita does not recognize him, but is strangely moved by the sound of his voice. The robbers make him sing to entertain them, and Leonarda also sings and dances in a grotesque fashion. The robbers conveniently retire into an inner cavern, in order that Alphonse may reveal himself to his wife; but Leonarda comes back and catches them embracing, so that they have to entrust her with the state of affairs. She promises to help them. The robbers come back, and Roustan makes an attempt to carry off Seraphita by force, but she is rescued by Rolando, who ends the act by holding the whole robber band at a distance with his naked sword.

Act III begins with a long chorus of the robbers, who swear allegiance to Roustan and are resolved to be revenged on Rolando. Most of them start off on another expedition, but it is understood that five are to remain behind to murder Rolando. Leonarda reveals the plot to him, on which he sings a long air to the effect that he repents of his banditry and would like to go home to his father like the Prodigal Son. He tells Seraphita that he will send her home; Alphonse reveals himself as her husband, and Rolando turns out to be Seraphita's long-lost brother. On that discovery there follows the siege of the cavern by the friends of Alphonse. The four principal characters sing a quartet on the stage, while two choruses, one of the robbers, the other of Alphonse's friends, are supposed to be fighting outside, singing at the same time, of course. Finally Alphonse's friends are victorious and enter the cavern, which promptly falls in at the back, revealing the forest behind it, whereupon all ends happily. Le Sueur suggests that, if it is not possible to sing the double chorus, the *allegro* of the overture should be played and the scene acted in dumb show.

The music is for the most part rather dry and mechanical. It has all the proper conventions of *opéra-comique, couplets, romance,* comic song, duets, trios, ensembles, etc. but there is nothing musically Romantic: the Romanticism is all in the play and the scenery. The only way in which we can regard the music as Romantic, taking the opera as a whole, is in the juxtaposition of so many incongruous elements – the serious emotions of Seraphita and Rolando, with the comic episode of the blind beggar and the old woman.

That, after all, constitutes a good part of the Romanticism of *Der Freischütz*: the Romantic attraction of that work lies very largely in its unexpected juxtaposition of serious passions with peasant scenes, popular dances, humorous songs and choruses. And we have all been brought up so systematically to believe that Romance is only to be found in the German forest, that we can hardly realize the possibility of a French Romantic opera with most of the corresponding elements, only French in their popular tradition and not German.

Le Sueur's next opera, produced in 1794, was *Paul et Virginie*. The original tale of *Paul et Virginie*, a boy and girl brought up on the French colony of Mauritius or Île de France, by Bernardin de St Pierre, a disciple of Rousseau, is one of the most famous products of the Romantic movement in literature. It is no wonder that it was seized upon by composers, though it does not really adapt itself very happily to operatic treatment. It had been set in 1791 by Kreutzer, whose music on the whole is trivial and uninteresting; but his opera has a certain historical interest, because the third act is almost continuous music from beginning to end.

In this act Paul has been separated from Virginie, who has just been taken off on a ship sailing for France. Paul, with the priest, watches the ship in the distance. A storm rises and the ship is wrecked. Paul throws himself into the sea to rescue Virginie, but the chorus imagine them both to be lost. Just as the storm subsides Paul and the negro slave Zabi are seen bringing Virginie in to land. The opera, needless to say, has to end happily, and Monsieur de la Bourdonnais, who was taking Virginie back to France, decides to allow her to stay on the island, Zabi being given his freedom.

The storm scene is much worked up, and there is an elaborate pantomime, or dumb-show, which is set out as follows:

Paul embraces his mother, raises his eyes to Heaven as if in prayer; he releases himself from those who surround him, mounts hurriedly to the top of the rock, and throws himself into the sea. The scene which follows is all in pantomime; only the orchestra occupies the audience and paints the storm in all its force. The thunder and lightning redouble. Madame de la Tour (the mother of Virginie) has fainted; the priest and Marguérite (Paul's mother) are attending to her. The officer appears with his troops, which he disposes along the shore so that the prospect of the sea is entirely visible to the audience. Sailors are on the rocks and throw ropes and planks to the people in the sea. In the distance is seen the ship of Monsieur de la Bourdonnais, at the mercy of the storm, without masts or sails. Virginie is standing on the poop, holding on with one hand and with the other making signs to those on shore. At her knees is a negro who seems trying to tear her away to save her. The stage is at moments brilliantly lit up by the lightning, at others in the most appalling darkness. A thunderbolt strikes the ship, which is broken to pieces, and Virginie is engulphed in the waves.

The storm dies down and the chorus sing:

> O vains regrets, soins superflus,
> La mort a terminé leur vie.
> Pleurons, pleurons, ils ne sont plus,
> Malheureux Paul et pauvre Virginie.

The sky clears, daylight returns, and a gay ritornello announces the arrival of Paul and Zabi bringing in Virginie. The priest exclaims (spoken) 'Les voici! ils sont sauvés!' During a gentle piece of music they carry Virginie to land; she is unconscious, and Paul takes her on his knees until she gradually recovers. Her first thought is to embrace him, but as they both catch sight of their mothers they run to them and fall on their necks. Monsieur de la Bourdonnais makes a speech, and the chorus bring the opera to a cheerful end.

The storm music consists mostly of scale figures within the key of D minor in semiquavers up and down, like pale reminiscences of *Don Giovanni*; but it is worth describing here, because it is certainly a Romantic conception, even if not very adequately carried out. It was not the first storm in French opera; in 1773 Monsigny had painted a storm in *La belle Arsène*, scored for two piccolos which represent the lightning, two bassoons, two horns and strings – not a very large orchestra for descriptive purposes.[5]

---

[5] There are similar storms in Monsigny's *Le Roi et le fermier* (1762) – as a link between the first two acts – Gossec's *Toinon et Toinette* (1767), and some of the operas of Rameau.

Le Sueur's opera is written on the same subject, but to a different libretto. It is characteristic of Le Sueur that the first act opens with a long chorus of savages singing a hymn to the sun, while Paul and Virginie listen in the background. The negro slave is here called Domingo, and he has a curious song in Act I which is evidently intended to be some sort of native melody. This act ends with the arrival of the French ship, a chorus of sailors and the despair of Madame de la Tour as the captain insists on taking Virginie to live with her hated aunt in Paris. Act II begins with a love duet between Domingo and Babet, a negress; it is not comic, but sentimental and idyllic. Next comes a *mélodrame hypocritique* as Paul and Virginie are seen descending a steep rock. Here again, as in *Télémaque*, Le Sueur directs the singers to make their movements in time to the music, but in such a way that it shall not appear to be conscious. After a duet they realize that they have lost their way, but they are rescued by Domingo and Babet, and the savages make a palanquin out of branches and creepers, in which they are carried home to the strains of a sort of religious march. Le Sueur again directs the chorus to make their movements to the music, but as if spontaneously, and he further insists on the religious character of the scene.

In Act III we see them arrive in the palanquin at Madame de la Tour's house. Everybody is in despair at Virginie's departure. Paul says he will swim after the ship as far as he can. They all make a last appeal to the captain, but he is inflexible and takes her away. Here the storm begins, first with 'la rampe à moitié baissée', and later 'la rampe baissée et nuit totale'. We see that darkness was produced at the Théâtre Feydeau by the gradual lowering of the row of footlights into a trough below the stage. The scene changes to the port, with a high rock on one side and half the ship arriving on the other. The soldiers carry the unconscious Virginie to the ship; savages pursue them into the wings, and the captain is seen to deposit Virginie on board, but the chief of the savages seizes her and throws the captain into the sea. Then, as in Kreutzer, a thunderbolt strikes the ship and sets it on fire; while it is burning, the savage chief is seen to carry off Virginie, followed by all the other savages helter-skelter. The remaining principal characters then come on in great surprise and delight, and the opera, as usual, ends with an ensemble and chorus of rejoicing. The music is all rather dry and the storm scene primitive, although there are mannerisms which remind one of Berlioz. At the same time one must admit Le Sueur's power of constructing long movements and of working up dramatic climaxes. The expression is to us conventional, and the music is utterly devoid of the sensuous charm of the Italian composers; but we are obliged to acknowledge its dramatic energy and force.

Another opera on *La Caverne* was brought out this year, composed by Méhul, but it does not appear to have been printed, and I can tell you nothing about it.[6] It was not Méhul's only opera in 1794, for he also produced *Mélidore et Phrosine*, which is a work of very Romantic character and one that is very characteristic of Méhul's peculiar charm.

The story of *Mélidore et Phrosine* is taken from a narrative poem of Gentil-Bernard; it was utilized not only by Méhul, but also by Guilbert de Pixérécourt as the subject of one of his melodramas. The scene is laid in Messina. Phrosine is in love with Mélidore, but her two brothers Aimar and Jule will not allow her to marry him, Aimar because Mélidore is supposed to be beneath Phrosine in rank, Jule because he himself is so devoted to his sister that he cannot endure the idea of her marrying anyone at all. Mélidore suggests that she should visit a pious hermit who lives on an island near Messina; he goes to the island himself and finds the hermit dead. He then annexes the hermit's cell and robes, and passes himself off as the hermit, in order to have meetings with Phrosine, who is an expert swimmer in the original story and swims to the island at night, guided by a beacon which is lit by Mélidore. Her brothers discover the affair; they extinguish the beacon on the rock, and deceive Phrosine by a false beacon on a boat; she swims after the boat until she is exhausted and drowned.

We see at once the resemblance to the operas about Paul and Virginie; we recognize our old friend the rock, and the character who leaps from it into the sea. We also remember that much the same thing happens in Wagner's *Der fliegende Holländer*, and we know that Wagner in his young days had a considerable knowledge of old-fashioned French opera.

For stage purposes, however, it was not convenient that the heroine should swim; the day of the Rhine-maidens had not yet arrived. Phrosine in Pixérécourt's melodrama rows a boat

---

[6] Méhul's *La Caverne* was given at the Théâtre Favart in December 1795 (not 1794); it was never printed.

instead; in Méhul's opera we are told that she swims, but we do not see her do so.

The opera begins with a very striking overture, rather in Cherubini's manner but with a great deal more passion and feeling. It ends in a strange way: the orchestra settles down to a diminuendo, which is followed by a sort of barcarolle movement in 6/8. The idea, no doubt, is to suggest the storm which plays so important a part in the last act, and the general atmosphere of the sea, which permeates the whole opera.

This overture does not lead straight into the first act; it comes to an end, and no doubt was applauded before the curtain rose on a garden in Messina. The back of the garden is closed by a railing and an iron gate; beyond, in the distance, we see the sea and an island. The act begins at once with a vehement air for Aimar, Phrosine's elder brother, a bass. He refuses altogether to allow Phrosine to marry Mélidore. After the air there is some spoken conversation in verse between him and Phrosine. The period in which the play is set may be gathered roughly from the fact that Phrosine remarks that Mélidore was victorious in the last tournament; we may assume a mediaeval or Renaissance background.

Aimar leaves Phrosine alone, and she sings a very charming *romance* of two verses, in the orthodox French *opéra-comique* style.[7] After more spoken verse she breaks into a recitative and cavatina, in which she expresses her confidence in the sympathy of her younger brother Jule, to whom she is much devoted. Jule enters, but to her surprise and disappointment he is anything but sympathetic. In the original poem he is supposed to be incestuously in love with her; but in the opera this is never made explicit.[8] He sings a long air, with occasional interjections from Phrosine. This method of allowing one character to interrupt another in the course of an aria is contrary to all correct Italian practice.[9] The orthodox theory was that a solo was a solo and a duet a duet; in a solo the singer had the stage to himself, and in a duet the music was equally divided between the singers. The only Italian example which comes at all near the method of Méhul is the aria

[7] The scoring – notably the almost exclusive use of stopped notes for the solo horn – is far from orthodox.
[8] No doubt to disarm the censor. It is certainly implied.
[9] There are a number of examples in the operas of Handel and Haydn, and in Gluck's French operas.

of Donna Elvira in *Don Giovanni*, where little remarks of Don Giovanni and Leporello in the background are interpolated at the ends of the lady's main phrases. This is one of the things that shows *Don Giovanni* to be a comic opera; and in any case the remarks of the two men do not interrupt the singer, whereas in this air of Méhul Phrosine directly addresses a remark to her brother. It is a case in which dramatic truth breaks down operatic convention, and we may take that as a sign of incipient Romanticism.

Jule leaves the stage, and it begins to grow dark. Mélidore enters and proposes a secret elopement. He suggests that they should get married by the hermit on the island, and then set sail in a ship for some other country

> Où l'homme, à l'homme égal, ne connoît de grandeur
> Que celles qu' aux vertus l'estime a consacrées.

The duet, as the situation demands, is agitated in the extreme. Méhul shows a remarkable power of expressive melody in the voice parts, though it is French conversation rather than Italian singing. He also has a very striking invention for instrumental figures and motives; these give his music great dramatic vitality, and contribute to the general sense of hurry and anxiety which is the background of this duet. In the middle there is a very strange modulation to the remotest possible key – from D major, the key of the duet, to A flat. The whole character of the music becomes dark and mysterious, as they sing:

> Sous les ténèbres les plus sombres
> Astres brillants, éclipsez-vous!
> O nuit, viens couvrir de tes ombres
> Et notre fuite et les jaloux!

The scene is now dark, and Aimar has entered unseen and observed the lovers. It is at this point that he joins in with remarks of his own, not heard by them. The music returns to the first key, for Méhul is still a slave to classical forms, and the subjects must be recapitulated. This leads to a slow duet in G, to which Aimar has to sing a bass part; this well illustrates the difficulty in which subsequent Romantic composers only too often found themselves – three or more characters are on the stage, uttering independent and very conflicting feelings, but being obliged to sing in vertical harmony together, and indeed to sing those conventional progressions which in classical times were considered necessary for the conclusion of any piece of music. It is this false situation, more than any other, which has made the whole idea of opera ridiculous to the ordinary person; and it is a vice of the Romantic Opera rather than of the old Classical one.

At the end of the trio Aimar, in recitative, makes himself known; he challenges Mélidore and they fight. Aimar falls, apparently dead; retainers of Mélidore force the gate and enter, singing a chorus in 6/8, followed by Jule with another chorus of *his* retainers, who sing (simultaneously) in 2/4. We notice such choruses (nearly always of male voices) in all these revolutionary operas, and they strike us as tiresomely conventional; but the public of that day no doubt found them very dramatic, especially when two sang against each other. It was a period when audiences were often noisy and ill-behaved; they would interrupt performances in order to insult singers whose political actions had made them unpopular, and they would join in uproariously in any song that they knew and liked. We can hardly imagine that the audience would want to join in these choruses of Méhul's, but they saw on the stage something of their own revolutionary demonstrations.[10]

Mélidore apparently escapes with his men; the others are left in possession and discover that Aimar is still living. To the mysterious sound of funereal chords played by four stopped horns, he is just able to say that Mélidore killed him and that Jule must be his avenger. A chorus of revenge ends the act. The second act shows us the island, with a view of Messina across the water. On the island is the hermit's cave, and one can just see some rough furniture inside it. Mélidore has taken refuge here. He is in despair of ever seeing Phrosine again, though he insists that Aimar met his death accidentally, and that he himself sought only to disarm him. He proposes to join the hermit in his solitary life, but finds him dead; he has thoughtfully left a letter, asking the first person who comes along to be so kind as to bury him in the grave he has already dug for himself, and inviting him to accept the hermitage and his small possessions as a reward for his services. Mélidore at once decides to take over the hermit's inheritance, and after an air goes into the cave to change his

[10] Staged versions of earlier public ceremonies were then common in Paris theatres.

74

clothes. While he is doing so a chorus of peasants arrives, with gifts of food and wine for the hermit. This is a charming little piece of music, quite in the manner of Auber. Jule now enters, in quest of the hermit, whose advice he wants about his family troubles. The chorus prevent him from searching the cave, as he at first very aggressively wishes to do; they tell him that the hermit is at prayer and must not be disturbed. Mélidore comes out disguised as the hermit, and neither the chorus nor Jule are in the least aware of his identity. At the request of Jule he sends the peasants away, and Jule explains the situation in spoken verse.

To a modern audience their conversation could only be unspeakably funny, but the author doubtless intended it to be perfectly serious, and a modern audience would take it seriously if it was set to music in the conventional Romantic style of recitative. Both singers and audiences – singers especially – are so accustomed to absurdity in opera that there is nothing they will not take seriously. The average opera-singer's point of view is that anything uttered by his own voice must *ipso facto* be serious, unless he is a professed comedian.

Jule is expecting Phrosine to come at once to seek the hermit's advice, and he hopes that the hermit, when he has learned from her the secret of Mélidore's whereabouts, will betray it to him. Here again Méhul treats the situation with very Romantic force. Jule and Mélidore are singing a duet; at the very end of it Mélidore suddenly tells Jule that he cannot pursue Mélidore, for he has been drowned and is no more. 'Mélidore is no more?' Jule repeats, as if unable to understand it; and just at that moment Phrosine enters, hears the fatal words and shrieks out 'Il est mort? j'expire moi-même!', whereupon the music stops abruptly on a discord. A long dialogue follows; Phrosine recognizes the voice of her lover, and almost betrays him, but Jule merely thinks she is delirious. He is determined that she should see the hermit; she protests, in order to make Jule the more obstinate, and finally, with apparent reluctance, she remains alone with him. In great haste, the lovers arrange that she shall cross the strait by night, guided by the beacon which he is to light on the top of the rock, to show her where to come ashore. They have a duet, which leads to a trio on the return of Jule; Jule is very angry, but it is not clear what he is angry about.[11] The sailors enter, to a lively

[11] He is tormented by jealousy and love for his sister.

hornpipe, almost in the English style, and Jules takes Phrosine to the ship; as the ship departs, the chorus sing a sort of barcarolle in 6/8 which ends *pianissimo.*

We notice in this act two very characteristic Romantic items, the chorus of peasants and the chorus of sailors. Both are in the nature of ballet music; it is possible that the peasants danced, and it is most probable that the sailors did. Méhul's music reminds us of Auber, who is more or less familiar to modern audiences; but it might equally well remind us of Rameau, and in most of Rameau's operas there are scenes of this type. The music strikes us as Romantic, because after the death of Rameau there was a break in the tradition; Gluck and the Italians who composed for Paris – Piccinni, Salieri and Sacchini – adopted French constructional principles, but not the native French feelings and sentiments. They could no more compose dances and choruses in this native French style than Handel could imitate the native style of Purcell.

Act III shows us another part of the island – a rocky site at the water's edge, with every suggestion of a dangerous approach. It is night, and Mélidore lights the beacon during a long instrumental introduction. He addresses the torch in an air, and follows this up with what Rousseau called *mélodrame –* instrumental music passing rapidly from one emotion to another, interspersed with spoken words. As in Kreutzer's *Paul et Virginie,* almost the whole of this act is continuous music. The *mélodrame* leads on to a storm, which is of gigantic length; it is a succession of three storms, for three times the orchestra dies down to nothing and then works up to *fortissimo* again. Sailors come on, apparently shipwrecked; Mélidore becomes anxious for Phrosine, and prays to Heaven for her safety: this is an early instance of Christian prayer in opera. Christian prayer would have been quite impossible in the old Italian operas; their librettists were always obliged to print a formal statement to the effect that such words as *God* or *Fate* were to be taken in a poetical sense only and that no offence was intended to Catholic consciences. The French Revolution destroyed the last vestige of scruples of this sort, and audiences came to regard a 'prayer' as a very effective piece of operatic business, not only in France, but in England and Italy as well.

In the course of the storm the beacon light is extinguished by the wind. Mélidore sees a small boat approaching, and hopes that it contains Phrosine, but the occupant is Jule. Here the music stops, while Jule tells a very long story of how Phrosine set out to swim to the island,[12] and he pursued her in a boat with a torch which she mistook for Mélidore's beacon. She succeeded in reaching the boat, but Jule refused to help her into it, and dashed his own torch into the water, leaving his sister to drown. Mélidore at once mounts the rock and dives into the sea; Jule remains on the stage, a prey to the last agonies of remorse. He calls on Heaven to destroy him, and the storm rises again; a thunderbolt marks its great climax as the chorus of sailors (off stage) cry out in terror. Mélidore's voice is heard from the waters calling on the sailors to save Phrosine. She is rescued and brought safely to land. There is a short spoken conversation in which Jule expresses his repentance and asks for pardon; even Aimar, who turns out to be still alive, is now reconciled to the union of the lovers. The chorus ends the opera with a movement in E major, 6/8, which has almost exactly the rhythm and style of Weber, as in the mermaid's song in *Oberon*.

I do not know how far German musicians were acquainted with this particular opera of Méhul, but even if it was never performed in Germany,[13] the score might easily have been studied there, as it was printed soon after the production, like those of almost all the French operas. The opera of Méhul which attained the greatest celebrity and popularity was *Joseph*; this work was occasionally revived as late as 1900 or thereabouts.[14] Both Weber and Wagner had the greatest admiration for *Joseph*, but I venture to think that one reason why it survived was because it was on a biblical story familiar to everybody, whereas the libretto of *Mélidore et Phrosine* was of its own age and country, and would after a certain time become out-of-date and rather ridiculous. *Joseph*, composed in 1806 and produced the following year, was the result of a discussion between various intellectuals in Paris over a play on the same subject which had received no great

---

12 This is not quite accurate. She bribed some sailors to take her over, but when they quailed before the storm she dived overboard and swam for the beacon.

13 *Mélidore et Phrosine* – like Le Sueur's *Télémaque* and *Paul et Virginie* – is not included in Alfred Loewenberg's *Annals of Opera*. The opening of the overture to *Der Freischütz* bears a striking resemblance to that of *Mélidore et Phrosine*.

14 At the Opéra (with recitatives by Bourgault-Ducoudray) in 1899, at the Opéra-Comique in 1910.

success. Alexandre Duval, a dramatist, maintained that the story of Joseph was perfectly suitable for a play although it contained no love-interest, and that there was no need to provide it with a fictitious love-interest. Méhul agreed to set the libretto to music, if Duval would write it for him.

It may seem inconceivable nowadays that an imaginary love-affair should be grafted on to the story of Joseph; but we may remember that Handel's oratorio *Jephtha* contains an imaginary love-affair for Jephtha's daughter.[15] Méhul's *Joseph*, one feels now, could only be put on the stage after the manner of William Blake's drawings, and on some occasion rather removed from ordinary operatic conditions. I cannot find it Romantic in spirit, but it certainly has elements which belong to Romantic Opera, notably the chorus of Hebrews singing their morning prayer at dawn. This must surely have been in the memory of Saint-Saëns when he wrote the analogous scene in *Samson et Dalila*. The most vivid dramatic characterization is shown in Méhul's treatment of Simeon, the eldest son of Jacob, who is maddened by remorse for his crime – the selling of Joseph into slavery in Egypt. Simeon is the great figure of the opera; Joseph and Jacob have a rather cold and Cherubini-like dignity.

If we compare Cherubini and Méhul, we see that Cherubini has much greater technical skill, owing to his thorough training in counterpoint under Sarti. He builds up large masses of sound and he can also construct extended movements; but when it comes to writing vocal music, he has neither charm nor any great invention. He relies a great deal, especially in the earlier operas, on the baldest Italian conventionalities, while he deprives himself austerely of any sort of Italian brilliance. Méhul, on the other hand, had little scientific training.[16] He makes little use of counterpoint, and his sense of form is not always equal to the difficult constructive problems which arise; it is extremely probable that he had no idea himself that there were any such problems, and allowed himself to be guided partly by tradition and partly by natural instinct. But Méhul has undoubted charm and considerable melodic invention. He aims, like all the French, more at truth of speech than at pure melody; he is concerned with the

---

[15] Handel's *Joseph and his Brethren* provides an even closer parallel.

[16] He studied for some years with the organist Guillaume Hanser, and with Edelmann in Paris.

study of character and the analysis of emotion, as expressed in the words; he has learned this from Grétry and Monsigny.[17] In the orchestra he makes interesting experiments, especially with the horns; the horn is evidently the instrument which fascinates him the most, for not only does he make it play unexpected solos, but he perpetually uses it, far more melodically than Mozart or even Beethoven, to enforce some particular inner voice of the orchestra. Mozart, in such moments, would have used the bassoon; Méhul knows that the horn will give him a peculiar quality that is fuller and richer than the bassoon, and at the same time far more penetrating and able to make itself heard through a noisy orchestra. He writes very carefully for the strings, and takes the greatest pains over accompaniment figures. Cherubini works accompaniment figures industriously, but he chooses very conventional ones; Méhul's are something new, neither Italian nor German, and point forward clearly to Berlioz.

Mélidore et Phrosine has in fact almost all the ingredients we look for in a typical Romantic opera; but perhaps we do not recognize them, because they are definitely French and not German. If that sort of descriptive orchestral writing which is called the 'music of Nature' is typically Romantic, we shall find that in Méhul too, at any rate as far as storms are concerned. As a Frenchman, he is concerned primarily with human beings and human feelings. The conception of man as the helpless victim of the invisible forces of nature, of man as something less than nature, was impossible for him, at any rate at this stage of his career. *Mélidore et Phrosine* ought to be as saturated with sea air as *Tristan und Isolde* or *Der fliegende Holländer*; we see the sea with our own eyes in every act, and we have the double choruses of sailors too; but apart from the general storm, Méhul gives us no musical seascapes, only sailors and boats.[18] But the French Romantic Movement is only in its infancy, and we shall find more exciting developments later on.

[17] And presumably from Gluck.
[18] This summary is scarcely fair to Méhul. Many of his operas, including *Mélidore et Phrosine*, show a strong preoccupation with descriptive music and the background of natural forces against which the action is set.

6

THE SCHOOL OF PARIS – III

In the same year as Méhul's *Mélidore et Phrosine*, 1794, Cherubini produced a new opera, *Elisa, ou le voyage aux glaciers du Mont Saint-Bernard.* This is the first opera in which the new Romantic interest in Swiss mountain scenery was illustrated.[1] In both acts the scene is the same, a part of the St Bernard pass, with the hospice and monastery of the monks and a precipitous snow-covered landscape. As far as one can gather, the period is that of Cherubini's own day. The first scene begins with the Prior and monks bearing lanterns and axes, looking for travellers lost in the snow. Next appears Florindo, the hero, a young painter, accompanied by his servant Germain, who is the usual faithful retainer, as in *Lodoiska*, considerably bored with his eccentric master's search for adventure. After Florindo's air, in which he speaks of his love for Elisa, Germain says to him

Vous verrai-je toujours romanesque, exalté?

Here we have the very word 'romanesque' occurring in an opera. The postman passes by and gives Florindo a letter which informs him that Elisa is betrothed to his rival. He is in despair, and the Prior attempts to console him. The day has passed even more rapidly than usual in operas, and although the scene opened in the early morning, the evening twilight is now coming on. The bell of the chapel rings, and the Prior tries to persuade Florindo to come back to the hospice with him; Florindo is at first unwilling, but finally yields. After he has left the stage we see the arrival of Elisa and her maid Laura, accompanied by a guide; Elisa is completely exhausted, but she is taken into the hospice by the attendants. This ends the first act.

The second act begins with a chorus of Savoyards on the way

---

[1] The credit for this belongs to Grétry, who anticipated Cherubini in *Guillaume Tell* (1791) – for which, according to Bouilly, he paid a special visit to Switzerland in search of local colour – and to some extent in the spectacular final scene of *La Rosière de Salency* (1773).

to France. Elisa in conversation with the Prior discovers that Florindo is staying at the hospice; she wishes to see him, but Germain enters and tells her that Florindo has gone, leaving a letter to say that after her betrothal to another he can only die. Elisa, Laura and the Prior sing a trio of despair, after which the usual operatic storm begins. The scene that follows is obviously modelled on the last scene of *Lodoiska*, except that whereas there we had a fire, here we have an avalanche. Florindo is seen crossing a bridge, which gives way; he is lost to sight, while Elisa looks on from the edge of a precipice, and a double chorus, half above and half below, sing alternately. Finally Florindo is rescued from the snow and all ends happily.

The music is remarkably picturesque for Cherubini; in fact this is the most consciously Romantic of all his operas. The opening scene, with the monks looking for lost travellers, is admirably written, and the woodwind have striking figures of rushing semiquavers which may be intended to represent winds. The arrival of Michel the postman is marked by a sort of 'march of mules', as the score calls it; it is really the introduction to Michel's ballad, the typical French ballad in 6/8, accompanied here by the bells and jingles of the harness. It is played by strings *sul ponticello*, with a characteristic solo for the piccolo. After he has given Florindo the letter bringing the news of Elisa's supposed elopement with his rival, Florindo has a long and very passionate air, which runs on into the arrival of the Prior. The duet which follows, the Prior gently but continuously persuading, and Florindo replying in short broken phrases, is extremely touching, and a great effect is made by the tolling of the monastery bell in the middle. This is truly in the Romantic spirit. The arrival of Elisa is curiously treated; she is accompanied by an elaborate horn solo, which goes on all through her scena. The chorus of Savoyards at the beginning of Act II is strikingly picturesque. Their guide sings a ballad in three verses, and they have another chorus, in 6/8, as they disappear into the distance. It is an excellent contrast to all the sentimental business of Florindo and Elisa. After hearing about Florindo from the Prior Elisa has a very fine air, which again is accompanied by a solo instrument, this time the oboe, which performs what one might almost call a concerto. Cherubini must have been remembering Mozart here, for I can think of no other composer who writes *concertante* parts in this style. The scene of the avalanche is well developed, and ought to be most exciting on the stage; but the finale, after Florindo has been rescued, is very conventional.

Cherubini's next production was *Médée* (1797), which is classical tragedy in the grandest manner. Unfortunately it follows the *opéra-comique* tradition, and has spoken dialogue, which to a modern reader seems to detract from its dignity. In Germany this opera used to be performed with recitatives by Franz Lachner, which are a good deal better than one might expect.[2] The plan of the opera is to some extent modelled on Gluck's *Armide*, and it ends tragically. There is a fine spectacular scene when Jason and Dirce are married in the temple with all solemnity, Medea looking on from the front of the stage and making furious comments. Berlioz must have known this, for it is very like the scene in *Les Troyens* where the Trojans bring the wooden horse into the city, Cassandra standing in the foreground and prophesying disaster. The main reason why *Médée* is never revived now[3] is because the vocal parts are so exhausting. Cherubini himself made several cuts and entirely recomposed the duet for Medea and Jason at the end of Act I, but even in this form the opera puts an impossible strain on the principal singers.

Médée was followed in 1800 by *Les Deux Journées*, the best known and the most popular of all Cherubini's operas. It is known in England as *The Water-Carrier*. The libretto was by Jean Nicolas Bouilly, who held an official post at Tours during the Reign of Terror; he came in for some appalling experiences and utilized them to make opera-librettos for his musical friends, of whom Cherubini was one. A fashion had arisen for operas based on contemporary happenings, and Bouilly announced on his librettos that they were *faits historiques*,[4] true stories; but he seems to have thought it safer to transplant them to some other country

[2] But they seriously distort Cherubini's design, which employs a graded method of dramatic expression (speech, *mélodrame*, string-accompanied recitative, set number with full orchestra) with striking originality, notably in the finale of Act II, the wedding scene mentioned by Dent.

[3] It was successfully revived, with Maria Callas as Medea, at the 1953 Florence Festival and subsequently given in many other cities. Most productions have used Carlo Zangarini's Milan version of 1909 with Lachner's recitatives, but a revival by the Palatine Opera Group at Durham in May 1967 restored the original dialogue form.

[4] Many operas of the Revolution period, usually of an ephemeral nature, had been so described.

and century, in order to avoid trouble with the revolutionaries at home. The story of *Les Deux Journées*, in which a gentleman is taken out of prison concealed in a water-cart, was based on an episode which Bouilly said concerned a relative of his own; but he transferred it to the seventeenth century. It is another opera of the rescue type, but in general style rather a regression to the older and more innocent form of *opéra-comique*; it has no storms and no melodramatic scenes of rescue from fire or water. It was immensely admired by Beethoven, as well as by many other German musicians; one probable reason for its appeal to Beethoven was that it was not at all sensational, but concentrated all interest on the simple human kindness and gratitude of the humble water-carrier.

Méhul had shown some indications of Romanticism in his first opera *Euphrosine, ou le Tyran corrigé*, which came out as early as 1790. It starts like a comic opera of the most frivolous type; although the scene is laid in a romantic castle of Provence in the days of the Crusades, the old doctor and the three charming sisters whom he has to receive are treated in quite an up-to-date manner. But the tyrant Coradin, owner of the castle and guardian of the three young ladies, although made fun of by the doctor and by the girls too, is treated more and more seriously as the opera goes on. The story is complicated, but offers a great many dramatic surprises. Euphrosine, the eldest of the three girls, sets herself to make a conquest of her guardian; but she has a bitter enemy in the Countess of Arles, formerly betrothed to Coradin and rejected by him, who is furious at the arrival of the three younger competitors. Through a series of complicated intrigues, Coradin decides to have Euphrosine poisoned, and the doctor is ordered to prepare the draught. He betrays the plot at once to Euphrosine, and tells her that he will give her a harmless potion, and that she must pretend to die in slow agony. Just as she has drunk the potion Coradin comes back in a great hurry, having changed his mind; he has to witness her apparent agonies and final collapse, to the delight of the Countess. Euphrosine is taken away, and Coradin launches out into the most wildly tragic air of remorse. Finally he requests the physician to prepare the same poison for him, but at this moment Euphrosine walks in perfectly well and happy. The Countess refuses to accept defeat, and is always ready with a new conspiracy, but finally the truth comes out, and she presumably goes back to Arles, as she merely leaves the stage, while the others celebrate the happy end.

Euphrosine is of some historical interest, for it has often been suggested that Weber and Helmina von Chezy were doing something quite new when they put together *Euryanthe*, a tale of mediaeval chivalry. It is quite obvious that they were merely trying to imitate Méhul, for whom Weber had the greatest admiration.[5]

Mediaeval chivalry is seen in full panoply in Méhul's *Ariodant*, composed in 1799 and dedicated to Cherubini in return for the dedication of *Médée*. The story is taken from Ariosto, and had been used by Handel in 1734. The scene is laid in Scotland, but it is the Scotland of Ariosto, not that of Ossian. It is a very good Romantic plot, and so like that of *Euryanthe* that we may well suspect Helmina von Chezy of deliberate imitation, though she was not very clever at it.[6] In Méhul's opera – it is unnecessary to compare it with Handel's – the scene is laid at the court of Edgard, King of Scotland, whose daughter is in love with the knight Ariodant. Her rejected lover, Othon, is wild with jealousy, and allies himself with her maid Dalinde, to bring about her ruin and blackmail her into marrying him.

The opera introduces us at once to the villain Othon, who is not a baritone, as one might expect, but a tenor. There is no long overture to this opera, which in many ways is curiously experimental and prophetic. The prelude begins with a slow movement for four violoncellos[7] (another Romantic device generally supposed to have been invented by a more celebrated composer), and this is gradually built up, but always in slow time, to a climax on the chord of the dominant, on which the curtain rises. Othon begins with spoken prose; to-day, he says, his fate is to be decided. The orchestra suddenly bursts in with a short and furious passage of diminished sevenths;[8] this recurs throughout the opera as a sort of *Leitmotiv* representing Othon's jealousy.

---

5   The most remarkable feature of *Euphrosine* is Méhul's use of a motive, first heard in the overture, to depict the corrosive effect of jealousy. See Winton Dean, 'Opera under the French Revolution', *PRMA* xciv (1967/8), 86.

6   The resemblance is more probably due to Weber's modification of the libretto, which in its original plan was less like that of *Ariodant*. Berton's *Montano et Stéphanie* (also 1799) uses the same story.

7   In fact three solo violoncellos, with a fourth part for unison string basses.

8   The decisive first chord of the motive is a dominant minor ninth.

At the end of his energetic air the orchestra suddenly changes to an entirely different mood, and then stops. This is Méhul's new device for introducing another character, in this case the maid Dalinde. The soft phrase is not a *Leitmotiv* to represent her: that is not the idea at all – Méhul, as we see consistently throughout this opera, wants to prevent a break of emotion at the end of an air, and to join it on to what follows as if the opera had continuous music and led into recitative. The phrase in question leads us to imagine that Dalinde will at once sing a recitative, but she does not; she begins in spoken prose.

Dalinde reveals that Ina, the king's daughter, loves Ariodant. A duet follows, Othon raging, Dalinde trying to quiet him; in the middle they suddenly sink to a whisper, as they watch Ariodant pass the length of the gallery at the back and enter the princess's apartments. Edgard enters and tells Othon that he will leave his daughter entirely free to choose her husband. Othon begins to concoct some sort of a plot with Dalinde, but it is purposely left vague, and we only gather that he may attempt to enter Ina's room at night, by the window. Ariodant comes on and has a solo, and then a duet with Ina, in the course of which there recur syncopated *sforzandos* for the orchestra alone, which the words make us interpret as depicting passionate embraces. Lurcain, Ina's brother, comes to warn them that Othon is approaching; Othon enters, makes a great scene, and wants to fight, but is prevented by the entrance of Edgard and the court; they all go into the palace for a feast. The act ends with a gradual diminuendo of the orchestra; this happens in several operas of this period – it was beginning to be the fashion.[9]

Act II shows us the garden, illuminated for the festivity; at one side of the stage we see Ina's balcony, with a small door underneath. The opening is very strange: one expects festive music of a conventional kind, but the orchestra begins with a slow and mysterious prelude. Some ballet music follows, very suggestive of Berlioz, and a chorus which is intended to be rapturous and erotic – just as in *Les Troyens à Carthage*. A bard (here is the first suggestion of Ossian in French opera) sings a song to the harp, with the most ridiculously conventional interludes between the verses. The harpist is directed to play an extempore prelude

[9] Compare Gazzaniga's *Don Giovanni Tenorio* (1787). (E.J.D.). Grétry had done this in Act I of *La Caravane du Caire* (1783), and there are other examples.

before he begins.[10] After this the chorus depart and Ariodant is left alone with Ina. She begs him not to go to his midnight duel with Othon, as she fears some snare. Ariodant asks her to buckle on his sword for him, which she does with a ribbon of her own – a truly Romantic moment! Ina has a very good air by herself, which is astonishingly like Weber, for it is ultra-'chivalrous' in style, mixing the Weber march rhythms with a violin figure in triplets that Weber would certainly have marked with his favourite word *lusingando.*

Lurcain enters with four friends who are to hide and defend Ariodant if Othon should play any trick on him. Ariodant, after singing a very charming little *romance,* not unlike some of Weber's songs, and with a typically Schubertian alternation of major and minor, meets Othon, who instead of fighting sets out to prove that he has access to Ina at night. He sings a sort of merry serenade, which must be meant to be malicious, rather like Mephistopheles' serenade in Berlioz's *Faust,* and a figure appears at the window; it is Dalinde, dressed in Ina's clothes. At this point begins a long and complicated finale.[11] Othon apparently has mounted to the balcony; Lurcain and his friends appear, and the chorus have a good deal to sing. Then they leave the stage, for Dalinde and Othon come down, with two guides who are to convey her to some distant place of safety. Edgard and Lurcain re-enter, go to Ina's chamber and bring her out; they find Othon's cloak and scarf, which they accept as proofs of her iniquity. This act, after mounting to a *fff,* dies down to nothing as the curtain falls; it is evidently becoming the orthodox ending for a second act.

Act III shows the hall of justice, where Ina is to be tried. Othon manages to have a private interview with Ina, in which he offers to save her if she will be his, and suggests that she should say that they are already secretly married, so that last night's visit would have been perfectly legitimate. She refuses. The guides come in and tell Othon that they have put Dalinde out of the way, and he rewards them; but they inform the audience that something has gone wrong with the plot and they have told

---

[10] A striking feature of this song (a popular favourite of the period) is the changed orchestration of each verse, copied by Weber in the first scene of *Euryanthe.*

[11] The finale has begun earlier than this, with a short trio for Ariodant, Lurcain and Othon before the latter's serenade.

Othon a lie. A march is played, more like Berlioz than like Gluck, and the trial begins. Dalinde, disguised and veiled, is brought in as prisoner, and is asked by Edgard to defend herself: she maintains complete silence, which according to operatic law at once involves her condemnation. Othon says she is his wife; she throws off the veil and says 'No!' She then explains the whole plot, adding that Othon intended to have her murdered by the two guides, but she was rescued by Ariodant. She appeals to the common-sense of the assembly, and asks how anybody could possibly have recognized her in the dark when the whole court has failed to recognize her by daylight. This brings the opera to its orthodox happy end.

The general resemblance to *Euryanthe* is very striking; it is not merely the similarity of plot and dramatic atmosphere, but the actual musical resemblance to the style of Weber. This is perhaps the best of all Méhul's operas, for it has consistency of style, and a plot which although wildly Romantic is not outrageously non-sensical and deals with very genuine human emotions. Moreover it is not dependent, as some of these operas are, on scenic effects such as storms and avalanches.

With Le Sueur's opera *Ossian, ou les Bardes*, produced in 1804, we are in the full flood of Romanticism. The poems of Ossian always had a deeper influence on the Continent than in England, for there was not so much scepticism about them. Le Sueur, as one would expect, took the whole thing quite seriously. The story of *Ossian* is rather like that of Purcell's *King Arthur*; Ossian is the hero of the Caledonians, who are making a patriotic struggle against their oppressors the Scandinavians under Duntalmo.

Le Sueur wished the whole opera to be dominated by the sound of the harps which the Bards are supposed to play. There are generally parts for two harps, and most theatres would consider this very extravagant to-day; but in a note at the end of the score Le Sueur directs that wherever the harps come in there should be no fewer than six firsts and six seconds, so as to dominate the entire orchestra and bring out the effect of the hundred harps of Selma. He makes many allusions to Selma in the score: several numbers are marked *chant de Selma*, but they do not sound like any Scottish music, as far as I can judge. They sound much more like Berlioz. The whole opera is on a very grand scale, with huge ballets, immense ensembles, and double choruses; it is quite clear that it must have been the model for Berlioz's *Les Troyens*, and most of it is much more like Berlioz than like Beethoven or Cherubini, except that Le Sueur is not always able to keep up his Romantic style, and at odd moments drops into the most anti-quated Mozartian formulae.

In the fourth act Ossian, who has been taken prisoner by the Scandinavians, is to be sacrificed to their gods. He is shut up in a place called the Circle of Brunco, a cavern in the rocks, but open to the sky. No sound is heard there, says the stage direction, quoting the poems of Ossian as an authority, except the howls and shrieks of phantoms. This is a considerable step forward from Cherubini's avalanche; Cherubini got as far as natural convulsions, but Le Sueur at last makes contact with the supernatural. The introduction to this scene is unmistakeably Romantic in character, and the clarinets and bassoons do their best to reproduce the ghostly moans and howls, though the spirits take no part in the performance. Ossian has a long mono-logue, and is then joined by Hydala, a friendly bard, who offers to change clothes with him and die in his stead; Ossian rejects this in what Le Sueur calls an 'air chevaleresque', and Hydala replies with an 'air romantique', after which they sing a duet. It is difficult to conjecture what Le Sueur actually meant by 'romantique' in this song, but it has great beauty and expres-siveness. In the fifth act there is a great chorus of mourning, and then the Scandinavians enter, dancing and singing, to a very curious march, played by strings only, with the triangle beating continuously and the big drum almost continuously. The general style of the march rather suggests a reminiscence of the Scythians in Gluck's *Iphigénie en Tauride*.

Stimulated no doubt by the outstanding success of *Ossian*, which had excited the cordial admiration of Napoleon, Méhul produced an Ossianic opera in 1806 called *Uthal*. This has become notorious in the histories of music, because it is scored for an orchestra without violins, the string band consisting only of violas, violoncellos and double basses. It has been suggested that the opera would for this reason be unbearably tedious, but, as Sir Donald Tovey has pointed out, *Uthal* is in one act only and quite short, so that its peculiar colouring would hardly have time to become oppressive.

The overture is quite as Romantic in character as any German music; it is full of mystery and wildness. It works up through very strange modulations to a great excitement of storminess, through which the voice of the heroine, Malvina, is heard shrieking the name of her father, Larmor. This apparently happens before the curtain rises;[12] the prelude goes on for some time longer without any further news of Malvina. It settles down to quiet, in the key of B flat, having started in C major: Méhul is not troubled by conventionalities of form. The curtain rises on a forest, with rocks and the sea; Malvina and Larmor are embracing. Uthal, the husband of Malvina, has risen against his father-in-law, a venerable and aged chief, and dispossessed him. Malvina flies to her father's help. Larmor is in a great state of indignation and has sent messengers to Fingal, who, he hopes, will send his warriors to devastate the country. Malvina is distressed; she had hoped that there would be no more war, and that her own charms would have more influence with Uthal than all Fingal's warriors.

Fingal's warriors are heard approaching – a distant chorus, accompanied by clarinets, bassoons, horns and harp behind the stage. They are headed by Ullin, who makes a long and quite unnecessary speech telling how Fingal has sent forces to the rescue. Larmor holds forth on his wrongs; it appears that Uthal has told him that he is too old for fighting and ought to stay at home and limit his activities to banqueting while Uthal goes to battle. The chorus wish to attack the palace, but Ullin holds them back: he will not start till daylight. However, they march away somewhere, in order that Malvina may have the stage to herself. A hymn to sleep is heard, sung by four bards; the warriors are apparently sleeping in the forest. Malvina decides to explore the forest in the hopes of finding some hero whom she may persuade to stop the war in the interests of the women and old people.

Uthal enters, and sings a recitative and air to explain that Larmor is a tiresome old man who will not sit quiet in his old age. He discovers the warriors, and also Malvina, whom he recognizes; but she does not recognize him. They converse, and she makes it clear that she loves her husband, on which Uthal takes off his helmet and reveals himself. The chorus break in, threatening Uthal, and he insists on fighting; Malvina, driven to

[12] Not necessarily: other French operas – for example Grétry's *Le Jugement de Midas* (1778) and Dalayrac's *Azémia* (1786) – demand some sort of *tableau vivant* during the overture.

a choice between husband and father, decides for the latter. She is left alone, and a bard comes and insists on singing to her, rather against her will. A battle takes place behind; Larmor re-enters to say that Uthal is a prisoner. Uthal, in chains, is condemned to banishment; Malvina says she will go with him. This is too much for his feelings; he collapses, and asks pardon of his father-in-law. Larmor of course forgives him, and the opera ends.

One of the most extraordinary productions of this period was Le Sueur's biblical opera *La Mort d'Adam*. Its first performance took place at Paris in 1809, but it seems to have been composed some years earlier, perhaps as far back as 1800.[13] The poem of this *tragédie lyrique religieuse*, as it is called, was written in imitation of Klopstock, and it is the same subject that William Blake treated in *The Death of Adam*. The whole opera suggests illustrations by Blake, though we may be fairly certain that Le Sueur had never heard of him, either as a painter or as a poet. But they had the same background – Milton, Klopstock and Young's *Night Thoughts* – and we see how much that we are inclined to attribute to the original inspiration of one artist is really common property. Le Sueur's full score is covered with annotations engraved wherever they can be squeezed in, partly in French and partly in Italian, making a reference on nearly every page to some book which he had the intention of publishing. He was firmly convinced that he was composing in the ancient Greek style, or else in that of the ancient Hebrews, and that conductors and performers must have a definite understanding of this in order to interpret his music in the spirit of the antique. The opera is laid out on a colossal scale, with vast choral scenes, more grandiose even than those of *Les Troyens*; it ends with a vision of Heaven and Hell, admittedly taken from *Paradise Lost*.

One more opera claims our attention – Cherubini's *Faniska*, which was not printed until after his death, at least not in full score. *Faniska* was composed for the Imperial Opera at Vienna in 1806, the year of Beethoven's first revision of *Fidelio* (performed on 25 February) with the overture Leonora No. 3. At that moment Cherubini was probably regarded all over Europe as the greatest active living composer. Haydn was still alive, the

[13] Much of it was certainly in existence by autumn 1801, when Le Sueur published a letter to N. F. Guillard 'sur l'opéra de la Mort d'Adam'. Guillard had written Le Sueur's libretto, and also that of Gluck's *Iphigénie en Tauride*.

patriarch of music, but he was now an old man, and had practically given up composition; Beethoven was producing some of his greatest works, but was by no means universally accepted. Rossini had not yet arrived, and Schubert was a boy of nine.

The French school of opera was well known in Vienna and very cordially admired; but Vienna had always remained loyal to the Italians. Salieri was still there, a personage of the greatest social importance; the German party had done their best to cast out Italian opera, but so far they had achieved nothing worth mentioning, except *Die Zauberflöte*, although the trivial operas of Weigl enjoyed considerable popularity.[14]

The full score of *Faniska* has Italian words only, although published in Paris, apparently about 1845. But it has no recitatives, and it is quite clear that there must have been spoken dialogue to connect the vocal numbers. If that was so, the opera must have been performed in German.[15] There are two episodes of *mélodrame*, but no words are printed with them; the mere presence of *mélodrame* excludes the possibility of *secco* recitatives, the only admissible form of dialogue in Italian.

The story of *Faniska* is much the same as that of Cherubini's earlier Polish opera, *Lodoiska*. The heroine Faniska is taken prisoner and held fast by a tyrant, Zamoski, who is in love with her, although she is a married woman with a family. Her husband Rasinski comes to rescue her, and introduces himself as a messenger to inform her of her husband's death; but he is betrayed by the indiscretion of his little daughter Edwige, and condemned by Zamoski to work in the mines. The plot is taken from *Les Mines de la Pologne*, a melodrama by Guilbert de Pixérécourt, and he no doubt took it from some earlier novel.[16] What happens in the second act is not very clear; Faniska and her child, accompanied by the servant Mosca, who in Act I was a rather unpleasant character, go to the mines to rescue Rasinski. There is evidently some sort of scenic effect in this act, but as the score gives no stage directions it is impossible to make out the course of events. The rescue is effected mainly through Rosno, a peasant or something

---

[14] The most successful German opera between *Die Zauberflöte* and *Der Freischütz* was Winter's *Das unterbrochene Opferfest* (1796).

[15] In a translation by Joseph Sonnleithner, apparently made after Cherubini had set the text in Italian.

[16] This has not been identified. The melodrama was staged at the Ambigu-Comique in 1803, with music by Gérardin-Lacour.

of the sort, who was helped long ago by Rasinki's father and is eternally grateful. Rosno is a typical figure of French Revolution opera. What happens in Act III is still more mysterious, but there are marches, presumably of soldiers, and in the end virtue is rewarded and tyranny punished.

Cherubini was evidently determined to give Vienna the best that he could produce, and to take advantage of the excellent Viennese orchestra. He had seen the performances of *Fidelio* in 1805, but he thought Beethoven did not know how to write for the voices. Cherubini's own vocal writing looks indeed far more singable than Beethoven's, and the score of *Faniska* is full of devices intended simply to show off a singer's voice, though always in a dignified style. But *Faniska* demands huge voices and singers whose physical strength can stand any sort of strain. As in *Médée*, every number strikes one as being much too long, and worked up with far too much grandiosity. Cherubini owes nothing to Beethoven; he was ten years older, and his own style had been completely matured before Beethoven began to be heard of.

What impressed the German composers in Cherubini's music must have been his handling of the orchestra. We must remember that in those days Beethoven was not a classic, and all his works were very severely criticized by his contemporaries. In our own day we have allowed symphonies to become more important than operas. This has been due, no doubt, to the incomparable grandeur of Beethoven's symphonies, which set a standard for the composers of the later nineteenth century. In the first half of that century the man who set the general standard of style was Cherubini. His operas may not have been much played,[17] but his overtures were, as the number of their editions and arrangements proves, and the overtures were almost symphonies in themselves. They had striking and original themes, even if they were less striking than those of Beethoven. Beethoven was regarded as too eccentric to imitate; Mozart was still a model for some, but on the whole was beginning to be found old-fashioned.[18] Cherubini had a more grandiose style of orchestration, and a more conscious technique of elaboration. His structural forms are not by any means orthodox, and it would be interesting, though laborious, to trace his methods of construction, and to

[17] They were far more popular in Germany than in France.
[18] But many Romantics regarded him as a prophet of the new style.

find out whence they were derived. He seems for instance to have adopted frequently Haydn's system of transposing his first subject to the dominant in order to make a second. I mention this, because I think the irregular forms of Weber, Mendelssohn and Schumann are probably due to following the example of Cherubini.

Another feature of Cherubini's music which appealed to the Romantics was his technique of passion and excitement. Beethoven can give us all this, it is true, and Beethoven in his greatest moments is of course incomparably greater than Cherubini. Besides, Beethoven, in spite of his notorious bad tempers – I speak only of his music – remains relatively calm, even in *Fidelio*, and more so in his non-dramatic music. Cherubini may have been a symphonist by temperament, but at this stage of his life – up to the age of about 50 – he was mainly a composer of operas, and for that reason passion had to be part of his stock-in-trade; it was indispensable to be able to keep up this atmosphere of excitement throughout long numbers, perhaps throughout a whole act of an opera. No doubt his passion often became mere *cliché*, and some of the exciting parts of *Faniska* are very dry and academic, notably the bits to accompany spoken dialogue. But he provided his followers with a technique, a technique based on rhythmical figures and modulations which were considered bold for their time, and a copious use of the diminished seventh.[19]

Le Sueur had no influence, as far as I can ascertain, outside France. He was an odd character who became odder as he grew older; a man very much cut off from the outer world, meditating in solitude, but at the same time devoted to teaching, and singularly beloved by his pupils. It is enough to say that Le Sueur originated many of the ideas and methods which have been credited to Berlioz.

Méhul deserves to be better known than he is at the present day. It is natural that *Joseph* should be the only one of his operas which is revived now, because Méhul's style has inevitably become antiquated, and it is generally felt that an antiquated style is suitable only for sacred music. But his influence on his own

[19] Other composers of the French school, notably Méhul and Berton, used more advanced chords and more experimental harmony than Cherubini, though they lacked his technical accomplishment in other respects.

day, and especially on the German composers, must have been considerable, and it is astonishing to see how much of the Romantic technique was invented by him.

The general effect of the French Revolution was to popularize the theatre, and make composers write for unsophisticated audiences. Hence the eternal insistence on the elementary virtues, gratitude, justice, generosity, respect for parents, etc – subjects which a modern audience finds rather ridiculous on the stage, even if modern spectators in their own private lives behave just as generously and honourably as those of the French Revolution. Audiences wanted to enjoy what had been the pleasures of the privileged classes, but they enjoyed them in a more childlike way; they were not concerned with passing themselves off as connoisseurs. The change in operatic life was partly due to a general lowering of social standards, but it did mean also a rise of standards in the humbler classes. Opera was being enjoyed by all and sundry instead of being an exclusively aristocratic entertainment; and this was only possible when the humbler classes reached a certain higher level of general education.[20]

[20] Opera was not an exclusively aristocratic entertainment in Paris before 1789 (there was much social mixing), and it is improbable that the general level of education rose during the Revolution, when the system broke down. Among the factors governing the increased popularity of opera were new laws easing restrictions on the theatres, the authorities' exploitation of their discovery that they controlled a powerful propaganda weapon, and the enthusiastic acceptance, by composers and audiences alike, of the ideals propounded by the Revolution.

7

SPONTINI

There is much about the Napoleonic period which does not strike us as Romantic at all, although it was contemporary with the most ardent Romanticism in other countries, and even, as we have just seen, in France itself. Spontini well represents the art of the Empire. In certain ways he resembles Lully; he produced operas for Napoleon as Lully did for Louis XIV, and his genius lay not so much in the making of beautiful music as in the architecture of colossal masses. Spontini is of all composers the most grandiose, and although that epithet may often imply distaste rather than admiration, still, there are occasions when the grandiose is in place, and it is right that a musician should understand the technique of it.

Spontini is best known by his opera *La Vestale*, but that was not the first that brought him to the notice of the Parisian critics. He had had a conventional Italian education, and had composed a large number of comic operas for Italian theatres which are now entirely forgotten. His first opera for Paris was *Milton*, a short work in one act.[1] It is amusing to an English reader, as it deals with an imaginary episode in the life of our great poet, and we see him dictating to his secretary the episode of Adam and Eve (before the Fall) in *Paradise Lost*. The music is rather trivial;[2] it is a not very successful imitation of the French *opéra-comique*. In 1807 he brought out *La Vestale* on a libretto which had already been refused by both Cherubini and Méhul: one wonders why, for it is extremely well written. It may be suspected that it was not nearly Romantic enough for Méhul; Cherubini might well have accepted it, for it is on much the same lines as *Démophoon* and *Médée*, and a careful study shows that it was planned on the

---

[1] Spontini's first work for Paris was *La Petite Maison*, a one-act *opéra-comique* produced 12 May 1804. *Milton* followed on 27 November the same year.

[2] For Berlioz's very different opinion see *Evenings with the Orchestra*, translated and edited by Jacques Barzun (Chicago and London, 1956, reissued 1973), p. 175. Berlioz's writings are full of enthusiastic references to Spontini's operas.

conventional scheme of the French 'rescue opera', although it is not generally classed in this category. The story is unusually simple. Julia, a Vestal Virgin in ancient Rome, is in love with a young officer, Licinius, who after five years' absence at the wars comes back to Rome to be given a triumph. He is horrified to find that Julia, who was previously free to marry, when he was young and unknown, has been compelled to take the veil for reasons of social ambition on the part of her father. At the ceremony of the triumph she has to place the laurel crown on his head; he manages to exchange a few words with her, and says he will meet her at night in the temple of Vesta. In Act II Julia is spending the night in the temple, responsible for guarding the sacred fire. Licinius comes, and in the excitements and raptures of love they forget all about the fire and it goes out. By some unaccountable means (unless the temple is supposed to be ex-posed to public view) the population of Rome at once become aware of the fact, and the priests and people burst in to arrest Julia and take her to prison. In Act III she is condemned to be buried alive. Licinius protests, arguing that Romulus himself, the founder of Rome, was the offspring of a Vestal Virgin; but no High Priest would listen to such casuistry for a moment, and the supreme pontiff is inflexible. Julia is condemned; Licinius tells the people that he is equally to blame, but she vehemently denies this. His followers start to make a disturbance. The stage sud-denly grows dark, and there is a great storm, during which the combatants are completely in disorder. A thunderbolt strikes the altar and re-lights the sacred flame, on which the High Priest, finding that his own authority is safe, thinks it wiser to allow the marriage of Julia to the popular favourite.

Here, as in *Lodoiska*, *Faniska* and many other operas, we have Julia, the captive, held enchained by the High Priest and the Head Vestal; her lover comes to release her, but in the second act has only made matters worse. The final rescue ought to be effected by his band of followers, but we are given a storm and a miracle too. A very characteristic stage direction comes immediately after the miraculous lighting of the fire; Licinius and his friend Cinna enter the tomb and bring Julia (who is unconscious) to the front of the stage. The heroine, as we have often observed, is always unconscious on these occasions, and she is always directed to be brought to the front of the stage.

A great deal of the opera is taken up with pageantry. Napoleon had a great admiration for Spontini's operas, and no doubt he approved of all this majestic glorification of ancient Rome, and of the authority of the State; it was probably for the same reason that *La Vestale* was chosen to be performed at Florence at the first Maggio musicale in 1934. Carl Ebert, who directed the production, said that it was hardly an opera but rather a *serenata* with dramatic episodes. It is not an opera that one wants to see often, but for a festival performance, in a very large theatre, with a sumptuous setting, it is still extremely effective and imposing, provided that the chief singers are equal to their very exacting parts. Spontini was not so well educated a musician as Cherubini, and he sometimes makes what one can only call clumsy harmony; but on the whole his pageant music is dignified, though it lacks the beauty of Cherubini's. The influence of Cimarosa is also apparent. If Cimarosa is remembered to-day, it is only for his *Il matrimonio segreto*, and he is generally described as having a genius for comic opera surpassed only by that of Mozart. But in his own day the opera for which he was most admired was *Gli Orazi e i Curiazi*, which the present age is certainly not likely to revive. *Gli Orazi* may be described as a typical old-fashioned *opera seria* treated very largely in the style of *opera buffa*. It is not intended to be comic in the least; it is not a libretto such as Casti used to write, in which great men of history were purposely presented in a ridiculous light. Cimarosa wrote this opera in all seriousness, and his audiences accepted it no less seriously; but the technical methods he employed were largely those of comic opera, and the result is something very like Rossini, with the regular Rossini crescendo thrown in, not to mention the Rossinian strings of thirds and sixths.

We find the same tricks in *La Vestale*; there is not much in the way of coloratura, but plenty of places where the voices or the instruments play pretty tunes in thirds or sixths. There are cases of the Rossini crescendo too, and many examples of the bass which rapidly alternates tonic and dominant. We notice also an inclination for melodies in slow 9/8 time, with a guitar-like accompaniment. The Italians of the next generation were to drench the world with sentiment in 9/8; but Beethoven himself had been before them, in his sonatas, and one finds the same sort of tunes, only more sentimental still, in the very interesting chamber music of Prince Louis Ferdinand of Prussia, who had been killed at the battle of Saalfeld a year before *La Vestale* came out.

These Rossinian mannerisms are probably enough to have secured the opera in the affections of the Italian public; it is not performed often, but it is certainly not dead, at any rate as far as Italy is concerned. And it deserves to live, for the dramatic episodes are sometimes magnificent; the whole of the second act, with the love duet between Julia and Licinius, and the going out of the fire, is extremely moving, even at the present day. So also is the third act, with Julia's *scena* before she goes into her tomb. The pageant music has become rather pale with the lapse of time, but at the present day that makes it sound all the more suitable as a background of antique ceremony, against which the human emotions stand out with greater vividness.

La Vestale can hardly be called a Romantic opera, but it is necessary to include it here, because the later Romantics learned so much from it. Spontini himself learned much from it, for it is recorded that he was always altering and revising it in the course of rehearsals. Composition seems to have been always a laborious matter with Spontini, as it was with his disciple Meyerbeer, but there can be no doubt that his operas owed their success and their long lives to his minute care for detail.

We notice too in this opera, and in a very marked way, the acceptance of certain conventions, characteristic of nearly all nineteenth-century opera, including at least the early works of Wagner. Opera has always had its conventions, and sometimes composers of strong character have destroyed them; but they have by that very act started the growth of new ones. Spontini seems to have been the inventor of that tiresome but universal type of ensemble movement in 3/4 time – it generally comes towards the end of a finale – in which the chorus is treated like a military band, and sings nothing but repeated chords on the beats / – 2 3 / 1 2 – / – 2 3 / 1 2 – / alternating tonic and dominant: if there is a second chorus, it sings the same chords a bar later, thus filling up the rests. We find this 3/4 movement in nearly all the big French and Italian operas – Rossini, Donizetti, Meyerbeer, Halévy, etc, and it drags out the finale to an interminable length.

Spontini's next opera, *Fernand Cortez*, was brought out in 1809 and revised for another production in 1817. Between those two dates came the fall of Napoleon, which meant the fall of Spontini too, as far as Paris was concerned. Spontini transferred himself to Berlin,[3] where he remained in charge of the Opera for some twenty years. This period of his life is historically of great importance, because although his later compositions were not very successful, his tenure of the Berlin Opera contributed much to the setting of a standard for performance in Germany, and indeed of a standard for style of composition.

Fernand Cortez is never seen on the stage nowadays; but it is mentioned frequently by writers on the history of music, though it may be doubted whether they have studied the score. Its chief reputation is that of being unbearably noisy; but it has many other qualities, good and bad, which make it worth while to describe it in detail.

First let me read you a paragraph from H. A. L. Fisher's *History of Europe*, in which he describes what Cortez actually did in Mexico.

With a mere handful of Spaniards, but with the invaluable aid of horses and guns, this resolute and resourceful commander had overpowered the Aztecs, a race of bloodthirsty cannibals who here maintained a curious and mutilated civilization, knowing nothing of coinage, of beasts of burden, of cows or of goats, had kidnapped their king Montezuma and made himself master of their capital city. There have been few clearer examples in history of the power of prestige in war. The Aztecs were as innocent as they were cruel. They found in the Spaniard a source of bewildered amazement. His fierce animal energy, his horses, his guns, were things outside the orb of their experience. They were ready to believe the fable industriously circulated by Cortes that the mysterious strangers who had suddenly dropped from nowhere with their uncanny attendant animals were demi-gods whom it was idle to vex or to resist.

Jouy, the author of the libretto, seems to have slightly confused the conquest of Mexico with that of Peru, for he makes the Mexicans hand over quantities of gold to the Spaniards, with the result that they wish to desert Cortez and go home. Gold was found in plenty in Peru; and it may also be mentioned that it was in Peru where the Spaniards, egged on by the missionary friars, carried out their most atrocious cruelties.

The author of Spontini's libretto knows nothing of cruelties

---

[3] Not immediately: he was engaged as chief Kapellmeister to the King of Prussia in September 1819 and settled in Berlin the following year after the failure of *Olympie* at the Paris Opéra in December.

SPONTINI

on the Spanish side; his Spaniards are the last word in nobility
and chivalry. There can be little doubt that the character of
Cortez was meant to suggest a resemblance to Napoleon himself,
and this was doubtless the reason why Napoleon admired the
opera.[4]

The opera opens with an overture, mainly in the military style,
but with a sentimental second subject; there are many passages
which at once remind us of Weber and of Schubert. The scene
of Act I[5] is the temple of Talépulca, the Mexican god of evil. It
is night, and the temple is strangely illuminated by the torches
of the priests and magicians preparing for a human sacrifice. The
voices of Spanish prisoners are heard, led by Alvar, the brother
of Cortez. They are prepared to die for their country, and
Spontini marks the score with the word *noblement* – a direction
which occurs two or three times in the course of the opera. The
prisoners sing a hymn in three parts unaccompanied – it is rather
like a German male-voice part-song, and at once suggests the style
of Meyerbeer. It is perhaps not surprising that the chorus of
Mexicans expresses a desire to tear them in pieces.

Montezuma, to the annoyance of the High Priest – that invariable High Priest of opera whom we have already met so often
– orders the sacrifice to be cancelled, or at any rate postponed.
Alvar, he says, being the brother of Cortez, is far too valuable
a hostage to be sacrificed. He is to be handed over to Amazily,
a Mexican princess who has become a Christian and so secured
some advantages for the Mexicans. The High Priest is of a
different opinion. Amazily enters, to the surprise of everybody;
she tells them quite plainly that it will be all up with Mexico if
Alvar is sacrificed: Cortez will follow the bad example of the
Mexican High Priest. She goes on to admit openly that she is in
love with Cortez and he with her, and further that she is a
convinced Christian.

Amazily's music is very striking, compared to anything that
we have previously encountered in Spontini's works. Her air is
forcible and concentrated; it has no coloratura, and no very
definite melody. It modulates freely, and has startlingly wide

[4] It is now known that Napoleon had a guiding hand in the whole project.
[5] Dent is describing the revised version of 1817. In the 1809 original Amazily,
who is not in love with Cortez, commits suicide by diving into a lake, and
Montezuma does not appear at all. The third act of 1809 was transmuted into
the first act of 1817.

100

intervals; it shows off the voice, but it makes no concessions to popular taste and always preserves a great dignity. Spontini here, and throughout the opera, shows a much more smooth and Italian line of melody than the French composers, but at the same time there is an almost German concentration on harmony; he has created the international style of the next generation.

Montezuma orders that the prisoners be taken back to prison and the oracle of the god interrogated. Amazily is left alone on the stage with her brother Telasco, one of Montezuma's officers. She reminds him that Cortez rescued her from a priest who had already murdered her mother: all this story is very inadequately explained. This conversation is interrupted by a general catastrophe – thunder is heard, the statue of the god is shaken and flames burst out all round it. Priests and people rush on and make a great noise; the High Priest naturally suggests that the god is angry because the prisoners have not been sacrificed. Montezuma however remains quite firm. A messenger arrives to say that Cortez is advancing to take possession of the city; Amazily, with Montezuma's approval, undertakes to see him and negotiate a truce. Here follows a quartet – one of those typical conventional operatic quartets in which the main object is to produce agreeable block harmony; but the characters all sing more or less different words, and the unfortunate High Priest, who has the bass part, can only repeat 'exterminez ces fiers guerriers' to the most uninteresting alternations of tonic and dominant. The chorus demand vengeance, and the act ends with a good deal of noise.

We see at once that the drama is not very clear, and that it is badly constructed owing to the need for alternations of solos and choruses. Spontini makes most of his effect with big choruses, and generally by dint of great crescendos working up to a climax.

Act II shows us the imperial tent in the camp of the Spaniards – the Emperor Charles V being represented by a throne, with his portrait above it. Through a half-open curtain is seen the lake with the Spanish fleet and a distant view of the city of Mexico. The soldiers and sailors are growing tired of the expedition, which they think is being carried on solely for the personal glory of Cortez himself. Cortez arrives and addresses them on the glory of the expedition; they become more rebellious and leave the stage. Amazily enters and informs Cortez that Alvar is to be set free; she then sings an affectionate air, which is one of the most attractive numbers of the opera. Telasco comes to negotiate peace terms; here there is a Mexican march, which is supposed to give local colour; at any rate it provides a great opportunity for pageantry – processions of Mexicans bringing gifts, etc. The curtains are drawn back and show the full stage, with the fleet and a place on land prepared for ceremonies, with the arms of the thirteen kingdoms of Spain. There follows an enormously long chorus of Spanish soldiers and Mexican women; the music is astonishingly like Meyerbeer; the voices are treated like military band instruments, and the phrases do not grow out of the words at all: in fact the words fit very badly.

Telasco wants peace, and offers gold in vast quantities, if the Spaniards will take ship and sail home. The sailors at once seize the gold; but Cortez disapproves. There is a long ballet, some of which must have been known to Schubert, for it contains suggestions of *Rosamunde*. After the ballet the cavalry and in-fantry of Cortez enter, all in revolt, singing their earlier chorus on a larger scale. Cortez makes a great speech, reproaching them for being mutinous when all Europe has its eyes on this expedition:

> Un monde était votre conquête,
> Encore un pas, vos noms victorieux
> Du temple de la gloire allaient orner le faîte.

He breaks into a chivalrous air of bitter invective; they take it up, and are at once converted to his side. They throw them-selves at his feet; others come in and there is a great march chorus. Cortez sends Moralez, one of his officers, on a whispered mission to the ships. Cortez demands the release of Alvar; Telasco is to be kept as a hostage, and the whole of Mexico sur-rendered to the Spaniards. As Telasco seeks to raise objections, Cortez points to the back of the stage:

> Télasco, vois s'il est facile de m'arrêter par des obstacles vains
> Et si jamais Cortez renonce à ses desseins.

At this moment the ships are set on fire; some explode, others go to the bottom. The Mexicans all depart in terror; the Spaniards are in great excitement, and Cortez starts them off on a quickstep which is quite obviously the model for the march in the overture to *Guillaume Tell*, to words which must have had a Napoleonic allusion:

Marchons, suivons les pas d'un guerrier invincible.
Cortez va nous conduire à des succès nouveaux,
À son génie il n'est rien d'impossible,
Et l'univers appartient aux héros.

They march off the stage, and are heard in the distance, the music dying down to nothing as the curtain falls. We are reminded not only of *Guillaume Tell*, but of *Fra Diavolo*.

Act III begins with a scene rather like the last act of *La Vestale*, the burial chamber of the Mexican kings, with the tomb of Amazily's mother in a prominent situation. The music starts with a march, which begins *pianissimo* and works up to a return *fortissimo* of the march and chorus which ended the previous act, as the Spanish soldiers climb the rocks and carry up their artillery. Some musical variety is provided this time by episodes representing an Indian tribe in alliance with the Spaniards. Telasco enters and observes these events, followed by Cortez, who sets Telasco free, as he says Montezuma has released the Spanish prisoners. Telasco is furious, but explains nothing. All this business is very obscure, and one wonders what any audience would make of it. Amazily comes on with Cortez and sings a long air, after which Moralez brings word that the Mexicans, stirred up by Telasco, have recaptured the Spanish prisoners and are demanding the surrender of Amazily. The High Priest naturally wants to have her sacrificed.

Here begins another distant chorus, accompanied by an orchestra of wind instruments and percussion on the stage. All the wind instruments except the flutes are muted, and no doubt the flutes would have been muted if Spontini could have thought of a way to mute them. Clarinets and oboes are tied up in leather bags. This orchestra plays a very lively military march, and the chorus are heard rejoicing at the liberation of the prisoners; they are accompanied by Mexican women, who seem always available to provide a soprano part. The chorus draws nearer and nearer and finally enters, with a great deal of dancing, only to be sent away again by Cortez because the news is false. Cortez and Amazily then sing a duet, which is all based on march rhythms, and just as we are beginning to get rather tired of this unceasing military music, Amazily, left alone on the stage, provides a contrast by invoking the spirit of her mother. She is however interrupted by the noise of battle, and takes refuge inside the tomb, directing her Mexican women and Spanish escort to follow her through its secret passages.

The scene changes to the vestibule of Montezuma's palace. The battle music still goes on, and we see Montezuma with Alvar and the Spanish prisoners and their guards. Montezuma says that he can defend the town no longer; he orders it to be set on fire and surrendered to the Spaniards. He also orders the prisoners' chains to be broken, as he does not wish to be cruel and prevent them escaping. They may join their brethren; but Alvar refuses to leave Montezuma. Montezuma mounts his throne to die there. The whole situation is very characteristic of what we may call operatic chivalry, descended from the operas of Metastasio, whose influence has not yet altogether died out. Amazily enters with her women. 'Non, vous ne mourrez pas', she says: Cortez has laid down his triumphant arms, and promises peace and prosperity to all. There is a great *marche triomphale*, to which Cortez enters on horseback with all his suite, to sing a chorus of satisfaction and watch an interminable ballet of the two nations. Here ends the opera.

Fernand Cortez is a significant production of the Napoleonic era, much more so than *La Vestale*, which is only a tentative beginning. *La Vestale* is the last descendant of the old-fashioned classical or mythological operas taken from Greek or Roman history. The pageantry with which it was surrounded was new to those who saw it; from a historical point of view it was not new at all, for as much pageantry and more had been seen in the Venetian operas of the seventeenth century. But those seventeenth-century operas, whether Italian or French, had not had the musical resources available to Spontini – his enormous orchestra and his accomplished choruses – for there is so much chorus work in Spontini that it could hardly be left to the ill-educated supers who learned their parts by ear in the older days.

Fernand Cortez may seem only a small advance on *La Vestale*. From a musical point of view the earlier opera is certainly far the better: that is, the quality of the music shows far more beauty, dignity and refinement, far more nobility of style and architecture. But if we admire it now, we admire it perhaps too much for its antique coldness and remoteness; it seems to belong to the age of Gluck, and differs from Gluck's operas only as Roman architecture differs from that of Greece. To us moderns both Rome and Athens are memories of an entirely remote antiquity.

Fernand Cortez belongs to what is officially called modern history, not to the Middle Ages, but to the Renaissance. If that history is put on the stage, it cannot be treated as a gallery of marbles; the characters must be flesh and blood, with human and super-human passions. The emotional standard is quite different from that of Gluck. To us, perhaps, the human emotion of Spontini's characters has become so remote that we are more inclined to be distracted by the pageantry, and in this opera pageantry seems to overwhelm everything. War is the background of the whole score; from beginning to end it is little more than a string of military marches, interspersed with a few dances in the polonaise style. The period of Beethoven is the age of the polonaise; it was not invented by Chopin.[6] The French had adopted it in the operas of Cherubini; *Lodoiska* and *Faniska* both show examples. It is highly probable that the Polish subjects were chosen because they offered the opportunity of introducing local colour in this form. But we meet with the polonaise rhythm everywhere; it is quite common in the earlier works of Beethoven, such as the Serenade for Flute, Violin and Viola; Weber wrote several pol-onaises, and so did Schubert. The style is continued by the Torch Dances (*Fackeltänze*) of Meyerbeer. And if we find polonaises in all the classical music of the epoch, still more do we find military marches. In a town like Vienna they must have been heard every day in the streets; people talked about nothing but war, and it was inevitable that even a deaf man like Beethoven should insert march-movements into his sonatas and quartets. I need not mention the copious output of Schubert in this style, whether he wrote the marches merely for pianoforte duet, that is, for dom-estic amusement, or to be scored for wind instruments and performed in the open air.

Spontini was the leader of all this musical militarism, and in his own day every musican knew it. Spontini too was the chief producer, though perhaps not the actual originator, of what the age of Mendelssohn called 'characteristic' music. The word is common among the titles of pianoforte pieces in Germany, and France too, in the Romantic era; to English ears it always sounds a little odd, for when we read the words 'characteristic pieces' on a title page, we imagine naturally that they mean 'character-istic of their composer'. They *are*, in most cases, for Mendelssohn

---

[6] J. S. and W. F. Bach, among others, had composed instrumental polonaises. The earliest operatic example appears to have been in *Lodoiska*.

cannot disguise himself; but their intention was to present something of a definite stage character – gipsies, sailors, huntsmen, or any of the other costumes in which the opera chorus can be dressed up, to come in and inform the audience at once who they are. They are about as genuine as the ladies and gentlemen at Flora's party in the third act of *La Traviata* who come in dressed up as gipsies, and tell her so.

All that comes mainly from Spontini, and most of all from *Fernand Cortez*. The weakness of the opera lay in a clumsily constructed libretto; it was Scribe, later on, who found out the right formula for constructing a political opera with the necessary solos, duets, ensembles and choruses. The influence of Spontini has in fact been disastrous to opera, not to its commercial success in the sumptuous days of the nineteenth century, but to opera at the present day. The public, thanks to Spontini, Meyerbeer, Wagner and perhaps to Verdi too, has become firmly convinced that opera is not worth seeing unless it is grandiose and spectacular, with the noise of an enormous orchestra. All this naturally costs a great deal of money, and under the conditions of the present day makes opera almost prohibitive as an entertainment to pay its way.

So much for what we may call the external influence of Spontini. But he has an internal influence too, that is, on music itself, on melody and harmony, and most of all on the dramatic style of singing – on the operatic style. It is difficult to analyse this without going into technicalities and printing a number of musical examples. Spontini, starting from the French style, avoids coloratura. Neither *La Vestale* nor *Cortez* has any noticeable amount of coloratura, and we must observe at the same time that both operas contain only one important woman's part. *Cortez* has in fact no other woman but Amazily; in *La Vestale* the senior Vestal Virgin is the only additional woman, and she is more or less the 'mère noble' – with a very short part too. Meyerbeer, Spontini's best imitator, generally has two or three important female parts, one a heavy dramatic soprano, another a coloratura-singer. By his time the vocal types have been sharply differentiated and divided into standard operatic categories. That subdivision always implies a conventionalization of opera, for composers are obliged to write, as a rule, for the standard types of voice.

SPONTINI

Spontini manages to achieve more genuine melodiousness than the French, Cherubini included, though he never seems to set himself to write deliberately pleasing melody. When he writes for chorus or ensemble, his melodies tend to become instrumental in character. Critics have often discussed what kind of music is 'vocal' and what not; we must admit that teachers of singing are always hostile to phrases and figures which are new or unfamiliar. But there is a type of vocal melody in Classical and Romantic operas which, although accepted because it occurs in what are called standard works of the great masters, is none the less unvocal and instrumental in conception, because it is not suitable to carry words and express the sentiment of words.

One discovers this best by trying to write words to music, as is the task of an operatic translator. Classical opera is not easy to translate, but once some principle has been found for the choice of words, translation is not impossible, and can even be satisfactory. There is not the least objection to coloratura of the Handelian type. But towards the end of the eighteenth century composers begin to treat their voices like instruments of an orchestra, or worse still, like those of a military band. They write recurrent figures, which simply cannot be thought of as the expression of words in any language. English is a very flexible language, and English words can generally be adapted comfortably and happily to any melodic phrase which is a good setting of the words in the original language, however widely that language may differ from English in its normal rhythm and accent. French, for instance, is peculiarly difficult to translate into English for music; but it can be done, and the more careful and conscientious the original composer is with his words, as Berlioz is, for example, the less difficult such adaptation becomes. But Spontini frequently employs characteristic military rhythms, derived from instruments and not from voices; and these rhythms are generally quite unsuited for words. A curious example stands out in my memory. You are probably acquainted with a Viennese operetta called *Das Dreimäderlhaus* ('Lilac Time'), made up out of popular fragments of Schubert. There is a vocal number – I think, a trio – on the tune of the well-known G major Ballet Music in *Rosamunde*. Sung by English singers with small light voices to clear-cut English words, this tune did not fit so badly, although one missed the clean attack of the violin bows.

But I once heard the operetta sung by an Italian company, the members of which felt it their duty to sing, not to talk, and to sing as if they were singing Mascagni. The result on this melody of Schubert's was indescribable. It is legitimate to quote this experience here, because Schubert was directly influenced by Spontini; he heard *La Vestale* at Vienna in 1812, and he was a thoroughgoing admirer of French opera. We can find many traces of Spontini in Schubert's symphonies, pianoforte and chamber music as well as in his operas.

The change of musical style which we notice in Europe about this time – the change that separates nineteenth-century music from that of Mozart – is due almost entirely to operatic influences, and enormously to Cherubini and Spontini. Some writers are always desirous of attributing all changes in musical style to the adoption of folk-music, songs or dances, into artistic music; they seem to have a certain political *parti-pris* which leads them to believe that all real musical inspiration comes from what they call the soil. I am inclined to suspect that a good deal of what is supposed to be folk-music, created by the communal inspiration of the agricultural labouring classes, is really no more than the dregs of Italian and other comic opera. However, it may reasonably be argued that these Italian comic-opera tunes came originally from the dregs of the population of Naples. The change I have mentioned is due largely to the adoption in chamber music and other concert-music of themes from the operas, including their marches and their dances. Nor did it stop at their adoption in the sonatas and symphonies; it influenced vocal music too, and especially in Germany it increased the production of songs based on very simple and square-cut metres and rhythms.

There is a certain type of 6/8 rhythm which became immensely popular all over Europe, especially in Germany and England, in the first quarter of the nineteenth century; a good example is the Mermaid's song in Weber's *Oberon*. The characteristic feature is that the bass stops while the treble goes on:[7]

$$1 - - - 5\ 6\ /\ 1 - - - 5\ 6\ /$$
$$1\ 2\ 3\ 4 - - /\ 1\ 2\ 3\ 4 - - /$$

[7] Dent noted 'Méhul, Ariodant!' in the margin. He may have been thinking of the finale of Act III of *Mélidore et Phrosine*, though the correspondence is not exact.

SPONTINI

I do not know who first invented it, but Spontini is the first standard composer in whose works I have found it. It is a rhythm not in the least typical of Mozart, though it may possibly be derived from an Italian source. It is still more characteristic when it proceeds supported by a tonic pedal, and in this form it is often to be found in Weber and Spohr. Tonic pedals are comparatively rare in Mozart, and when they do occur, they are generally very short, or else come at the end of the movement, as a coda. In Romantic music they are extremely common.

It has been necessary to consider Spontini in some detail, because although his music may sound to us Classical rather than Romantic it contributed very largely to the establishment of an operatic convention, and this convention became fixed in the minds of musicians, whether they wrote operas or not. Some, like Halévy and Meyerbeer, accepted the convention whole-heartedly, and wrote their operas in it, developing a style of their own which was not only conventional; it was supremely accomplished and effective. Others, like Schumann and Mendelssohn, would have liked to make a success on the stage, but hesitated about the convention. They professed to despise it, and started that school of thought which regards opera as an inferior form of music altogether – a doctrine which Mozart would never have tolerated for a moment, and which Beethoven would probably have rejected with equal energy. But the anti-operatic set were not quite honest about it; they never made a success with their own operas, and the reason can only be that they had not sufficient inspiration and imagination. Their imagination, in fact, was only good enough for chamber music and symphonies, in which some faint echoes of the opera-house gave them what we now regard as a Romantic charm.

8

ROSSINI

We must now retrace our steps for a short distance and consider a few minor composers of the Italian school. The first who claims our notice is Giovanni Paisiello, a Neapolitan. He has already been mentioned as the composer of Casti's *dramma eroi-comico*, *Il re Teodoro in Venezia*, but the opera which made his fame all over Europe was *Nina pazza per amore*. He had had considerable success in Vienna with *La molinara* (1788); Beethoven wrote variations on two of its themes. Andrea Della Corte, author of a careful study of Paisiello,[1] considers *La molinara* to be his best work. He admits that Paisiello had many limitations: he was not a well-educated man, and he seems to have had a rather narrow outlook on life and literature. He bears in fact a considerable resemblance to Pergolosi – a composer whom he himself criticized very severely! The attraction of Paisiello lies in his delicate sentimentality. He had none of Mozart's skill in the handling of the orchestra; the orchestra for him was merely an accompaniment to the voices, and his whole inspiration is concentrated on the voice-line. And, as Della Corte admirably says, it is concentrated in the opening bars of his arias, for beyond writing a charming initial phrase he has no idea how to amplify it and carry it on. We shall find that this limitation of inspiration to the initial phrase is the curse of many Italian composers and of some Germans too. They had the best of all models in Mozart, but they preferred to run after the more fashionable Italians such as Paisiello.

The libretto of *Nina*, which came out at Naples in 1789, was adapted from the French, like so many comic operas of its time. The original story came from a novel, *Les Délassements d'un homme sensible*, and had been made into a *comédie en prose mêlée d'ariettes* by Joseph Marsollier de Vivetières for the French composer Dalayrac; in this form it was first produced in 1786. Dalayrac is

---

[1] *Paisiello.... L'estetica musicale di P. Metastasio* (Turin, 1922).

a composer of a certain charm, but hardly of outstanding genius, and Paisiello certainly made more of an opera out of this subject. The play is sentimental comedy at its worst. Nina is a young lady who has fallen in love with a young man of whom her father does not approve. He is involved in a duel, and is supposed to have been killed. Nina goes out of her mind, and remains out of her mind until the young man comes back and is allowed by the father to marry her, since the father would rather see her married against his will than permanently insane. It would hardly be legitimate to class this little opera as Romantic, but its sentimentality is a step towards Romanticism. Its sentimentality is to modern ears perfectly unbearable, and we cannot understand how the whole of Europe was reduced to tears by these infantile melodies. But whatever we may think of them, we cannot afford to neglect their historical influence, for Paisiello's tunes were known all over the world, and there was hardly a composer of the time who was not to some extent affected by them.

Another Italian composer who was much performed in Germany at the turn of the century was Ferdinando Paer. Like Paisiello, he was much in Paris during the Napoleonic period,[2] and although his name is now almost completely forgotten, he had a considerable share in the formation of the Romantic style. Paer's most successful opera was *Camilla*, first produced at Vienna in 1801. Like *Nina*, *Camilla* had been taken from a French opera, based on a story by Madame de Genlis. The French opera was another work of Dalayrac – *Camille, ou le souterrain*. The very title suggests something Romantic, and the opera, as set by Paer, is as absurd a story as one could wish. Like *Lodoiska* and others of the French school, it is a 'rescue opera', and follows the usual formula. Camilla is the wife of an eccentric Duke, who shuts her up in a cellar in his castle in the Apennines for some ten years, because he supposes her to have been unfaithful. The overture represents a storm; this is the first case I have come across in which the storm appears so early,[3] though there is a rather feeble storm as prelude to the prologue of Salieri's *Tarare*. When the curtain rises we see a scene which by this time has become very

---

[2] Both composers were summoned by Napoleon and given official appointments, Paisiello in 1802–4, Paer from 1807.
[3] There are previous examples in the overtures of Grétry's *Le Jugement de Midas* (1778) and Gluck's *Iphigénie en Tauride* (1779).

familiar – a forest, with rocks at the sides of the stage, and an ancient castle, apparently half in ruins. Two travellers are lost in the storm; we have met them before, under other names. This time they are called Loredano, who is a romantic young gentleman, and Cola, who is his servant – and of course (in the Italian version of the story) a Neapolitan, who takes the earliest opportunity of singing a typical *buffo* song all about Naples.

An old gardener, or something of the kind, called Gennaro, comes out of the castle and gives a lurid account of his mysterious master, and we also make the acquaintance of a peasant woman, Ghitta, the wife of Gennaro, and much the same sort of person as Leonarda in Le Sueur's *La Caverne*. In the second act we meet the Duke, and we see him go to the secret staircase which leads to Camilla's prison. She is kept alive by food sent down in a basket on a string; but as she has not touched the food for some days, the Duke wonders if she is dead and goes down to look. He finds, however, that she is merely on hunger-strike, and he has to have her up and let her talk to him and inform the audience of her sufferings. She is particularly annoyed at being separated from her son, who is one of the first of that race of operatic children who become more abundant in subsequent generations. Adolfo is brought in to make her acquaintance, but he is not told that she is his mother; the Duke's idea is that if Adolfo spontaneously recognizes her as his mother, it will be taken as evidence of her innocence. Adolfo is quite old enough to sing a small part, like Edwige in *Faniska*, and if he does not commit himself to a definite statement, he is at any rate mysteriously moved by the sound of Camilla's voice. Camilla, during the interval in which the Duke goes to fetch Adolfo, sings a recitative and rondo which must have been very popular in its day, for occasional copies of it are found separately. It is certainly a very attractive song, and it is interesting to compare it with Dalayrac's setting of the same situation. Dalayrac's music is pretty, but it does not amount to very much. Paer's is quite obviously in the comic-opera style and not in the least like grand opera, but it has great charm, and is also brilliant without being aggressively showy. The child's feelings are expressed in a trio which he leads off, the other parts being taken by Camilla and the Duke. This is also a most charming little piece, rather in the innocent style of Paisiello; it is a round, in which each character repeats the same subject, the other voices combining with free parts, and the orchestral accompaniment is very elegantly scored. The round is a favourite operatic form at this date, found frequently in Mayr and Rossini as well as Paer. The classical example is that in Beethoven's *Fidelio*; but it had been used by Mozart in the supper scene of *Così fan tutte*, and it is generally supposed that he was following an Italian model, perhaps Cimarosa or Paisiello. Certainly there are very similar rounds composed by Padre Martini of Bologna, but who first introduced them into an operatic ensemble I am quite unable to say.

In the third act Camilla is rescued by soldiers who come to arrest the Duke for some misdemeanour. The music of the opera is not very Romantic, except in the introductory storm (for I think we must regard all operatic storms as Romantic); but the sentimental style of the songs and ensembles is worth considering, for it becomes clear that the new sentimental manner which we find in so many composers of the 'early Beethoven period' was based on the operatic melodies of Paer and other Italians. It is a style which we cannot ignore, although the chief exponents of it are the second-rate composers such as Dussek, Prince Louis Ferdinand, and Spohr; for it is observable also, if only at certain moments, in Beethoven himself, as well as in Weber and Mendelssohn.

It is the characteristic style of another composer of Italian operas, Simone Mayr. Mayr was not really an Italian at all; he was a German from Bavaria, but he went in his youth to Italy, and remained there all his life, composing operas for Rome and Venice, and making his home chiefly in Bergamo, where he trained Donizetti and finally died. Mayr's operas have been analysed and described in detail by Ludwig Schiedermair of Bonn; his book fortunately gives copious musical examples, for scores of Mayr's operas are scarce. In London I was only able to find (in the British Museum)[4] a selection of favourite arias arranged for pianoforte solo, published in England about 1825, from an opera on an English subject, *La rosa rossa e la rosa bianca*,[5] which may have something to do with the Wars of the Roses but

---

[4] The British Museum possessed scores of Mayr's *Ginevra di Scozia* (1801), *Adelasia e Aleramo* (1806) and *Medea in Corinto* (1813) long before Dent's time.

[5] This opera (1813) was revived at Bergamo in 1963. *Medea in Corinto* was staged in New York in December 1969 and at the Wexford Festival in October 1974, and has been recorded. See also p. 130, note 8.

is merely a sentimental comic opera of the usual type. Mayr's arias were bound up with similar selections from Weber, Auber and other composers of the 1820s, and when I read them through, without any words, they all seemed very much alike, shocking as it may seem to say so. But one saw in this way how universal that particular idiom was. It seems to have made a peculiar appeal to the Germans, for Spohr adopted it completely, even before Weber did, and we can find plenty of traces of it in Schubert too.

It is important to realize the characteristics of Paer and Mayr, obscure as they are to-day, because much of their style has been credited to the genius of Rossini. Rossini was always a great enthusiast for German music; he was himself sneered at for being too German, and although he wrote disparagingly of Beethoven in 1816, he was always an ardent worshipper of Haydn and Mozart, and in late life of Beethoven and J. S. Bach too. But I suspect that the formation of his solid style, a style conspicuously different from that of Cimarosa and Paisiello, although influenced by them, was due mainly to the study of Paer and Mayr, more particularly of Mayr, who always showed a thorough German conscientiousness in the details of his workmanship, and a German understanding of the emotional resources of harmony. The Romantic style was in fact the outcome of the German–Italian alliance, initiated at Vienna – the marriage of Italian melody to German harmony. As Paisiello remarked to one of his pupils, the Germans were mostly bad singers and therefore concentrated mainly on the study of harmony to produce their musical effects, whereas the Italians, being singers by nature, had no need of harmony – their melody could express anything.

I do not intend here to pursue the career of Rossini in detail; I am concerned with him only as a contributor to the Romantic Movement. We shall have to consider him in two aspects – as one who was at times Romantic in himself, and as the cause of Romanticism in others.

To read through one opera of Rossini is exhilarating; to read a dozen is depressing and wearisome. The only source of amusement is the discovery that Rossini frequently used the same music in different operas: thus 'Io sono docile', the lively section that follows 'Una voce poco fà', sung by Rosina in *Il barbiere di Siviglia*, is given a year or two later to Queen Elizabeth of

England.[6] Romanticism, generally speaking, was entirely foreign to Rossini's whole temperament, and to his conception of opera. It was perfectly reasonable for him to transfer songs from one opera to another, for although some of his operas may be outstandingly better than others, they are all written in exactly the same style, with the exception of *Guillaume Tell*,[7] which belongs to the end of his career, and is moreover a French opera, not an Italian one.

The nearest approach to Romantic feeling in Rossini may be seen in *La donna del lago*, which being taken from Sir Walter Scott was in itself Romantic, and in *Otello*, where Shakespeare could not fail to inspire him to his greatest heights. There is a distinctly Romantic feeling about Ellen's first song in *La donna del lago*, though it is perhaps more of a Venetian barcarolle than Scottish; and this song must have struck Rossini's audiences as Romantic, for we can trace its influence in many other composers. Schubert remembered it in *Rosamunde*, Auber in *Fra Diavolo*, and Spohr, for all his disapproval of Rossini, could not help remembering it several times.

The supernatural made no appeal to Rossini; the only occasion on which he had to find music for it was in *Semiramide*, where the ghost appears, and he wisely turned to Mozart for a model and copied the disappearance of Don Giovanni. But in *Otello* – an opera in which he must have set himself to give his best all the way through – the human emotions provided by Shakespeare compelled him to be Romantic, and he suddenly thought of an addition of his own, not in Shakespeare, which is the most Romantic touch of all. It is in the last scene, where Desdemona is preparing to go to bed and, in Shakespeare and Verdi, sings the Willow Song. Rossini gives her a song too, but before it he makes her hear, from the canal below, the song of a gondolier. It is said to be the melody, traditional in the time of Rossini and Byron, to which the gondoliers were supposed to sing stanzas from Tasso, but Rossini substitutes a few lines from Dante, a poet who was just beginning to be talked about, and possibly even a little read, in Italy of the Romantic period. In Voltaire's time, as

---

[6] This is incorrect: like the overture, it was composed for *Aureliano in Palmira* (produced December 1813) and transferred first to *Elisabetta, regina d'Inghilterra* (October 1815), then to *Il barbiere di Siviglia* (February 1816).

[7] Rossini's other Paris operas must also be regarded as exceptions, at least in part.

you probably remember, Dante was talked about, but certainly never read. Byron, in *Childe Harold*, says,

> In Venice Tasso's echoes are no more,
> And silent rows the songless gondolier.

It does not matter whether the music is traditional, or whether it was composed by Rossini; it fulfils its purpose. The whole of that scene is a wonderful piece of music. Verdi has killed it, and probably it will never be put on the stage again;[8] but it is worth reading and studying.

Rossini has been called the Napoleon of music, and the comparison is not altogether absurd, for Rossini too conquered the world and did not enjoy his conquest long, though he survived his age, as Napoleon did at St Helena. Before Rossini, Italian music had always been local and provincial, Neapolitan or Venetian; Rossini made it Italian and universal. And Rossini was one of the really great masters of his time; one cannot feel that there is any true greatness about Paisiello and Cimarosa, or Paer and Mayr. To all of these he was indebted, and he could never have created a style of his own – as he undoubtedly did, limited though it was – without their materials.

Rossini's style is chiefly a product of the warlike age in which he lived. He is the first musician who seems to compose everything with the military band in view. Many great composers have had, or appear to have had, some favourite instrument which dominates their entire outlook on music. J. S. Bach was dominated by the organ; whatever he writes, whether for voices or for instruments, is conceived as organ music. Purcell seems to have been haunted by the sound of the trumpet, Beethoven by that of the string quartet. With Rossini the inspiring instrument seems to have been the clarinet, though he did not play it himself. The clarinet had just begun to be popular. Rossini thinks of it not as the delicate, tender and sentimental voice of the music Brahms composed for it; Rossini's clarinet is the military instrument, taking the place of the violin in outdoor music, sharp and penetrating, with an unmistakeable attack and clear articulation in the rapidest passages. All Rossini's vocal flourishes seem to

---

8 Rossini's *Otello* was staged at the Camden Festival in London in May 1961, and at Rome in 1964, Berlin in 1966, Wexford in 1967 and New York in 1968. It had a concert performance in New York in 1955.

have been imagined for the clarinet; in his overtures, those second subjects with rattling triplets do in fact sound much better on the clarinet than on the violin. We may note that Schubert too was curiously fascinated by the same instrument; the Octet, especially the variations, is a conception for a military band. All Rossini's quick movements are in the style of a military band; he has two types of march-movement for his arias, one in which dotted quavers and semiquavers are perpetually kept up, the other, much imitated by Verdi, in which the accompaniment reiterates chords in crotchets, often played by pizzicato strings. The orchestra, by such means as these, drives the voices along. Rossini only once travelled by a railway train, and that was for a short distance from Antwerp; but although nothing would ever induce him to enter a train again, he was curiously obsessed by the triplet rhythm which is so characteristic of a railway journey. Schubert uses it in the finale of the C major symphony, and it is obviously from Rossini that he got it. Rossini derived a good deal of this from Spontini, but most of his rhythms must have come from observation of the life all about him. In every opera they are the same, and they thus give to every opera, even the most trivial, an extraordinary vivacity and energy – the qualities for which we have no suitable English term: we are obliged to borrow such words as *élan* and *brio*. This driving force of Rossini is what made him irresistible; the most commonplace flourishes became fascinating when they were fired off at this pace. Rossini is cynically indifferent to local colour, as a rule, or to any sort of real characterization. His characters are just the operatic categories, *prima donna*, *primo uomo*, *basso cantante*, and so forth. They have no personalities, only voices, and that is why Rossini's music is almost unsingable at the present day. We have plenty of intelligent singers, who make the most of their personalities; they have to do so, because they have no voices to speak of.

Rossini has a style of his own, but he makes no attempt to distinguish between the serious style and the comic. That is one reason why we are justified in calling him a Romantic. In Mozart's day the two styles were sharply differentiated, because generally speaking singers concentrated on the one or the other. Rossini has no scruple about giving chattering quavers to the most imposing characters. His serious operas contain no intentionally comic figures, but that is really the only distinction he makes.

Beethoven told Rossini, when he visited him in Vienna, that he ought to stick to comic opera and nothing else; in some ways Beethoven was right, for *Il barbiere di Siviglia* is almost the only one of Rossini's operas which has survived to the present day. In this aspect of his music he differs from his immediate predecessors and contemporaries of the Italian school. The Romantic style had been initiated very largely because composers and audiences insisted on taking seriously what the poets and dramatists had intended to be comic. This is a fundamental aesthetic question of music. We have to ask outselves, as we must always be asking ourselves, what our own reactions to music are. There have always been a good many people who would say with Jessica in *The Merchant of Venice* 'I am never merry when I hear sweet music.' I have no intention of discussing here the question of whether that is the right attitude to music or not; it is a point everybody has to think out for himself. Another difficult question is that of humour in drama or literature. Our own age, at any rate in England, is inclined to take everything possible in a humorous spirit, especially the open expression of emotions, and of simple emotions. It is conceivable, indeed it is almost certain, that audiences in the early nineteenth century were less sophisticated, and that they were ready and willing to be moved to tears by things which we to-day find simply comical. It is often recorded in Romantic days how people, both men and women, were so much affected by hearing music as to lose complete control of themselves and become almost hysterical in public places.

For these reasons it is very difficult for us to assess the right value of music at this time, and particularly to realize the influence on musicians all over Europe of music which to us seems completely dull and uninteresting. It is unthinkable that any of Rossini's earlier serious operas should be revived now, although *Il barbiere* remains unassailable in the current standard repertory, and *La Cenerentola* has proved attractive to modern audiences. It might be possible to revive *La gazza ladra*; but otherwise the earlier Rossini may be dismissed as dead and buried.[9] The most famous of the serious operas were *Semiramide* and *Mosè in Egitto*; both of them are hopelessly artificial and unreal. They were

[9] At least 26 of Rossini's 37 operas, eleven of them serious, have been revived on the stage since 1950, most of them with conspicuous success.

composed with a view to quick popularity, and they have paid the penalty of it.

It is a very different matter when we come to consider *Guillaume Tell*, the last and greatest of Rossini's works for the stage. *Guillaume Tell* stands in a class by itself, apart from all the other operas of Rossini, and indeed apart from all contemporary operas. It was composed to French words for performance in Paris in 1829; hence it is a considerable way outside the period of history I am discussing in this lecture. In many ways it owes much to Rossini's acquaintance with operas which I shall have occasion to discuss in subsequent lectures; but in spite of that I propose to deal with it here.

The story of William Tell had been treated in opera very nearly 40 years before by Grétry (1791), and here I may remind you that Schiller did not begin his play on the subject until 1803. The libretto of Rossini's opera was written by Jouy; it is rather stiff and old-fashioned in style, and Rossini had it revised for him by a writer called Bis. It bears little resemblance to Schiller's drama. Grétry's opera seems a very small affair as compared with Rossini's, but it is interesting as an early example of Swiss local colour in music. Grétry makes much use of the celebrated *Ranz des vaches*, and the sounds of the Swiss cow-horns and so forth; the first act especially is full of little songs dragged in merely to give local atmosphere.

Rossini's *Guillaume Tell* must have owed much to Auber's opera *Masaniello* (*La Muette de Portici*), which came out in 1828. Historians and critics have hitherto been completely at a loss to account for Auber's suddenly producing this extremely serious and at the same time exciting work, when the rest of his career had been and was still to be devoted to comic opera of the lightest and most elegantly charming type. But the seriousness of *Masaniello* lies mainly in its subject – the Neapolitan revolution of the seventeenth century. It was a performance of this opera at Brussels in 1830 which started the Belgian revolution against the Dutch; and one can well imagine that if the Belgian audience were in a state of mind to be inflamed to revolution by the music of an opera, it would be Auber's stirring military march rhythms that would bring about this effect. We know these military march rhythms only too well from *Fra Diavolo* and other comic operas of Auber. They were no less suited to comic opera than to serious; and in any case, they were derived originally from the earlier operas of Rossini, in so far as they did not owe their origin to the common stock of military marches all over Napoleonic Europe.

They are indeed conspicuous in *Guillaume Tell*, but only in situations where they are appropriate, and herein lies the contrast between *Guillaume Tell* and the earlier operas of Rossini. The overture is too well known to require description, though I may point out that the use of Swiss local colour, and also of four solo violoncellos, which has often been described as an invention of Rossini, can be found in operas by several earlier French composers long before him.

Grétry's opera opens with preparations for the wedding of Tell's daughter to young Melktal; the wedding is suddenly abandoned because news is brought that old Melktal, his father, has had his eyes burnt out by order of the Austrian tyrant Gesler. Rossini's opera starts with three weddings; this of itself shows the generous scale on which the opera is conceived. In none of the three is young Melcthal concerned: young Melcthal, whose name here is Arnold, is far too important a character to marry a peasant girl, as he is the principal tenor. Old Melcthal does not have his eyes put out; in fact he comes to bless the three weddings, so that we may make his acquaintance comfortably before we receive news in the second act that he has been executed.

Rossini starts with a pretty little rustic chorus, after which the essentially Romantic atmosphere is established by the song of Ruodi the boatman, a typically Rossinian barcarolle, but derived of course from the popular folksong characteristic of all the older Italian and French comic operas. Here is serves a dramatic purpose, for Tell himself, at the end of the first stanza, makes his own comments on it and contrasts the happy carelessness of the boatman with the miseries of the Swiss people groaning under the tyranny of the Austrians. Tell's very first bars have character and set the tragic tone of the opera. It is pure Rossini, but it is a new Rossini, with an unwonted seriousness and depth of feeling. Tell does not say much: the boatman starts his second verse, and comments are suppied by Tell's wife Hedwige and his son Jemmy; it is the usual 'conversation piece' of Rossinian opera, rather like the opening scene of Tchaikovsky's *Eugene Onegin*, where the two girls sing a song to the harp while their mother and nurse carry on a separate conversation in the garden. More time is taken up with local colour – the *Ranz des vaches* and a chorus of peasants going home from work. Rossini writes, like Spontini, for a huge stage, on which large crowds can move about at their leisure and single figures approach slowly from long distances. Melcthal, who is apparently blind from old age, comes on guided by his son Arnold, to give his blessing to the three couples. Here a very large ensemble and choral movement is built up. In the older operas such a movement would have been left to the end of an act, but it is characteristic of this Romantic period to introduce the chorus at the outset and to give them frequent movements on a large scale. The result is not always satisfactory; these operas are rather overweighted with their choruses, even if we cannot sympathize with old Lord Mount-Edgcumbe, who detested Rossini because he had so many noisy ensembles instead of leaving everything to the solo singers.

Tell takes Melcthal into a châlet for a rest, in order that Arnold may have the stage to himself and explain that he is in love with the sister of the Austrian governor – Mathilde, who is the chief soprano part. Everything in this act is very leisurely, and perhaps with good dramatic reason; the excitement can be worked up later on. Thus Arnold's recitative is interrupted by the sound of Gesler's hunting party at a distance: this gives Rossini the chance of writing a longish movement for four horns on the stage. The horn is always supposed to be a particularly Romantic instrument, and the German composers soon came to regard it as something peculiarly their own, associated with the German forest, which is the background of their most Romantic feelings. But the fact remains that the horn had already been utilized very skilfully by the French; it had its century-old tradition of the hunting-field in France, probably before it was introduced into Germany at all.

Tell comes back and has a magnificent duet with Arnold, in which he tries to make Arnold confess the secret he is hiding. This is an admirable piece of dramatic music; it is constructed with all the classic formality of Cherubini, but that does not prevent the sharp differentiation of characters, nor, in Tell's case, the careful and incisive declamation of words. Tell is inclined to speak almost more than to sing: Arnold, whose emotions are more lyrical, has a rapturous burst of melody. It is a classical sonata movement, with a first and second subject, just like the great duet in Cherubini's *Médée*; and at the same time it is intensely expressive and dramatic. The duet is followed by the wedding processions, which provide a charming contrast; Rossini's music has served for over a century as the model for all kinds of 'rustic music'. After the rather lengthy benediction of Melcthal Tell has a vigorous recitative in which he warns the people of the necessity of throwing off the Austrian yoke; this becomes very dramatic as the horns of Gesler's hunting-party are heard coming nearer and nearer. But Tell is not yet ready for revolution, and he bids the people continue their rejoicings so as to disguise the true state of their feelings from the tyrant. There is a chorus and a long ballet, after which the main action at last begins with the entrance of Leuthold, a shepherd, whose daughter has been ravished by one of Gesler's men; he has killed the man and is being pursued by Gesler's soldiers. His only chance of escape is to get himself ferried across the lake. Ruodi the boatman says that the rocks and current are too dangerous, but Tell volunteers to make the attempt. Rodolphe, the captain of Gesler's bodyguard, enters with soldiers, and as the Swiss people refuse to betray Tell he arrests Melcthal and has him carried off, the villagers being unable to resist as they have no weapons. All this is carried on in an enormously long ensemble and chorus, in the manner of Spontini. It seems extraordinary to us that audiences should have enjoyed these interminable noisy finales, but no doubt they were interested in the spectacle on the stage and excited by the mere sound of the full orchestra and chorus.

Act II begins with a long chorus of huntsmen, with another chorus of shepherds; this is all to give atmosphere and set the stage for the appearance of Mathilde, who has escaped from the hunting-party in the hopes of meeting Arnold. Mathilde and Arnold, being the principal soprano and tenor, are treated very much in the grand operatic manner, with airs and duets to show off their voices to the greatest advantage. There is a curious difference between their music and that given to Tell and the other characters. Tell and the humbler characters have music which is really dramatic and human; Arnold and Mathilde seem to be opera-singers and nothing else, although it must be admitted that their music has considerable dignity and nobility of style. With Mathilde's departure the music begins to be really dramatic again. Tell and Walter Furst, his father-in-law according to

Schiller, enter and convince Arnold that he must join their revolutionary plan. He hesitates at first, but is persuaded on being told that his father has been put to death. All this scene is full of genuine feeling: we are made to realize the affectionate sympathy of Tell and Furst as well as their intense patriotic ardour. Rossini's military rhythms come in very useful on such occasions; in fact one may say that the regular technique of chivalry in opera is to give an exaggerated energy and brilliance of rhythm to some rather commonplace theme. The finale now begins; it represents the gradual assemblage of the men from the three cantons along the lake – three separate male-voice choruses. Rossini has succeeded very well in contrasting the three different groups. Tell makes a great speech to them, and they all solemnly swear to rid Switzerland of the tyrants. This finale is much more dramatic than the first; it is not too long and is admirably built up.

The third act begins with a scene in a ruined chapel, where Arnold and Mathilde have another meeting and the usual series of airs and duets. Then comes the great scene at Altdorf, where all the Swiss people have to make obeisance to Gesler's hat on a pole. Grétry treats this very ingeniously as a sort of entr'acte in dumb show, separate from the act which follows. Rossini treats it as a great scene of festivity, in order to bring in a huge ballet, after which we have the main episode of the legend: Tell refuses to salute the hat, and Gesler orders him to be arrested and made to shoot an apple from the head of his little son. All this is worked out very effectively; the conversation of Tell with the child is one of the most moving scenes in any opera. He shoots the apple successfully, to the delight of the people, and then admits that his other arrow was intended for Gesler, if he had killed the child with the first. Gesler orders him to be thrown into chains, but at this moment Mathilde arrives and pleads for mercy. Gesler refuses, and orders Tell to be taken to prison at Küsnacht on the lake; Mathilde at any rate succeeds in taking charge of the child. There is the usual enormous finale, one chorus cursing Gesler and the other praising him, but it is obviously impossible to distinguish any words in the midst of such a tumult.

The fourth and last act begins with a short soliloquy for Arnold before his ancestral home; the Swiss patriots enter, and he provides them with arms from some store of his own; in this act the marching rhythms grow more and more insistent. The scene changes to the lake-side, with Tell's cottage: a storm is rising.

Mathilde brings the boy back to his mother. This provides an excellent opportunity for an episode which contrasts with all the noise and excitement of the previous act. Mathilde here becomes more human, and there is a beautiful trio for the three sopranos, Mathilde, Hedwige and Jemmy, in the form of a round. The storm begins to rise again; the women sing a prayer, and Tell is seen rowing across the lake. He lands safely: Gesler and his men are on the top of a rock. Tell shoots Gesler with an arrow, and he falls into the lake; we observe the reappearance of the familiar rock and the familiar leap into the water that we remember in several of the old French operas – *Paul et Virginie* of Kreutzer and Le Sueur, *Télémaque* of Le Sueur and Méhul's *Mélidore et Phrosine*. The Swiss patriots assemble with shouts of triumph; the storm clears, and the opera ends with a great stage effect of a gradually brightening landscape showing the lake, with boats, and the mountains shining in the far distance, while the principal characters and the chorus hail the reign of liberty. Rossini in the last pages of this opera quite achieves the sublime; Wagner must have remembered this scene when he wrote the last scene of *Das Rheingold* with the rainbow bridge and the entry of the gods into Walhall.

Guillaume Tell is not only Rossini's masterpiece; it is one of the great masterpieces of music, in spite of some rather conventional pages. It is an astonishing work, because although it is full of the Romantic spirit from beginning to end, it is severely Classical in its construction, and makes Weber's operas seem curiously amateurish by comparison. It has immense dignity, and dignity is a quality we do not usually associate with Romanticism. It is unfortunate that we have few singers nowadays who are capable of singing music of this kind; *Guillaume Tell* is very rarely seen on the stage, especially as it requires huge choral resources and elaborate scenic effects. Modern singers, and modern conductors too, are hardly capable of realizing its amazing grandeur, for grandeur is a quality seldom met with in even the best operas of the current repertory. We may find something of it in Verdi's *Otello*, or in Bellini's *Norma*, and there is grandeur of another kind in Wagner's *Ring des Nibelungen*. *Guillaume Tell* rises far above the purely personal element – it is the story not merely of a hero but of a whole country, and indeed of an ideal which transcends the limits of any one country.

9

BEETHOVEN AND SCHUBERT

When we look back from the present day to the first quarter of the nineteenth century it is difficult for us to see anything except the colossal figure of Beethoven, with perhaps Schubert standing humbly beside him. If we had lived in Vienna during that period we should in all probability have taken a very different view of the situation. Quite possibly we might never have even heard of Schubert; Beethoven would have been known to us as a strange and eccentric personality who wrote symphonies which were completely unintelligible.

Our modern view of the classical era has been so much formed by the accumulated reverence for Beethoven that we accept without question the doctrine that the symphony is of all musical forms the most important, the one into which a composer must inevitably pour all his mightiest inspirations. That certainly was not the view of Beethoven's own period. The generation which had just lost Mozart and had exalted his memory to a place amongst the gods was inclined to regard operas and concertos as far more important than symphonies. The concerto was obviously a more important form than the symphony, because it was an occasion for watching the composer himself apparently in the very act of composing. It is difficult for us to imagine a period of musical history in which there were no classics, and in which all interest was concentrated on the newest production. The English, by commemorating Handel in Westminster Abbey in 1784, had taken the first step towards establishing a cult of 'the classics' in music, and this cult of Handel had just begun to spread from England to Germany. Johann Sebastian Bach, who for us to-day is the great classic of the eighteenth century, was practically unknown outside Leipzig. The only works of Bach which Beethoven is likely to have known were the Forty-Eight Preludes and Fugues;[1]

---

[1] This is misleading; a number of Bach's other works had been printed: see Max Schneider, 'Verzeichnis der bis zum Jahre 1851 gedruckten (und der geschrieben im Handel gewesenen) Werke von Joh. Seb. Bach', *Bach Jhrb* 1906,

Forkel had just begun to awaken interest in Bach's music, and hardly any of it was accessible in print.

It is necessary to emphasize this state of musical knowledge in or about the year 1805, in order to visualize a musical society so remote from our own that people were interested first and foremost in new music and not in that of a hundred years before, as people are to-day. When Beethoven first produced *Fidelio* in that year 1805, it was just one new opera among many. The tendency of recent times, guided by the teaching of such writers as Sir George Grove, was to regard all opera as an inferior form of music, but to respect *Fidelio* because it was by Beethoven. It was admitted that *Fidelio* was not a very successful opera; to have made it successful would have been to admit that it had the same attractions as *Carmen* or *La Traviata*, which would have been blasphemous. It was an unlucky venture on Beethoven's part, for it was universally agreed that he had no understanding of the stage.

Much the same thing was said about Schubert, except that in his case it was considered politer to ignore his operas altogether and forget that they had ever existed, just as was done in the case of Handel. The fact remains that for a great part of his life Beethoven was intensely interested in opera and desirous of composing for the theatre; and exactly the same thing must be said of Schubert, who composed not one single opera but a dozen. It cannot be denied that both these composers of great classical symphonies put some of their very best work into music for the stage, and it is merely a stroke of ill-fortune that the operas of Beethoven and Schubert have not, generally speaking, enjoyed theatrical success.

Fidelio, or as the opera was originally called, *Léonore*, was a story of the French Revolution. The author of the first libretto on this subject was J. N. Bouilly, a man of letters, most of whose life was associated with his native city of Tours. During the Reign of Terror Bouilly held an administrative post there, and found himself in frequent difficulties with the Terrorists because he was a profoundly humane character and more inclined to help those in difficulties than to hand them over to torture and death. He was interested in music and a friend of musicians; towards the

84–113. Beethoven subscribed to the so-called *Oeuvres Complettes* in 14 volumes (Vienna, Leipzig, 1801–6).

end of the eighteenth century he was engaged to the third daughter of Grétry, Antoinette, who died before she could be married to him. The tale of *Léonore* was an absolutely true story which had happened in Tours within Bouilly's own experience; he had known the lady in question and had personally assisted her to the best of his powers.[2] When he made the episode into an opera libretto he thought it wiser to transfer the story to Spain in the sixteenth century, for fear of getting into trouble with the authorities at Tours if the characters were recognized. In this shape, as *Léonore ou l'amour conjugal, fait historique espagnol*, the story was set to music in 1798 by Pierre Gaveaux, one of the lesser musicians of the French Revolution. The best than can be said of Gaveaux is that he was an imitator of Cherubini.[3] The opera is constructed on the regular French model; it belongs to the class of 'rescue operas' of which we have already discussed so many. Dom Florestan, a Spanish nobleman, has been unjustly thrown into prison by the tyrant Pizare; his wife determines to rescue him and for that purpose disguises herself as a man, and manages to enter the prison as an assistant in the service of Roc the jailer. She is so successful in her disguise that Roc proposes to marry her to his daughter Marceline, who is violently in love with the supposed young man, to the despair of Jacquino, the porter, who is in love with Marceline. In the course of the first act Pizare arrives, and makes an arrangement with Roc which is not divulged to the audience. The prisoners are let out for an airing, but Florestan is not among them. The first act ends with the chorus of prisoners who come out of their cells and go into the garden of the prison.

The second act begins, just as it does with Beethoven, in the dungeon where Florestan is confined in almost total darkness. Roc and Léonore come down, having received orders to prepare a grave for Florestan in an old disused well. As soon as they have cleared the opening of the well Roc is to give a signal, and an unknown man in a mask will enter the dungeon and murder Florestan. Léonore has helped to dig the grave and tries to make out whether the prisoner is her husband or not, but it is too dark

[2] His account is in *Mes Récapitulations* (Paris, [1836]), II, 81ff.

[3] This judgment seems too severe. Berlioz, though concerned to play down Gaveaux's remarkable treatment of the horns in *Léonore*, praises several features of the score: see *A Travers Chants* (Paris, 1971), 94.

127

for her to see him. She determines to rescue him whoever he is; this decision of hers provides one of the great moments of Beethoven's opera, and it is interesting to note that it was a feature of Bouilly's original libretto. Very probably it was part of the true story, as told to Bouilly by the lady herself. The man in a mask comes down, and reveals himself as Pizare; he is about to murder Florestan, but is prevented by Léonore, who points a pistol at him. At that moment the trumpet signal is heard outside, informing us that the minister Dom Fernand has arrived to inspect the prison; Pizare is obliged to go at once to meet him, being the governor of the prison and responsible for it. Roc accompanies him, but first snatches the pistol from Léonore's hand as she falls unconscious. Léonore and her husband are now alone in the dungeon; Florestan tries to approach and comfort her, but he is held fast by a chain and cannot reach her. She recovers consciousness, and they both realize that their danger is worse than before, for she has lost her only weapon. A noise is heard outside as of men approaching: a chorus is singing. Léonore and Florestan naturally suppose that they are guards coming to arrest them and have them both put to death; but when they burst in, they prove to be rescuers, led by the Minister, who comes to set Florestan free, and all ends happily.

In view of Beethoven's version of the story it is important to remember certain episodes which are treated differently by his librettists.[4] First, Bouilly gives the love-affair with Marceline much more prominence. The opera of Gaveaux begins with a song for Marceline in the Spanish style – an interesting case of an experiment with Romantic local colour in opera. Marceline thus explains to the audience that she is in love with Fidelio before Jacquino comes on to sing his duet with her and be treated very unkindly. Further on Marceline has a duet with Fidelio, in which she dilates on the expected joys of marriage, and tells us that she is going to have a large family; there is an amusing and almost Mozartian discussion between the two as to whether the first word

---

[4] Dent deals throughout with the third (1814) version of Beethoven's opera. The original version of 1805 is much closer to Bouilly's libretto, of which Sonnleithner's is almost a straight translation, with additional musical numbers. Marzelline begins the opera and is prominent throughout; her duet with the embarrassed Leonore is included (without the 'Papa'–'Maman' dialogue); and the entire action of Bouilly's dungeon scene is retained. Beethoven's finale on the parade-ground dates from 1814.

which their first baby will utter is to be 'Papa' or 'Maman'. All this is very embarrassing to Léonore, who has to keep up the situation as best she can while explaining to the audience in asides how uncomfortable she is.

In Beethoven's opera Pizarro explains the whole plot to Rocco on the stage in a duet; Bouilly's original version is more dramatic, because we are kept in the dark until Pizare arrives in the dungeon. In the second act the entire scene of the rescue – Léonore's threatening Pizare with a pistol, etc. – is conducted in spoken dialogue, not set to music, as with Beethoven. The situation after Pizare's departure is much more exciting and dramatic in the original than in Beethoven's version, if we consider the work as a play. The French opera, in fact, is much more what we should now call a 'melodrama'; it was an intensely thrilling dramatic story in which the music was a comparatively secondary affair. Gaveaux retains the old French tradition of the *romance*, generally in 6/8 time; thus Léonore has a *romance* of this kind in which she explains her intention of rescuing her husband – the moment at which Beethoven has the great *scena* 'Abscheulicher, wo eilst du hin?' followed by the aria about hope. And Florestan when he is discovered in his dungeon begins with a very dramatic recitative, but follows it up with another *romance*.

Gaveaux's opera was performed in Paris and Brussels (1799), never in Vienna; but it is very probable that Beethoven saw the score, as it was printed at once, like nearly all the French operas of that time, and copies were doubtless available in Vienna.[5] Gaveaux's music has curious premonitions of Beethoven; but the probable truth is that these passages which remind us of Beethoven were just the ordinary commonplaces of the whole French Revolution school.[6]

The libretto was promptly seized upon by other composers. Ferdinando Paer had it translated into Italian, and his setting was produced at Dresden (3 October 1804) and Prague (1805). Paer's

[5] Beethoven's library at his death contained printed scores of French operas by Gluck, Salieri (*Les Danaides*), Cherubini (*Médée*), Méhul and Dalayrac. Apart from Mozart, Dalayrac was the only composer represented by more than one opera.

[6] It seems more likely that Beethoven developed the rudimentary ideas he found in Gaveaux's score; some of the parallels are striking. See Winton Dean, 'Beethoven and Opera', in *The Beethoven Companion*, ed. Denis Arnold and Nigel Fortune (London, 1971), 343–4.

opera has a fine *scena* for Leonora corresponding to Beethoven's 'Abscheulicher', but most of the work is very Mozartian. The duet between Marcellina and Giacchino is obviously imitated from *Figaro*. The second act opens with a long introduction for the orchestra and a fine *scena* for Florestan; the grave-digging duet is not very interesting. There is no music for the rescue episode, and apparently Pizarro had no arias to sing at all. The duet for Leonora and Florestan after the rescue is quite different from Beethoven's, simply because the situation is different,[7] as has already been explained.

Yet another Italian setting of the story exists, in the shape of a *farsa sentimentale* in one act by Simone Mayr, whose *L'amor conjugale* came out at Padua in July 1805.[8] We may be fairly certain that Beethoven had no acquaintance with it. The story is much compressed, and the names of the characters are all changed, as the scene is transferred to Poland, no doubt in imitation of Cherubini's *Lodoiska*.

The history of Beethoven's *Fidelio* is so well known that there is no need to go into it here in detail. It is however worth noting that there was difficulty with the censorship at Vienna over the libretto. The first German version had been prepared by Joseph Sonnleithner, who was secretary of the Imperial Opera. But as late as 2 October, 1805, seven weeks before the first performance, Sonnleithner had to write to the censorship to beg for the removal of the ban which had already been laid on *Fidelio*. The reason for this was no doubt political; Florestan represented the type of man who got imprisoned by the authorities for his revolutionary opinions, and at the end of the opera he was rescued by his revolutionary friends. The final entrance of the chorus was too much like the capture of the Bastille. Sonnleithner brought forward several arguments in favour of the opera. The first was that the Empress herself had greatly admired the original libretto; the second was that Paer's opera on the same story had been given with great success in Dresden and Prague, where no objection had been raised at all; thirdly, Beethoven had been at work on the opera for a year and a half; fourthly, good librettos were extremely scarce.

---

[7] Different from Beethoven's 1814 version; not from that of 1805.

[8] Mayr's *L'amor conjugale* was revived at a London concert in March 1973, Paer's *Leonora* on the stage at Parma later the same year. Mayr's opera has been recently published in full score.

There is a story which has often been repeated on the authority of Ferdinand Hiller, that Beethoven went to a performance of Paer's opera with Paer himself, and in the course of the performance said to the composer 'Ah, comme c'est beau ça; il faut que je compose cela moi-même.' Although it is said to have been told to Hiller by Paer himself, the story is apocryphal: Beethoven did not go to the performances either at Dresden or at Prague, and it is evident from Sonnleithner's letter to the censorship that Paer's opera had not been performed at Vienna, or he would have mentioned that as a fact. There was a meeting between Beethoven and Paer in Vienna, in 1803, and as Paer's opera had not yet come out, it is possible that Paer himself told Beethoven the plot, and that Beethoven then made the remark attributed to him.

The first performance of Beethoven's *Fidelio* took place on November 20, 1805. It was universally regarded as a failure, and with great difficulty Beethoven was persuaded to shorten it for performance in 1806. The first version was in three acts; but that merely meant that Bouilly's first act was divided into two separate scenes, one in Rocco's house and the other in the courtyard of the prison. For the revised production (29 March 1806) three numbers were sacrificed altogether,[9] and the opera was played in two acts; the scene of Act I being so arranged that a change of scene was not necessary. This arrangement is very often made nowadays for the sake of economy.

The third version of *Fidelio*, performed in 1814, was considerably altered. The libretto was remodelled by Treitschke with the object of providing more opportunities for music,[10] so that *Fidelio* became more of an opera and less of what we should describe as a play with songs. This distinction is most important to bear in mind for the whole development of Romantic Opera, because Romantic Opera evolved entirely out of comic opera, and chiefly out of French comic opera with spoken dialogue. It is very

[9] This statement, often repeated, is not true. Only Rocco's aria was cut; many movements were shortened, some drastically, and their order was changed. The libretto was revised by Stephan von Breuning. The reduction of Act I to a single scene dates from 1814. For the complex history of the text in all three versions, see Dean, *op. cit.*

[10] This had been Sonnleithner's aim in 1805; Treitschke's was quite different. He strengthened Act I by reducing Marzelline's part in the plot and tightening the finale, but seriously weakened the dramatic motivation and characterisation in Act II.

urgent to realize that the general background of a Viennese opera-goer in the days of Beethoven was almost exclusively a background of comic opera, whether French, German or Italian, and that however low the standard of the Italian operas might be, that of the German comic operas was a great deal lower. Antiquarian-minded musicians of to-day and German patriots may be inclined to admire the comic operas of Dittersdorf, Weigl and the rest, but their songs are very slight and trivial as compared with those of Anfossi and Cimarosa, and far below the quality of such now forgotten Italians as Paer and Mayr.

It is not in the least surprising that *Fidelio* was found far too serious and complicated. The first audience of November 1805 consisted mainly of French officers; if they were at all musical, they would be pretty sure to prefer the style of Gaveaux and Dalayrac to that of Beethoven.

Beethoven's models were Mozart and Cherubini. There is very little Mozart in *Fidelio*: that is, very little that we recognize at once as a reminiscence of Mozart. The operas of Mozart which had impressed themselves on Beethoven's mind were *Don Giovanni* and *Die Zauberflöte* – both of them mainly in their most serious moments. Mainly, but not altogether, for it is strange to find very noticeable recollections of the duet between Papageno and Papagena in the duet between Florestan and Leonore. Florestan and Leonore, as I have said in my book on Mozart's Operas, are like Tamino and Pamina grown up and come down to real earth after fairyland. The part of *Die Zauberflöte* which did most to form the style of the German Romantic composers was the scene of the fire and water, especially the dialogue between Tamino and Pamina which precedes the trials. From the moment when Tamino and Pamina meet in the presence of the Armed Men, the music takes on a new dramatic style which is of the aria type, not in the least like recitative or even arioso, but at the same time free from conventional restrictions, completely flexible and serving a dramatic purpose. If that style has any affinities elsewhere, it is in France; we find it most conspicuously in Méhul. It is probable that it was French in origin, and that both Méhul and Mozart evolved it out of the style created by Grétry and Dalayrac.

The weakness of *Fidelio* as a work for the stage is due to various causes – first, to the German librettists. Sonnleithner in his anxiety to provide Beethoven with more opportunities for music, and to elevate the general tone of the play,[11] forgot that Bouilly had seen his characters quite clearly and given each of them his or her own individuality. In Beethoven's opera Leonore was exalted out of all proportion and, as years went by after Beethoven's death, she became more and more monumentalized, thanks largely to the influence of the overture known as *Leonore No. 3*, which has had many more performances than the opera to which it was once unfortunately attached. The result of monumentalizing Leonore was that Rocco, Marzelline and Jaquino retired more and more into the background and became almost negligible puppets. Marzelline's love-affair with Fidelio must have been amusing as well as harassing to the first French audience. The motive of a woman dressed as a man and causing other women to fall in love with her was nothing new; it was one of the stock situations of the older Italian comic operas, and consequently it was one which nobody took very seriously. No one in those days would have found anything offensive about it. After the complete disappearance of the male soprano the attitude of the public naturally began to change, and we live now in an age when the mere sight of a woman dressed up as a man is either ridiculous or positively unpleasant. It is only in the half-antiquarian and conventionally absurd world of opera that it is possible at all. A straight modern spoken play in which a woman is disguised as a man is now pretty well inconceivable.

Beethoven's Marzelline begins to interest us seriously because, being Beethoven, he has given her such beautiful music to sing; after the first scene she practically disappears from the opera, though she has to be settled with at the very end. One's impression is that she is very scurvily treated, both by the other characters and by the poet and the composer. Bouilly managed things more neatly; in place of Beethoven's huge finale there was a general clearing-up in spoken dialogue, so that Marceline had time to come to the front and demand some sort of 'settlement'. And Bouilly makes a settlement that is effective and characteristically French: Léonore, no longer a humble jailer's assistant but a Spanish lady of the aristocracy, pleasantly suggests that Marceline might as well marry Jacquino, and says that she herself

---

[11] This 'elevation' was the work of Treitschke (and Beethoven) in 1814. The Leonore of 1805 was a more human, less idealized character.

will provide a handsome dowry. In the land of *mariage de convenance* what could be more satisfactory?

This all hangs together with the fact that Bouilly quite clearly made Roc, the jailer, a typical French peasant whose mind is concentrated on money and nothing else. He is honesty itself, but he will do anything for money; that shows what a good father he is – his one wish is to provide properly for his daughter. The German translator either did not understand this, or disliked it,[12] and the tendency of the German theatre has been to play Rocco as a kindly old dodderer – a forerunner of Hans Sachs and Gurnemanz; and it is probable that German opera-singers, who judge all new parts by some conventional one that they have learned, when approaching the part of Rocco, explain it to themselves, or have it explained to them, as a sort of minor Hans Sachs.

Beethoven was not really a composer for the theatre, because he never seemed to see his characters as real persons, in the way that Mozart did. He was more interested in moral qualities. The Italian composers, one must admit, were not much concerned with the delineation of individual character; but they were intensely and indeed almost exclusively concerned with the expression of human emotions. Metastasio's characters might be conventional puppets, but they went through every conceivable phase of human feeling – love, timidity, passion, filial devotion, paternal affection, paternal severity, jealousy, rage, despair – there is no end to the range. With Beethoven human feeling is strangely remote as compared with his intensity of expression where moral abstractions such as hope, liberty and personal devotion are concerned. This type of expression is what we all feel to be typical Beethoven, whether early, middle or late; we have come to imagine that it is his own creation. It is not; it was the creation of Cherubini and the composers of the French Revolution.

Was Beethoven a Romantic? This is a difficult question to answer. If we consider him historically, we shall certainly agree that he stands nearer to Cherubini than to Weber. The Romantic generation of German musicians – Schumann, Wagner and their

[12] The softening of Rocco's character was also due largely to Treitschke. He is not a dodderer in the 1805–6 versions, in which he deprives Leonore of her pistol.

contemporaries – certainly regarded him as a Romantic. Every generation sees in Beethoven what it wants to find in him. The criticism of Beethoven is particularly interesting to-day, because there is a violent reaction against the adoring attitude of the disciples of Grove. Those of us who were brought up on Grove's writings and have been worshippers of Beethoven for half a century often feel uncomfortable when the younger generation say that they have little use for him; but we must face the situation calmly and allow Beethoven to pass into the category of 'old music', along with Haydn, Mozart, Handel and Bach – music which has to be understood on a historical basis.

Schubert, likewise on the authority of Grove, has been venerated as a pure classic, and especially as a composer of quartets, sonatas and symphonies. Probably few of Schubert's adorers could even state the name of one of his operas. Yet he was even more devoted to the theatre than Beethoven. There can be no doubt that he was closely in touch with the operas of his day. We know that he saw Spontini's *La Vestale* at Vienna in 1812; he was a keen student of the scores of Gluck and saw *Iphigénie en Tauride*, probably in April 1815. It was about that date that he was known to prefer the music of Salieri to that of Beethoven; and if he admired Salieri, it must have been primarily for his operas.[13] Schubert's own first opera was *Des Teufels Lustschloss*, composed in 1814 at the age of seventeen, and in the following year he composed, or at any rate began, no fewer than seven operas.[14] These operas, however, were all *Singspiele*, plays with spoken dialogue and songs, many of them in one act only. It was in 1817 that Rossini visited Vienna, and Schubert, like everybody else, fell a victim to the Rossini fever. But in 1819 we hear of him going to see a French opera, *Sémiramis* by Catel, which is a work of great dignity, with remarkable premonitions of Romanticism.[15]

It was in 1820 that Schubert composed incidental music for a wildly Romantic play, *Die Zauberharfe*. The overture is frequently to be heard at modern concerts, but the rest of the music has remained in oblivion, although printed in the complete edition

[13] Or perhaps for his learning. Schubert's humility in this respect is confirmed by his late counterpoint lessons with Sechter.
[14] Only four, two of them in one act, can be dated positively to 1815.
[15] Catel's *Sémiramis* was first produced at the Paris Opéra on 4 May 1802.

of Schubert's works. The overture is obviously imitated from Rossini, and is so good an imitation that it is in some ways more like Offenbach. The story, as far as it can be made out, is as Romantic as anything in Weber. Ida, the rightful heiress to the Duchy of Brabant, gets lost in a magic forest while on a hunting party. She rescues a white dove from the clutches of an eagle. There is another claimant for the Duchy in the shape of the young son of Arnulf, who is on bad terms with his wife Melinde, who appears to be a sort of enchantress, very much dominated by an evil spirit named Sutur. There are long scenes in the enchanted forest, in which Melinde and Sutur address violent remarks to each other to the accompaniment of music that is quite as Romantic as anything in the operas of Weber. Schubert in fact knew all Weber's technical tricks for creating Romantic effects, and could write Weberish music that from a purely musical point of view was far better than anything of Weber's own; but Schubert had little sense of stage action and no understanding of the time required to do certain things in the theatre, with the result that most of his numbers are much too long.

Alfonso und Estrella, the first of Schubert's two really important operas, was composed in 1821–2. The libretto is decidedly Romantic in character, though modelled to some extent on the French rescue-opera system. The scene is laid in mediaeval Spain. Alfonso is the son of Troila, the wrongfully deposed king of Leon, who has gone into retirement as a hermit in a secluded valley. Alfonso is strictly forbidden to leave the valley, and knows nothing of his origins. By accident he makes the acquaintance of Estrella, the daughter of Mauregato, the king who has usurped his father's throne. He does not know who she is, and of course falls in love with her. Adolfo, a warrior on Mauregato's side, claims the hand of Estrella as his reward for placing Mauregato on the throne. Mauregato is willing to give her to him, but seeing her evident distress says that she can only marry the man who brings her a lost family relic, the chain of Eurich. Adolfo starts a conspiracy against Mauregato, from which he and Estrella are rescued by Alfonso and his men. Troila at the end makes the supreme self-sacrifice of forgiving his ancient enemy and allowing Alfonso to marry Estrella and mount the throne. The chain of Eurich has been saved by Troila, so that Alfonso is able to present it to Estrella. This is Schubert's only opera without spoken dialogue; as in Weber's *Euryanthe* and Spohr's *Jessonda*, composed about the same time, the music is continuous.

It is obvious that a story of this sort offered opportunities for all the kinds of Romantic music which very soon became stereo-typed; the chorus of huntsmen with horns, the choruses of war-riors, the marches, the songs to the harp, and so forth. The hermit is a well-known Romantic figure; we have met him in Méhul's *Mélidore et Phrosine* and we shall meet him again in Weber's *Der Freischütz*, to say nothing of certain operas of Bellini and Verdi. It is interesting to know that hermits were no ima-ginary creations of the operatic librettists; Spohr describes in his autobiography how he met one living on the bank of the Danube about 1820. The weak point of Schubert's opera is that it is long-winded and monotonous; and here we must analyse the music and find out exactly why. The real weakness lies not in the music, which is astonishingly beautiful, in Schubert's most Rom-antic manner, but in the libretto. Musical historians have often condemned operas of this period for their unsatisfactory librettos, and readers of histories of music might well imagine that the badness lay in the actual plots and arrangement of the scenes and what happens in them. That is not generally the case; the se-quence of events and the arrangement of scenes is as a rule no worse than it is in such an opera as *Il Trovatore*, notoriously the most unintelligible of all librettos – and one of the half-dozen operas which are indispensable to the repertory of every opera-house in the world at this present day. The weakness of *Alfonso und Estrella* is not dramatic but metrical. The poet cannot get away from the perpetual rhythm of 8.7.8.7. This metre is quite suitable for a German song, and indeed it is one of the favourite metres of German songs; but it will not do for a whole opera. The consequence is that Schubert, who had already written hundreds of *Lieder*, inevitably composed the arias of the opera as if they were *Lieder*, and the poet even used this same metre both for the highly emotional utterances of the characters and for the more or less commonplace pieces of information which an Italian would have set in plain recitative. This fault is very notice-able in some of the operas of Spohr. The result is, even in the case of Schubert, that the style of the German *Lied* is not strong enough for the emotional crises of the arias, and it is not dramatic and concise enough for what ought to have been recitative.

In 1823 Schubert was commissioned by the famous manager Barbaja to compose an opera for the Theater an der Wien. This was *Fierrabras*, described as a 'Heroisch-romantische Oper'. It was never performed in Schubert's lifetime. We see from the title that Romantic Opera is now an officially recognized form. Like Cherubini's *Faniska*, which is the standard model for all these operas, *Fierrabras* has spoken dialogue, but there is not very much of it. Opera had moved a long way from the idea of a play with songs, a *comédie mêlée d'ariettes*, and it is only the very shortest of steps to continuous Romantic Opera in the manner of *Euryanthe*.

The scene is laid in the eighth century. Emma, the daughter of King Charlemagne, is in love with Eginhard, a poor young knight. After a victory over the Moors, the King sends Eginhard with other knights to offer them peace if they will all become Christians. At this point Fierrabras, one of the Moors, is brought in as a captive. Emma is distributing wreaths to the victors; Fierrabras sees her and at once falls in love. Fierrabras is the son of the Moorish king; four years before, he and his sister Florinda had been on a visit to Rome, where each of them had fallen in love with some unknown person whom they had never seen again. The lady of Fierrabras's Roman adventure was Emma, and the gentleman with whom his sister fell in love was Roland, the very knight who has just captured Fierrabras. Roland is equally in love with Florinda, so both are delighted at the situation, and Roland and Fierrabras swear eternal friendship. Fierrabras says that Roland can safely go to the Moorish camp and demand Florinda in marriage.

Eginhard now comes on to serenade Emma, who admits him to her apartment. They are pursued, and try to escape, but are intercepted by Fierrabras, to whom they appeal for help. Fierrabras, being a hero after the Metastasian manner, agrees to help them out of pure self-sacrifice, and after a long trio Eginhard flies, leaving Emma to talk to Fierrabras – the chorus all this time raging in the distance. Fierrabras promises to keep Emma's secret, and is just leading her back to the palace when they are met by the King and his suite; the King is horrified, and sends for Eginhard. In the meantime they join in a very agreeable trio, in which all three sing different words and express different sentiments to what is substantially the same music. We need not blame Schubert for this; it has by this period become a regular convention, one of the authorized absurdities of opera. Eginhard is brought in, much embarrassed. Here we have a quartet, and another conventional situation of Romantic Opera: the King hands over Fierrabras to Eginhard to be dealt with as he will. Fierrabras is on the point of explaining everything, when Emma and Eginhard stop him with the words 'Ha, schweig!' At this moment trumpets are heard announcing that it is time for Eginhard to start on his mission of peace; the chorus of knights enter, dawn breaks, and they set off for their diplomatic expedition. This ends the first act.

Romantic Opera, we see, is based on a system of manners by which everybody acts on immediate impulse, without ever stopping to think what the consequences may be. Everybody makes the rashest promises of silence, and the stage is a tangle of unrevealed secrets which have to be kept up until somebody lets the cat out of the bag at the end of Act III. The situations arise not so much because the characters are so strict in keeping their secrets – very often they are not – but because nobody is ever allowed time for explanations. This all hangs together with the musical construction, the desire of the composers being to develop the lyrical numbers, especially the ensembles and symphonic pieces, to the greatest possible length, at the cost of recitative, which they wish to minimize at all costs. That, really, is why there is never time for explanations, with the result that the audience is completely bewildered as to what is going on.

Hasty behaviour, rash vows of secrecy, impulsive actions, were not created by the Romantics. They go back to the days of Metastasio and Zeno; we can find endless examples in the operas of Scarlatti and Handel. But in those old Italian operas there was at least a little more time for dialogue, and there were no ensembles, so that the audience had a clearer understanding of things, all the more so as most of them must have known Metastasio's dramas by heart. The German librettists were very hazy as to how to write a libretto; they leant now to French models, now to Italian; they were bored with recitative, because they did not understand the foreign languages fluently, and as a result they got thoroughly entangled, as the notorious Helmina von Chezy did, in their dramatic complications. If the Romantics had stuck to the good old Italian plan of concentrating on the direct emotions of the principal characters, all would have been well;

but they were always wanting to introduce pageantry – choruses of knights and huntsmen and so forth – with the result that they were constantly losing the direct thread of the story and of the emotions concerned.

Let us return to Act II of *Fierrabras*. It opens in the country, near the French frontier; there is a mountain, over which the various choruses can go up and down. The Frankish knights come over the hill in the early morning and have a rest in the valley while Eginhard sings them a song to the harp with a chorus. The words are 'Grüss ich zum letzten Male dich teures Vaterland', and as one might expect from this the style of the music is thoroughly Schubertian. It is a most attractive movement, but wholly German and in the *Lied* style. After some talk the knights go away, as Eginhard wants the stage for a soliloquy; he says he will catch them up later. This unfortunate desire to hold the footlights is Eginhard's ruin, for before he can begin his aria Brutamonte, a Moorish warrior, appears with a chorus of Moors. (These operas of Cherubini and Schubert all seem to demand, as Spontini's do also, a very large supply of male chorus singers. We must remember that we are in the period of the Napoleonic wars and the immense enthusiasm for male-voice part-songs all over Germany, so that no doubt the theatres could get men singers more easily than women.) Brutamonte is very suspicious of Eginhard; he has seen the other knights in the distance, and he now takes Eginhard prisoner, refusing to believe in his explanations. There is an enormously long chorus, in which far too much time is wasted on the musical effects of horn calls on the stage answered by horn calls from behind the scenes. After the Moors have at last left, the Frankish knights come back to look for Eginhard, and the curtain falls on their vain endeavours. This first scene, we observe, contains a great deal of music but very little drama; the old Italians would have got through the business much quicker. They might indeed have left the whole scene out, and explained the capture of Eginhard later in a recitative; or they might have had just a short scene in which he came on alone to sing his song and be captured by Brutamonte single-handed.

The second scene represents the tent of the Moorish prince, whose name is Boland. The Romantic poets had little sense of humour, or they would have seen the obvious absurdity of naming two opposing warriors Boland and Roland. Florinda has

an exquisitely beautiful duet with her confidante in A flat, 6/8
– both key and time are characteristic of Schubert and his
Romantic style. She talks about Roland. Brutamonte brings in
Eginhard, who confesses how Fierrabras was first set free and
then arrested again through the treachery of a friend, to wit
himself, as he admits. All this is carried on in a very fine quintet,
after which the deputation of knights arrives, and Florinda
recognizes her old admirer Roland. Roland says that Fierrabras
has become a Christian, which makes the Moorish King very
indignant. Florinda in vain begs for mercy; the Moors surround
the knights and take them away to prison. Florinda, left alone,
sings a great aria in which she determines to rescue Roland; it
is a thoroughly ineffective piece of music, with unsuitable vocal
writing and heavily over-scored.

Again the scene changes: the third scene of this act represents
the prison where the Frankish knights are confined. They are
very depressed, and, as one might expect in a German Romantic
opera, they pass the time singing a long unaccompanied part-song.
Eginhard confesses his whole story, at which they are horrified.
There is a noise outside and a scene of *mélodrame*, i.e. spoken
dialogue through music; after much difficulty the door is opened
and Florinda comes in, carrying a light and a sword. This is just
like an opera of Handel; she faints, recovers, and joins in a duet,
followed by a chorus. There is a great deal of trumpeting outside;
the fortress is being attacked. Florinda shows the knights a secret
store of arms, and they go out to have a battle which she watches
from a window and describes to the audience. The battle, however, is rather a failure, for the knights come back saying 'Oh
Missgeschick!' and collapse in despair as the curtain falls.

Act III has three scenes too; *Fierrabras* is an expensive opera
to put on the stage. We begin with Emma's apartments, having
lost sight of her since the first act. She and her maidens are
preparing a welcome for the knights. The King enters and is
rather anxious about them; Emma makes a full confession of her
adventure with Eginhard. Charlemagne at once orders Fierrabras to be released and brought in. After a fine duet between
the King and his daughter Eginhard enters in great disorder and
distress to announce the capture of the knights. The King decides
to send an expedition to release them, and Fierrabras, who is a
perfect monster of chivalry, says that he will defend Eginhard.

The scene ends with a trio characteristic of Schubert in his rather tedious *Lied* style. We now return to the inside of the tower where the knights are imprisoned. Florinda, who is apparently staying on as a sort of Florence Nightingale, sings a charming song with male chorus; then we hear a funeral march in Schubert's best manner, and one of the knights looks out of the window and says that Roland is being led to the stake with a long procession. Florinda at once hangs out her scarf as the white flag of surrender. The scene changes for the last time to the outside of the tower, where her flag is seen hanging out of the window, and below it a pile of faggots for the execution of Roland. There is a march of Moors, a trio and a chorus, all much too long; Florinda as usual begs for mercy. Trumpets are heard off, the Frankish knights (second instalment) enter and after a great battle defeat the Moors altogether. Charlemagne arrives with Emma, and there is the usual happy end – Roland marries Florinda and Emma marries Eginhard. Only one mistake is made; the unfortunate Fierrabras, who has given his name to the opera, is left out in the cold, after having behaved with·incredible chivalry and heroism, and having even wasted his energies on becaming a Christian for nothing.

Fierrabras is a good example of the complete muddleheadedness shown by the Germans, both poets and musicians, as soon as they attempted to write the kind of opera that had been manufactured to standard pattern hundreds of times by the French and the Italians. The successful type is generally credited to the genius of Weber, but it ought to be pointed out here, first, that of Weber's Romantic operas only one is still in the regular German repertory – *Der Freischütz. Oberon*, which contains his best music, is considered quite impossible in England, the country for which it was written, and for the German stage it has had to have additional music composed by later musicians.[16] *Euryanthe*, in spite of the admiration which critics and historians have lavished on it, is regarded by all stage managers as impossible. From time to time an attempt is made to put it on the stage, but it is always a complete failure. For practical purposes *Euryanthe*, the supposed masterpiece of the man who was born in the theatre and had all the tricks of the stage at his fingers' ends (according to popular musical history), is just as dead as the

[16] Today *Oberon* is not always given with additional music.

operas of poor Schubert, who naturally had no idea of writing for the theatre at all. As regards the practicability of Weber and Schubert for the stage, there is really not much to choose between them, for anyone who has worked in a theatre knows that even the much admired *Der Freischütz* is a horribly difficult problem for the producer, unless he is content to accept all the old conventions and absurdities and trust simply to effective singing and the universal popularity of the separate numbers. It cannot be too often repeated that Schubert's operas are of a far higher musical quality, generally speaking, than anything of Weber's, and that they have, at their best, all the essentially Romantic character that is generally supposed to have been the creation of Weber.[17]

Schubert is perhaps the easiest of all composers to enjoy, and the hardest to understand – to understand, I mean, in the sense of historical analysis. Few composers among the great masters can have absorbed subconsciously so much bad and commonplace music from his daily surroundings. His modern admirers talk of him as if he were the purest of pure classical symphonists. In reality his mind must have been a jumble of church music – church music which the more pious among modern Catholics repudiate with horror – military music, street music, gipsy music, dance music, operatic and theatrical music of all sorts, and, worst of all, that type of music which is called *volkstümlich*. I asked Alfred Einstein the other day how it was possible that Schubert could have written what we all feel to be divine masterpieces and at the same time songs that touch the lowest depths of bourgeois commonplace. He replied simply 'Schubert was a *petit-bourgeois* himself, and lived in that sort of society; he was very good-natured, and he wrote numbers of songs just to please his friends.' That is the simplest explanation of Schubert's musical variability. One can thus well understand his quarrelling with Weber, for Weber was not at all a simple soul who was perfectly happy in the humble society of Schubert's surroundings. Schubert no doubt had the

---

[17] This paragraph, misleading in 1937 (which saw a successful production of *Euryanthe* at the Salzburg Festival), has been further overtaken by events. The principal British opera houses have hitherto fought shy of *Oberon* and *Euryanthe*, but each has been produced several times in Britain since the war, and they are not dead in Germany. Schubert's operas have very seldom been staged anywhere, and never successfully. Dent does not grapple with the reasons for this.

same inward feelings and passions that may come to any man and develop into tragedy or exaltation; but his social world was of the narrowest, and his only escape from it seems to have been into the theatre. Weber, on the other hand, had lived through his most impressionable years in an extremely aristocratic society to which, despite his alleged noble birth,[18] he did not really belong, so that he must have acquired the regular habit of posing, if the word is not too offensive, in order to hold his place. It is this pose of aristocracy that we find in all his music – this affectation of dashing chivalry, which is so effective on the stage, and now sounds so hollow and artificial in his pianoforte sonatas and concertos. We are so remote from it that we can find it amusing; but it is amusing perhaps only to sophisticated people.

Schubert's music has lasted longer; but with both composers we have to eliminate and select what is worthy of survival. That is a question I cannot discuss at this point; but I shall have something to say about it when I come to my last lecture and to a review of what Romantic music is and how much it owes to the music of the theatre.

[18] Weber's noble birth is a myth invented by his father: see John Warrack, *Carl Maria von Weber*, 2nd edition (Cambridge, 1976), 23ff.

10

WEBER AND
HIS CONTEMPORARIES

By the time that Weber appears on the scene the Romantic style in music has been pretty well established. When we come to analyse Weber's operas in detail it is difficult to say that there was anything which was specifically his own creation; he was just as much of an eclectic as Handel, and like Handel he adopted the current methods of his own day. In considering the position of Weber in the history of music we ought to investigate the reasons why he is now regarded as a pioneer and a man of genius while his contemporaries have fallen into oblivion. Weber, it is assumed, is one of those great masters whose works are still in the universal repertory. To what extent is this true? In Germany performances of *Der Freischütz* are still numerous; it can certainly be said that for that country *Der Freischütz* is as indispensable to the stock repertory as *Carmen* or *Faust*. But that is all; *Oberon* is revived at rare intervals, *Euryanthe* may be exhumed once in twenty years and then buried again. In other countries it is rare to see even *Der Freischütz*; England and France, at any rate in our day, do not demand it as they do the works of Mozart and Wagner. In the concert-rooms of all countries the overtures to the three great operas are convenient make-weights where a short and effective opening number is wanted, one too that any symphony orchestra can play without rehearsal. The symphonies and concertos, except for an occasional performance of the *Koncertstück*, are utterly forgotten, even in Germany. It is evident, then, that what keeps Weber's reputation alive on the German stage is the essentially German and national quality of *Der Freischütz*. Germany's affection for it is an irrational one, based mainly on associations of childhood; every child who learned the pianoforte was taught to play the simpler tunes from it, and it was always regarded as the appropriate opera to which children could be taken for their first visit to the theatre. It is an opera 'for the people', and for the German people; and for this reason a non-German musician has, so to speak, to become spiritually naturalized as a German, if he is to enjoy the work thoroughly. Many non-German musicians, otherwise saturated with German music, educated perhaps in Germany and with the most whole-hearted sympathy and devotion for Schumann, Brahms, Bruckner and Pfitzner, none the less sometimes feel that *Der Freischütz* is simply unbearable.

In all probability they take it too seriously. We have been brought up to too profound a reverence for the 'great masters'; and we of the nineteenth and twentieth centuries have also absorbed the idea that all music was written for immortality and must be heard as the bearer of an ethical 'message'. Let us try to put ourselves back into the days of Weber, and into the mentality of himself and his friends.

First, let us recall Weber the man, and most especially Weber the young man. He was the son of a strolling actor and manager who when it suited him claimed the right to a baronial title. His more respectable cousins, the Webers who come into Mozart's life (and their respectability was none too remarkable), made no claim to it whatever. Old father Weber must have been something like a mixture of Mr Crummles, Mr Jingle and Mr Micawber: that is the only way in which I can suggest his portrait to English-speaking listeners.

Carl Maria has sometimes been compared to Byron, and in the matter of genius it is perhaps no unjust parallel; in private life he was more of the type of Thomas Moore. Some biographers have laid stress on the dissipations of his youth; but it would seem that he was merely a hanger-on of dissipated society rather than a rebel against social conventions like Byron and Shelley. The important factor in his career is that for several years he was the modern equivalent of a court jester, something like the Clown in *Twelfth Night* as Granville Barker interpreted him – the kind of young man who is perpetually invited to stay in the houses of the great because he can dance and sing and amuse the company with a certain elegance and refinement of style. Weber sang a little, and played the guitar; he also played the pianoforte with remarkable fluency. In that sort of society it was natural that some of the young noblemen should write vapid little poems about the ladies, and that Weber should set them to music on the spur of the moment. Such elegant trivialities came easy to him; the shape was that of the German lyric, the musical style a mixture of the French conversational manner with an occasional Italian cadence. It is the infancy of the 'drawing-room song' of the nineteenth century; the 'Adieu' attributed to Schubert is the classical example of it, and late Victorians and Edwardians can remember its decrepitude. Weber was always being called upon to play the pianoforte; what had he to play? The sonatas of Hummel and Woelfl, perhaps; the chamber music of Dussek and Prince Louis Ferdinand; but probably what he most often did was to improvise on memories of the popular operas of the day. It was the great age of pianoforte variations; we know the huge output of Haydn, Mozart and Beethoven in this form, or rather, we know very little of it as a rule. What the great men wrote the little men wrote too; and they wrote variations, as some other composers, from Rameau to Chopin, wrote fantastic preludes, because it was the fashionable thing to extemporize them. Those who had the necessary inspiration might extemporize, or possibly pretend to do so; the unfortunate amateurs who could not raise even that much inspiration bought their improvisations ready-made.

I emphasize this phase of Weber's life, because there is so much of his printed work, especially in the operas, which sounds like Rossini remembered by ear at the pianoforte, with the lapses of memory covered up by conventional flourishes.

It was in 1813 that Weber settled down to steady work as conductor at the opera in Prague; let us review the list of the operas he conducted. The first was Spontini's *Fernand Cortez*; after that came Catel's *Les Aubergistes de Qualité*, Méhul's *Joseph*, Spontini's *La Vestale*, Cherubini's *Les Deux Journées* and *Faniska*, Méhul's *Uthal*, Isouard's *Le Billet de Loterie* and *Cendrillon*. The first German opera Weber conducted was *Carlo Fioras* by one Fränzl,[1] which was a failure; later on he produced *Fidelio* without much success, as well as *Don Giovanni* and *Così fan tutte* – this last with a new libretto. Weber was evidently too Romantic to appreciate the wit of Da Ponte.

In 1817 Weber became conductor at Dresden, where his

[1] This and Benda's *mélodrame Medea* came between *Le Billet de Loterie* and *Cendrillon*. Weber's Prague repertory also included *Le nozze di Figaro*, *La clemenza di Tito*, three operas by Boieldieu, two each by Grétry and Dalayrac, and one each by Berton and Gaveaux. For a full list, see Z. Němec, *Weberova pražská léta* (Prague, 1944).

energies were concentrated on the development of German opera in opposition to the Italian opera conducted by Morlacchi. What was his repertory at Dresden? Méhul's *Joseph* for his *début*: then followed much the same French operas as he had produced at Prague, with the addition of Mozart's two German *Singspiele*, Cherubini's *Lodoiska*, Spontini's *Olimpie*, and in 1822 Rossini's *La donna del lago*. The repertory had to be French and Italian, because there were no German operas worth performing except those of Mozart and Beethoven.

But three other German composers came into Weber's life, and it is interesting to observe his relations with them. The first is Louis Spohr, venerated by the nineteenth century and despised by the twentieth. Spohr was in every way a complete contrast to Weber. He was bourgeois and eminently respectable; he was a man of immense physical strength who at a comparatively early age settled down to matrimony, whereas Weber was always frail and delicate and did not marry until he was over thirty. Spohr first met Weber about 1808, and it is hardly surprising that he thought very little of him. Even in later years Spohr always regarded Weber as an amateur, and although it is customary to laugh at Spohr's judgments on his contemporaries, it must be admitted that, from his rigorously orthodox and professional point of view, he was not far wrong. Posterity has associated Spohr mainly with oratorio, but in his own day he was a composer of operas as much as anything else, and above all things he was a violinist. The violin dominated everything he wrote; his life, indeed, seems to have been one perpetual violin concerto. It is the violin which betrays him in his opera *Jessonda* (1823), an extremely competent piece of work, modelled mainly on Cherubini, but without spoken dialogue: it is sung all the way through. The style is astonishingly like that of Weber. The story, the scene of which is laid in Malabar, is Romantic in the manner of *Fernand Cortez* and was obviously the model for Meyerbeer's *L'Africaine*; it turns on a love affair between Tristan da Cunha and an Indian widow. It was an opera that in Germany could remain for a long time in the orthodox repertory; but it has now dropped out entirely. If exotic scenery is wanted, Meyerbeer's opera is more grandiose and showy; *Jessonda* has no appeal to popularity, and could never delight the multitude which enjoys the village humours of *Der Freischütz*. Its respectability has killed it; it is so admirably finished in every detail that it is hardly possible to be surprised by anything which happens in it. Like so much of Spohr's music, it has the correct manners of the man who has acquired them by industry and not by inheritance.

Heinrich Marschner, another composer still much respected in Germany, though seldom performed, is often described as a follower of Weber, but he is a follower only in a chronological sense. He came into Weber's life in the year 1819 and became his assistant at Dresden. Weber at first disliked him; he was ill-mannered and tactless in conversation. He was obviously a very German provincial type, physically strong and aggressively virile; it is interesting to note that Weber subsequently became much attached to him. It was always characteristic of Weber to require friends of the virile type on whom he could lean for support. In music Marschner was more of the school of Spohr than a disciple of Weber. If it is difficult for the non-German to enter into the spirit of Weber, it is still more difficult for him to swallow Marschner. Marschner's subjects are as Romantic as could be wished; he is always raising spirits. But his supernatural music fails to frighten us, and his humorous rustic scenes, though still admired in Germany, are as boring as the back numbers of an old comic paper.

It is necessary to mention Spohr and Marschner, and especially their very German operas, such as Spohr's *Der Berggeist*, because we must try to find out what technical elements cause them to be so tedious. It is quite clear that this tediousness is due to monotony of rhythm; and the monotony of rhythm is in the first place the fault of the librettist. Weber, when he corresponded with Planché in London about the libretto of *Oberon*, observed very properly 'that the composer looks more for the expression of feelings than the figurative; the former he may repeat and develope [*sic*] in all their graduations; but verses like:

> Like the spot the tulip weareth
> Deep within its dewy urn,[2]

must only be said once.' The German librettists never seemed to realize that the composers would want to repeat their words over and over again. They adopted the metres suitable for short songs

---

[2] These lines occur in the finale to Act I of *Oberon*. Weber disposes of them in seven bars of quick tempo.

or for long ballads; they had no metres suitable for recitative. Blank verse, which German poets had adopted from Shakespeare, makes a rather cumbrous medium for recitative – it is too uniform in rhythm.

Both Spohr and Marschner soon become tiresome with their uniform melodiousness and their monotonous rhythm-patterns. They are about the first composers to warn us – though the warning was entirely lost on their successors – of the fatal danger that results from trying to construct operas which shall be all aria and no recitative, like a pudding which is all plums and nothing else.[3]

The third composer who influenced Weber was E. T. A. Hoffmann, better known as a novelist. Weber met him at Bamberg in 1811. Bamberg at that time had a very good theatre, in which Hoffmann both conducted and painted scenery. Weber himself seems to have had some knowledge of scene design, if not of the actual painting. It is perhaps characteristic of the Romantic epoch that a composer should interest himself actively in the visible as well as the audible aspects of the stage.

Weber's relations with Hoffmann were not always cordial; Hoffmann must have been a very difficult character to be on friendly terms with. He had exactly the same ideals of a Romantic German opera as Weber himself; moreover, he had the same sort of amateurishness, and his accomplishment in musical technique did not really fall very far short of Weber's. But in the long run Hoffmann was a man of letters, and music was a side-issue for his versatility. Weber wrote verse and prose as a side-issue, but he was perhaps less accomplished in letters than Hoffmann was in music.

In 1816 Weber met Hoffmann again, this time in Berlin, where Hoffmann's opera *Undine* was produced. Weber was very cordial in his appreciation of it. 'I thought the music full of character and effect', he wrote in a letter, and when the opera was repeated at Prague in December of the same year he wrote about it in enthusiastic terms. Yet he was quite aware of certain defects, especially some mannerisms imitated from Cherubini. We see again that it is always Cherubini who is regarded in Germany as the standard of perfection for operatic writing. Hoffmann's *Undine* was revived a few years ago in Germany, and the vocal

[3] See p. 137 for Dent's similar criticism of Schubert's operas.

score printed; but it has not held the stage. Like all these early German Romantic operas, it suffers from a badly written libretto, which forces the composer to make the words ludicrous by repetition. This is one of the faults of Cherubini; whenever Hoffmann – or indeed Weber – tries to write an extended movement, he adopts certain mannerisms of the conventional symphonic style, certain well-worn formulae that we now regard as classical, and it is these which make the music sound old-fashioned and undramatic, because the German words cannot possibly fit them naturally. They are survivals from a French or Italian style of a much older generation. Hoffmann had little melodic invention; he could acquire the routine tricks of the symphonic style, but when it came to creating melody, the best that he could do was something in the German ballad style, which we now associate chiefly with the later songs of Carl Loewe. It was not even a very pure German style, for it had at an early period absorbed something of the Italian manner.

Like all the German Romantics, Hoffmann was much fascinated by the possibilities of the orchestra. He is really the initiator of the doctrine pursued later by Weber, Spohr and Marschner, and brought to its highest development by Wagner, that the orchestra, as Adolf Weissmann well said, represented the supernatural and mysterious forces of nature against which humanity vainly struggles. As far as one can judge from a vocal score, it looks as if Hoffmann often allowed the noise of the orchestra to overpower the singers; but his orchestral sounds are never more than mere conventionalities. Spohr never set out to do anything more than compose practicable operas, as a carpenter might make practicable chairs and tables. Hoffmann may at least be credited with the desire to create works of imagination, to seize the unseizable and set it down in musical notes; unfortunately his musical technique was not adequate to the expression of his fantasy. The German audiences of his day were thrilled by the ideal of Germanism in music – a new experience for them, as the nationalism of some modern English music is for us of to-day; but nationalism has no merit for the world in general, unless it be that of the picturesquely exotic.

It is fairly obvious that Germanism of this type was only a passing phase for Weber. He utilized it to the furthest possible limit in *Der Freischütz*, but wisely saw that that was a thing one could only do once. There is no trace of it in *Euryanthe* or *Oberon*. In later years Weber came almost to detest the opera which had brought him fame, for wherever he went the popular numbers were played in his honour. Those were just the numbers in which there was least of his own genius.

It is interesting to know that in 1814 Clemens Brentano had suggested *Tannhäuser* as a subject for Weber, and had actually written a good deal of a libretto on the legend. Weber never attempted to set it to music, for at that time his mind was concentrated mainly on *Der Freischütz*. It was the supernatural element that appealed especially to his imagination; he seems to have foreseen the doctrine of Busoni that the supernatural is the realm in which music for the stage is most at home, because, as Busoni says, music can make it credible. When he first discussed the libretto of *Euryanthe* with Helmina von Chezy, he insisted that the supernatural element should be brought in, and so it was, but with disastrous results. Many writers have encouraged the opinion that Weber was, so to speak, born in the theatre, and that he could not help being an efficient composer for the stage. He knew instinctively what would be effective, and made the fatal mistake of trusting to instinct, which in his case, as in most people's, meant relying on routine. Anyone who has worked in a theatre knows only too well that Weber's operas present the most horrible problems to a producer and stage-manager. Perhaps they are difficult to produce nowadays because Wagner has taught us new ideals of stage presentation. The Dresden Opera in Weber's time must have been very different from what it is now. For one thing, it was almost impossible to obtain female chorus singers; the female chorus parts were sung by boys from the Kreuzschule, and not much trouble was taken in dressing them up. *La Vestale*, in which the female chorus is very much to the fore, was a dangerously grotesque exhibition. The acting in old Italian and French comic opera was naturalistic, as far as one can ascertain, but with the growth of ensembles during the period under discussion naturalistic acting must have become impossible. Audiences settled down, as many eye-witnesses have told us, to accepting an operatic convention which is not yet dead; the naturalistic treatment of the choral masses can hardly have begun before the great days of the Meiningen Theatre in the 1860s, which set a new fashion for the performance of

Shakespeare, and gradually began to influence the production of opera.

A curious light is thrown on *Der Freischütz* by the recent publication of a manuscript version of the play in English by Washington Irving. He had seen the opera in Dresden, and began to make his adaptation at the end of May 1823 during a tour in Silesia and Bohemia. He made final corrections to the manuscript in Paris in the autumn of 1824. Irving had collaborated anonymously in a play about Charles II produced by Charles Kemble in London in October 1824; he was therefore to some extent familiar with the conditions of the English theatre at that time.

The interesting thing about Irving's play *The Wild Huntsman*, as he calls his version of *Der Freischütz*, is that he evidently had no conception of the work as an opera, in the way that we now understand the word – that is, as a complete work of art in which the music is the most important thing and the personal creation of a distinguished artist. To Irving it was merely a play, a Romantic play with incidental music. The music, in fact, was so incidental that he seems to take it for granted that any numbers can be left out, or new numbers inserted. This was the regular practice on the English stage, where comic operas were always pasticcios made up from music by various composers. To-day we are accustomed to regard the Wolf's Glen scene as one of the world's masterpieces of continuous dramatic music; Irving evidently saw it merely as a pantomimic spectacle to which any sort of music would do as a background. If his version were to be adopted now, it would make the play so long that there would be hardly time for any music at all. Considered simply as a remodelling of the play, without regard to music of any kind, Washington Irving's version is certainly an immense improvement; it keeps the supernatural element well in the foreground and makes the whole play seem haunted by it. It clarifies many points which the German, as now spoken, leaves rather obscure, and by the bold stroke of transferring all the business of casting the magic bullets to Kilian instead of Max, it leaves Max completely innocent at the end and thus able to marry Agathe at once. Kilian consequently has to be developed into a character of some importance; he is induced by Caspar to join in the pact with the Devil because he is by nature vain and boastful, as well as dissipated and given to drinking.

In the course of Weber's unfinished and very fragmentary novel, *Tonkünstlers Leben*,[4] there is a discussion on the subject of opera – 'opera, I need hardly say, as a German wants it to be'. German opera, says Weber, must be a complete and organic work of art, in which all the associated arts combine to make a whole which presents us with a new world. But he admits that in actual practice it is generally isolated features which attract the spectator and ensure success. Such in fact was the fate of *Der Freischütz*; it had a certain number of episodes which at once captivated the unsophisticated public, and that is probably the reason why it still holds the stage. Weber's supposed genius for the theatre was not an understanding of continuous drama; he had merely a practised eye for isolated theatrical effects, for all those gestures and attitudes which provoke an immediate response from an audience. He can always invent the most ravishing initial phrases, but they are almost always instrumental and not vocal. They sound exquisite when played by the solo instrument which starts the introductory symphony, but very often they will not fit the words which the voice has to sing. In some numbers Weber simply gives up the attempt, the solo instrument delivers the attractive phrase, and the voice has to go on as best it can, until Weber suddenly thinks of some French conversational way of treating the words that brings out their sense for a flash in the most illuminating way. Those are Weber's great moments, moments of direct expression which are indeed his and his alone; but he is incapable of constructing a well-balanced piece of music.

Euryanthe was the opera which he himself loved best; it was meant to be a work of idealism, a work of art as a whole, with no concessions to popular taste. On the stage it has always been a failure, and the fault is always laid at the door of the unfortunate librettist. Let us consider the opera carefully for a moment, and see if we can find out exactly where its weaknesses lie.

The story is absurd; that is universally agreed. But it is not more absurd than many other plots, some of Shakespeare's included. Shakespeare's absurdities are compensated for by the beauty of his language, and by the truth of human feeling which he presents; in many cases too there is picturesqueness of environ-

[4] Weber's prose works were edited by Georg Kaiser (Berlin and Leipzig, 1908). A modern selection, including *Tonkünstlers Leben*, is available in paperback, ed. Karl Laux (Leipzig, 1969).

ment to add to the illusion. These are all features of Romantic Opera, allowing for the new aesthetic values introduced by music. In assessing the value of an operatic libretto we have to consider it from various angles. A libretto may have the common fault of ridiculous language, language which perhaps sounds all the more ridiculous when it is sung, and yet have quite a good plot, as far as the skeleton of the play is concerned. It may have picturesque scenes, with no proper motive for their introduction; on the other hand, it may have words of literary distinction but unsuitable for setting to music. Helmina von Chezy's libretto suffers mainly from its verbal absurdities; these might be done away with by translation into another language, that is, by taking the situations as they stand, and writing appropriate words suggested by the shapes of Weber's music.

It is easy to make fun of the situations and motives, but in an opera there is no more need for logic and realism than in a fairy-tale or legend. It is a commonplace of Metastasian opera that the characters are always in too much of a hurry to allow misunderstandings to be explained until the situation becomes so complex that a general *dénouement* – an untying of knots – has to be made at the end of the opera. It is conceivable that in the Middle Ages, when people were more impulsive and violent in their manners, and had a less flexible language in which to explain themselves, they actually did act in what we should call a Romantic operatic manner. The scene of *Euryanthe* is laid in France in the year 1110. At the court of King Louis VI Count Adolar, a rather languishing young troubadour, sings about his betrothed, Euryanthe of Savoy, who is living in retirement while he is at court. Count Lysiart makes fun of him and suggests that the lady is as frail as any other. Adolar wagers his castle and estate in her defence; Lysiart boasts that he will prove her infidelity (compare *Così fan tutte*). Such behaviour may seem shocking to modern people, but it would have appeared quite reasonable to Shakespeare. The ordinary musical critic never thinks of adopting a Shakespearian outlook; he starts from what he has read in many books, that *Euryanthe* foreshadows *Lohengrin*, and he therefore starts with the assumption that the five chief characters in Weber's opera must be exactly the same as those of Wagner's. They are not. The King, to be sure, is a lay figure in each case; he has no personality at all. Euryanthe bears a superficial resemblance to Elsa, but her situation is quite different. Elsa claims property; she is not concerned with love, until Lohengrin appears quite unexpectedly. She is asked to keep a secret, and cannot do so; in this she resembles Euryanthe, but Elsa never has the chance of showing heroism and self-sacrifice, as Euryanthe does in the third act. Adolar is not in the least like Lohengrin; Lohengrin is a quasi-supernatural character, who fights to defend Elsa, but never seems very much inclined to marry her, and is very glad to seize on the first excuse for making his escape from her. Adolar is an adoring lover from the first, and Weber makes clear, if his librettist does not (although she certainly suggests it), that Adolar is the gentle, artistic, troubadour type of man, as contrasted with Lysiart the ultra-virile and aggressive warrior. Lysiart is not evil to begin with: he is driven to evil by passion, and encouraged in his wickedness by Eglantine. The fundamental motives of both Lysiart and Eglantine are absolutely clear and natural: Lysiart is the rejected suitor of Euryanthe, and Eglantine is desperately in love with Adolar.

Eglantine is under a cloud, and living in retirement with Euryanthe, because her father has been a rebel; if all this had been more clearly explained, there would have been no difficulty in understanding Eglantine's state of mind.[5] She is evidently young, hot-blooded and passionate in temperament, contrasting with the rather chilly nature of Euryanthe. Passion, too, is the dominant motive in the character of Lysiart. Unfortunately the subsequent developments of the German operatic stage lead everyone to expect that Adolar, being the tenor, will be heroic at all costs in manner, especially if not so in appearance; that Eglantine will be corpulent and motherly, like most interpreters of the part of Ortrud, and that Lysiart will be an elderly singer with much conventional experience and a large heavy voice. A Wagnerian interpretation of the opera would be its ruin; we must see it as the descendant of the French Romantic Opera of Cherubini and Méhul.

The absurdity of the plot begins with the futile attempt to find some device which will compromise Euryanthe's reputation in the eyes of the stage characters while preserving it for the audience. Here Weber himself is to blame, for it was he who insisted on the introduction of some supernatural element. Helmina von

---

[5] She explains it in her first recitative with Euryanthe, in Act I Scene 2.

Chezy accordingly invented the ghost of Emma; Emma, whom we never see, even as a ghost, was the sister of Adolar, and committed suicide long before the action begins because her lover was killed in battle. If Emma only haunted the play like the Ghost in *Hamlet*, we could believe in her easily enough, and ask no questions about the reason for her walkings; at the present day suicide seems an inadequate ground for so much worry and trouble. In Weber's day, and in a Catholic country, suicide was probably taken more seriously. Eglantine has found out (she admits that she is inquisitive by temperament) that Euryanthe pays secret visits to a vault where she prays for the soul of Emma, and she manages to steal a ring from the tomb – the poisoned ring by which Emma brought about her death. Lysiart produces the ring at the court of King Louis, and it is accepted as proof of Euryanthe's fall from virtue. Euryanthe is apparently too much bewildered, as well she might be, to defend herself; but in any case there is really nothing contrary to operatic practice in her being condemned without further ado.

In the third act Adolar conducts her into the wilderness with the intention of slaying her; death is to purify her from sin. In the first version of the story a lion appears; Euryanthe offers to allow herself to be devoured in place of her former lover, and for this kind action he agrees to leave her alone and give her a sporting chance – we might call it a Shakespearian chance – of surviving. As lions were never encountered on the soil of France, even in the Middle Ages, Weber insisted on the animal being changed to a serpent, perhaps remembering the first scene of *Die Zauberflöte*. The serpent is really an even more absurd idea than the lion; but I suggest that if we were to make the beast a dragon, the sense of probability would no longer be outraged. The opera is a romance of brave knights and fair ladies, and in that environment dragons are as much at home as cats and dogs in our own. The appearance of a dragon would at once set the atmosphere of legend, and then almost any motive of conduct can be accepted.

Adolar slays the dragon, after which he rewards her offer of self-sacrifice by leaving her to starve or die of exposure. She is then discovered by a hunting party, which provides the usual male-voice chorus with a quartet of horns indispensable to all Romantic operas. The King arrives, and this time he has leisure enough to listen to her explanations, which are extremely summary, but apparently quite convincing. After an ecstatic aria Euryanthe falls unconscious, and is carried back to the seat of the court, the sound of the chorus and the horns dying away in the distance. The next scene is at Adolar's castle, where a rustic wedding is taking place. This makes an attractive contrast, with its ballet of peasants, and affords the opportunity of showing us how Adolar is adored by his local vassals, and how horrified they are at the property passing into the hands of Lysiart through Adolar's foolish wager. At this moment the wedding procession of Lysiart and Eglantine arrives, and the much abused poetess has given Weber a magnificent opportunity for dramatic music by making Eglantine almost insane with remorse; she thinks that the ghost of Emma rises before her and demands the return of the ring. Adolar reveals himself and threatens vengeance; Lysiart is prepared to fight, and the chorus lustily support the cause of Adolar. The fight is prevented by the entrance of the King; Adolar appeals to him, saying that Euryanthe was a paragon of virtue – a statement for which he has no evidence whatever. The King informs him that Euryanthe has been found, but has died of a broken heart, and Eglantine at once bursts out with a cry of triumph.[6] She rejoices at the death of her rival; she reproaches Adolar for his coldness towards herself, and in order to intensify his agony she confesses openly that she stole the ring from the tomb and that Euryanthe was completely innocent. Lysiart is enraged at this confession; Eglantine tells him contemptuously that he was nothing more than the miserable tool of her own revenge. Lysiart at once kills her; the King orders him to be seized and put to death, but Adolar intervenes, taking all the blame on himself and accusing himself of the murder of Euryanthe. Just as he collapses in remorse, the huntsmen are heard shouting behind that Euryanthe lives, and she rushes on to an immediate embrace with Adolar, after which Adolar suddenly says that he is in some mysterious way aware of Emma, and that her spirit is finally at rest. The opera ends with the usual chorus of rejoicing.

I can see no reason why *Euryanthe* should be remembered as a standard masterpiece, though a neglected one, if Schubert's two great operas are entirely forgotten. It seems to be generally

[6] Compare the Countess of Arles in Méhul's *Euphrosine*. (E.J.D.)

agreed that for Schubert's operas there is not the smallest vestige of hope; *Euryanthe,* however, is periodically revived by enthusiasts, although it is never successful. For sheer musical beauty Schubert is incomparably superior to Weber, and there is no aspect of the Romantic technique which Schubert had not made completely his own. The main difference between the two is that Weber has hardly any sense of musical form. He can invent the most fascinating initial phrases, but he cannot balance them; his music tails off in interest just at the very moment where it ought to become more interesting. He tries to save the situation with a coda and a conventional high-note-effect; in some of his arias, notably in those of Eglantine, he is so determined to be passionate that he piles one climax on another. He is quite incapable of planning the form of a number and holding a climax in reserve. He trusts to luck and to the occasional moment when individual words can be brought out with an effect that certainly is at times overwhelming. It is a curious paradox that the man who in his critical writings asserted so firmly the essential principle of making an opera an organic whole should have won his popularity by that attractiveness of isolated numbers which he himself so emphatically condemns.

The fault of *Euryanthe* lies in its formlessness and in its want of proportion. There is much too much time wasted on mere picturesqueness; the choruses are dragged in for no dramatic reason, and most of them are too long. One can well understand Weber's reasons for this. The old Italian opera which he detested had been essentially an opera of soloists; the presence of the chorus contributed to a certain national feeling, as if the chorus represented that new consciousness of the nation which he wished to express in his music. Male-voice choruses were springing up all over Germany; they were singing Weber's own patriotic part-songs. A good male chorus was easily obtained for the theatre, and it always had a popular appeal. It has still, in Germany; the huntsmen's chorus in *Der Freischütz* invariably fetches rounds of applause.

The result of all this preoccupation with the merely incidental and picturesque is that very little actually happens in the course of the first two acts; *Euryanthe* in this respect offers a pitiful contrast to Méhul's *Ariodant.* The story of *Ariodant* is not much less absurd, but it is crowded with incident, and each dramatic situation arises naturally out of the preceding one. We can see, too, that the contrast of Euryanthe and Eglantine is probably derived directly from the contrast between Ina and Dalinde in *Ariodant*, and also from the contrast between Euphrosine and the Countess of Arles in Méhul's earlier opera. It is only in the final scene of *Euryanthe* that dramatic incidents come thick and fast, and even here, as in the very similar operas of Cherubini and Schubert, the action is perpetually obstructed by the long-windedness of the choruses.

Weber's last opera, *Oberon*, contains perhaps his most delightful music, but it stands rather outside the main stream of operatic history, because it was planned for performance in London, as an English opera based on an entirely local convention. Planché, the author of the libretto, was a typical Englishman of what we may call the 'neo-Gothic' period. The English theatre was at its lowest ebb, and Planché supplied it with plays, farces and extravaganzas by the hundred. His autobiography shows us that he attached no great value to any of them. What he really loved was the society of titled people, and that naturally led him to the study of heraldry and archaeology. As regards his qualifications as a librettist, he was Englishman enough to be familiar with the favourite plays of Shakespeare. For the book of *Oberon* he drew liberally on *The Tempest* and *A Midsummer Night's Dream*; and those works were at any rate a more useful source of operatic inspiration than any which were at the disposal of continental librettists. Planché aimed frankly at conventional stage effects and nothing else; in the first place, scenery, in the second, ballet, then chorus and finally a few soloists. *Oberon* illustrates the mechanics of Romanticism, as far as the libretto is concerned. It survives in Germany through the beauty of its music. I could wish that it might be revived in England, with its original English spoken dialogue; it is certainly absurd, but with the inconsequence of a child's picture-book.

To most historians of music Weber is the typical Romantic composer and indeed the creator of the Romantic style. These lectures will have shown you, I hope, how very little of that style was really the creation of Weber. The real initiators of Romantic Opera were the French; the French and Italian operas met on the common ground of Vienna, and from that union there developed a general Romantic phraseology which is common to most German composers between about 1800 and 1820. It was Weber's good fortune to have been born in the theatre, and he was fortunate in later life in being regularly employed as a theatrical conductor at Breslau, Prague and Dresden. It is obvious that this experience must have been of value to him in the composition of operas; it is perhaps less obvious, but for all that extremely probable, that his position of eminence and influence as conductor in an important opera-house must have made it all the easier for him to get his own works successfully produced elsewhere.

11

BELLINI

If these lectures had been designed merely to survey the origins and first developments of the Romantic Opera, they would have come to their appropriate end with the study of Weber. But it was my intention from the first that we should study Romantic Opera not so much for its own sake as for an understanding of its influence on all subsequent music, and for that reason it is indispensable that we should give consideration to the operas of Bellini.

In the course of these lectures I have had occasion to speak of Pergolesi and Paisiello as the typical exponents of the sentimental – indeed I might say, of the namby-pamby – style in opera. One would hardly expect this to produce a composer of undeniable genius; but the fact remains that Vincenzo Bellini formed his style on that of these two Neapolitan sentimentalists, and demonstrated that even sentimentality can be intensified to a degree that makes it still convincing.

We know so little about Pergolesi, and his life was so short, that it is difficult to say whether we ought to call him a gifted amateur or an inefficient professional. Paisiello is certainly professional, and his vapidity is part of his slick professionalism. Bellini managed to live a few years longer than Pergolesi, and he certainly achieved a decided maturity of style; but his technical accomplishment was always amateurish, and his amateurishness strikes us now as being more noticeable than that of Weber, because the subsequent history of music has led people to expect a German outlook on harmony and orchestration which came natural to Weber and was completely foreign to the Italian tradition in which Bellini was brought up.

I mentioned some time back[1] that the Italian school of the early nineteenth century was divided into two groups, those who

---

[1] The reference is presumably to the beginning of Lecture 8, where however Dent does not make precisely this point.

adopted French methods and encouraged the use of ensemble numbers, such as Paer, Mayr and Rossini, and those who remained faithful to older Italian conventions, such as Guglielmi, Fioravanti and others now quite forgotten. Bellini, born in Sicily and sent in adolescence to be trained at Naples, was naturally cut off from what was then the modern world of music, a world centred in Paris and Vienna, with a subsidiary centre at Milan. It is not surprising, therefore, that Bellini's first attempts at opera were in the old-fashioned style of sentimentalized *opera buffa.*

Adelson e Salvini is Romantic in so far as the scene is laid in Ireland, a country as mysteriously picturesque to an Italian as Sicily is to us. We find it a little difficult to believe in Lord Adelson, whose title suggests that he must have been raised to the peerage in consideration of financial assistance rendered to the Prince Regent, and that his original name might have been something like *Adelssohn.* The plot is mainly sentimental, but there is the indispensable Neapolitan comic bass, who is the servant of the Italian painter Salvini, on a visit to Ireland. The music is a curious mixture of styles, as one might reasonably expect from a very young composer living rather remote from the fashionable world; there are reminiscences of Paisiello and Cimarosa, and of Pergolesi as well, with occasional clumsy attempts to reproduce the chromatic harmonies of the modern French school. Bellini's third opera, *Il pirata*, is more aggressively Romantic in story; we have choruses of fishermen and pirates, as well as a mysterious gentleman known as *il solitario*, a nobleman in retirement and disguise, exactly like our old friend the Duke in Paer's *Camilla.* From a historical point of view the most notable thing about *Il pirata* is that there is no *recitativo secco*; we are definitely in the Romantic style of continuous opera.[2] To our ears the choruses are rather feeble stuff; but we must try to hear them in the spirit of their first audiences. Old Lord Mount-Edgcumbe detested modern opera, as exemplified by Rossini; choruses, in his experience, were always abominable, for they had to be sung from memory by bad singers, and how could such a chorus ever learn anything at all complicated? The Italian chorus, even more than the German chorus, had to sing in the style of

---

[2]   Mayr in *Medea in Corinto* (1813) and Rossini in *Elisabetta, regina d'Inghilterra* (1815) had dispensed with *recitativo secco*, as had Bellini in *Bianca e Fernando* (1826).

a military band on the stage, the violins playing the really important tune of the movement.

Bellini is the great exponent of what we may call the barcarolle style, which became the rage of all the drawing-rooms of Europe in the early part of the nineteenth century. It has survived to our own day in the songs of Denza and Tosti. How far it was genuinely folk-music only an Italian could tell us; by Bellini's time it seems to have become a recognized commercial product. It was this mixture of styles in opera which roused the wrath of Lord Mount-Edgcumbe; at the same time one cannot condemn the barcarolle style as unworthy of serious opera, for Mozart had given us the loveliest possible example of it in *Idomeneo* – 'Placido è il mar, andiamo.' But our sense of fitness may well be offended by such a movement as that in Bellini's later opera, *La straniera*, where the chorus relates a narrative in quick chattering semiquavers, almost like a patter-song. This was derived from Cimarosa, who had already begun to treat serious opera in the trivial style. We can find many examples of this type of choral writing in the operas of Donizetti and Verdi. The older composers would have given us all this necessary information through the mouth of some subordinate character, telling us the story in *recitativo secco*; the Romantics wanted to avoid *recitativo secco* at all costs, and the devices that they utilized were either the ballad for a single voice (much favoured by the Germans) or something like a ballad sung by the chorus. The most familiar instance is that of the opening scene in *Il trovatore*.

The influence of the military band on choral music in Italy is seen not only in the rub-a-dub-dub-dub for the brass instruments which so often assaults our ears at the most inappropriate moments, but still more in the sudden alternations of *pianissimo* and *fortissimo*, especially those violent *sforzandos* on a single chord, followed by a *pianissimo*, quite regardless of the sense of the words. Rossini, in *Mosè*, had already made his sensation with the crash of big drum and cymbals on the second beat of the bar.

Bellini's genius was for pure melody. Modern listeners can hardly realize how exquisitely subtle and expressive that melody is, for the art of singing it is almost lost nowadays. We hear Bellini more often in the circus than in the opera-house, or perhaps played by the local wind-band (and often very expressively played) in the public square of some Italian city. But it is inevitably coarsened in performance, and if we cannot hear Bellini sung as he ought to be sung, we must study his melody by ourselves, preparing our imagination first by a course of Chopin and Field. Chorley, writing in 1850 or so, spoke very severely of the *largo cantabile* airs in 9/8 or 12/8 which Verdi so often wrote, saying that they were only fit for singers with long breaths and powerful voices who had never acquired the true art of singing, of modulating the voice expressively; their songs, he says, gave only the outward appearance of feeling. We often find these songs of Verdi beautiful at the present day, but they are undoubtedly conceived for singers with voices like trombones, and they never sound better than when played by a military band. The airs of Bellini, on the other hand, demand a delicacy and refinement for which modern singers have not the technique. It is not that they are unable to cope with the execution of the coloratura; the female singers of to-day, at any rate, can often sing coloratura with amazing assurance and accuracy. Bellini requires a different technique, the technique of subordinating coloratura to expression, and cultivating the subtlest elegances of nuance and phrasing. It requires a standard in these matters which has almost passed out of knowledge among singers and is now regarded as the province of violinists and pianists.

The weakness of Bellini, especially in these early operas, is that he seems to have no sense of general dignity of style. At one moment he will write melodies that are deeply moving, and on the next page we shall find trivial vulgarities which modern musicians find either disgusting or ridiculous. In reading these things we are obliged to accept the taste of the age, and we have to remember the conditions of the Italian theatre in Italy itself. The best examples of Italian opera, as regards performance, were at that time to be found in Paris or Vienna, perhaps also in London. In Italy, the opera was becoming more and more democratic; it was the entertainment of the lower classes as well as of the aristocracy, and in a few years the opera-houses were destined to become hot-beds of revolution.

Bellini's early operas belong to the 1820s; Rossini was at the height of his fame, and Weber had begun to be known outside his native country. It is very difficult to decide how far Bellini was influenced by German music; it has been suggested by recent Italian critics that he knew such works of Beethoven as the Sonata in C sharp minor,[3] and that he was well acquainted with *Der Freischütz*. It is much more probable that he drew his inspiration from the common stock of popular Italian music of the day; I do not mean from folksong, if such a thing exists, but from all the commonplace music, dance music, church music and military music, that he would hear in the streets and in private houses.

The first opera in which Bellini achieved some sort of unity of style was *La sonnambula*, produced at Milan in March 1831. It is still popular in Italy, and it formed part of the current repertory in Paris not many years ago. The same can be said of his two later operas, *Norma* and *I puritani*; in an international book about Bellini published in 1936 in honour of the centenary of his death, Jean Chantavoine gives statistics of the Paris performances down to 1909. The other operas of Bellini disappeared from the stage in Paris about 1840–50.

La sonnambula, considered historically, is a very curious opera. It is in two acts only, and short as compared to the average opera; in Milan or Paris to-day it would probably be given along with a ballet or some other work in order that the audience might get full value for their entrance money. It belongs to the class of *opera semi-seria*: that is, it is fundamentally a comic opera, but treated sentimentally. The libretto seems to bear no affinity to the standard French type, though it is probably based on some short story of the period.[4] The scene is laid in Switzerland, which, as we have seen, was a country much favoured by the Romantics, and the plot turns on a case of somnambulism. It would be interesting to investigate the circumstances which had suggested this subject to Felice Romani, Bellini's librettist. Somnambulism had been observed in England more than two hundred years earlier in the well-known case of Lady Macbeth; and it is possible that the revival of interest in Shakespeare had drawn Romani's attention to it.[5] Bellini had already composed an opera on the subject of *Romeo and Juliet*. The plot of *La sonnambula* is, how-

---

[3] He must certainly have known the 'Moonlight' Sonata as there is a longer reminiscence of it in *La straniera* which was afterwards incorporated in *Norma*. (E.J.D.) The earlier reminiscence is in Act II, *Bianca e Fernando*.

[4] It is based on the scenario for *La Sonnambule, ou L'arrivée d'un nouveau seigneur*, a ballet-pantomine by Scribe and Aumer with music by Hérold. This in turn was derived from *La Sonnambule*, a comédie-vaudeville in two acts by Scribe and Delavigne.

[5] Somnambulism comes into several operas and ballets of the period; the idea probably originated with Lady Macbeth. (E.J.D.)

ever, very far from Shakespearean in character. The inhabitants of the Swiss village begin the opera with a chorus in praise of a peasant girl, Amina, who is about to be married. Her rival, Lisa, who keeps an inn, and is in love with Elvino, Amina's young man, at once declares her jealousy to the audience, while the chorus go on shouting 'Long live Amina!' Here we have the typical Romantic opera, with its opening chorus, and its insistence throughout upon the importance of the chorus. Amina enters with her beloved mother (who in this case is not her mother at all, but merely her adopted mother); Italian operas of this period make great effect with mothers, whose principal occupation seems to be prayer; they are often blind, and sometimes already dead, but they go on praying all the same (compare *Rigoletto*). Elvino comes on; he too has a mother, but she is one of the already dead; he has just been praying at her tomb.

The betrothal is solemnly witnessed by a notary, and it is arranged that the religious rite is to take place the next day.[6] The sound of horse-hoofs is heard outside, and Count Rodolfo, the local squire, arrives, having been absent from the village for a long period. As his castle is some way off, he decides to stay the night at Lisa's inn; he does not, however, reveal his identity, and nobody knows who he is. Evening falls, and Teresa, the old woman who has adopted Amina, warns Rodolfo to go in, as the local ghost will soon be walking. Rodolfo is somewhat sceptical, but the chorus and principals, including Amina herself, assure him that the ghost of a figure in a winding-sheet is seen every night. The chorus leave the stage, and the Count, after a little mild gallantry towards Amina, retires to the inn. Elvino is inclined to be jealous, but after a not very serious tiff he and Amina sing an affectionate duet in thirds and sixths.

The scene changes to the Count's room at the inn. Lisa intimates to him pretty plainly that she is quite ready to respond favourably if he should care to make advances to her; but at this moment there is a noise outside. Lisa runs away, and Amina, walking in her sleep, enters by the open window, dressed in her night-gown. She is still thinking about Elvino, and imagines herself to be going through the marriage ceremony, supported

---

[6] Stage weddings were very numerous at this period, and considered effective; but there were great difficulties in Catholic countries owing to the impossibility of putting the actual church service on the stage. (E.J.D.)

by her mother. This is all cast in the form of a duet between the unconscious Amina and the Count, who takes care to impress upon the audience that he realizes the situation and has no intention of doing any harm to the sleep-walker. The chorus, meanwhile, come softly in to serenade the Count, who seems to have slipped off to bed in another room, leaving Amina alone on the stage. The chorus see the white figure, but do not take it for a ghost; they recognize it as a woman. At this moment Lisa brings in Elvino, telling him that Amina is paying a nocturnal visit to the strange gentleman of her own free will. The chorus in their astonishment make such a noise that Amina awakes, and a long ensemble of recrimination follows. Elvino is in too much of a hurry to listen to explanations, and Amina is indeed not capable of making any; the Count is apparently sleeping peacefully in spite of all the tumult in the next room.

The scene of Act II is a wood between the village and the Count's castle. The Count has apparently revealed himself in the morning and has gone home; a chorus of villagers, unwilling to believe Amina guilty, are on their way to the castle to beg the Count to explain what has happened. Amina and Teresa come on, and there is another scene of recrimination with Elvino; the chorus return, saying that the Count has assured them of Amina's innocence. Elvino does not think much of the Count's evidence, and still refuses to have anything to do with Amina. We now return to the village, where Lisa tells her former admirer Alessio, a peasant, that she is going to marry Elvino; Alessio is much annoyed and threatens trouble. The chorus, who in this opera are very seldom absent from the stage, enter and inform Lisa that Elvino is ready to marry her instead of Amina.

Elvino appears, and makes rapid arrangements for the marriage in language which is both elegant and precise, but hardly impassioned; this is interrupted by the entrance of the Count, who insists on the innocence of Amina, and proceeds to give the assembled villagers a little lecture on the phenomenon of somnambulism, a thing of which they have never heard. People like Amina, he tells them (and he is careful to say it twice over) are called somnambulists because they walk and sleep at the same time:

E chiamati son sonnambuli dall' andar e dal dormir.

The Swiss villagers are not going to be taken in by that sort of nonsense; to walk and to sleep at the same time is obviously a sheer impossibility. Teresa, the old mother, begs the chorus to be quiet for a little, as poor Amina has gone to sleep and is in sore need of rest. Lisa boasts of her new conquest, and also of her virtue; Teresa produces a garment of hers which was found in the bedroom of the Count. This is very embarrassing for Lisa, and Elvino naturally does not know what to do. It is obviously the moment for a great ensemble, at the end of which the Count draws their attention to the fact that Amina is again walking in her sleep. She crosses a little bridge by the mill, and it gives way under her, but she just manages to save herself. This little episode, which of course offers the chorus great opportunities for emotional comment, suggests that Bellini's librettist was not altogether ignorant of old French opera; we remember the bridge in *Lodoiska* and *Elisa*. Amina is naturally given a considerable scene here; she reaches the front of the stage, says her prayers and protests her devotion to Elvino. Elvino, now completely convinced, very ingeniously stages an elegant tableau; he approaches Amina, puts the ring on her finger again, arranges Teresa behind her ready for an affectionate embrace, and himself falls at Amina's feet. At a signal from the Count the chorus wake her with a loud shout, and all ends happily.

Bellini was fortunate in his librettist; Felice Romani was a poet who could combine elegance of diction with simplicity of sentiment. His verses are commendably free from literary affectations, and he is acknowledged by all Italian critics to write in a very pure and distinguished style. It is a style which naturally appears old-fashioned to the modern reader, but when set to music, and especially when set to the sensitive music of Bellini, it has a very touching sincerity of emotion. The result is that this opera can still appeal directly to the feelings of an audience, especially of an unsophisticated audience; Bellini's characters, silly as their behaviour may seem to us, do really say the things an ordinary person would say in similar circumstances. Moreover, the whole interest of Bellini's music lies in the vocal melody, and experience of opera-going shows us that that is really the secret of any opera's power to hold the stage.

Bellini's vocal forms are of the simplest. He never attempts the Mozartian form of the aria; indeed that survived only in

Guillaume Tell. It was a form for the grand manner; Bellini's audiences wanted something more elementary. Almost every one of Bellini's airs is in the form represented by A A B A – a first strain, the repetition of it, a contrasted strain and then yet another repetition of the first (as in *The Vicar of Bray* and *The British Grenadiers*). It is the form preferred by Weber also; it had the advantage that it required only the minimum of inspiration and it secured the maximum of satisfaction to an audience, because the tune, or at any rate the essential part of it, could so easily be remembered. The applause of the audience was secured by the addition of a coda, sometimes of several.

In the following season, that is, in December of this same year 1831, Bellini produced what is generally acknowledged to be his masterpiece – *Norma*, described as *tragedia lyrica*. It is one of the first operas to end with the death of the heroine; but it should be pointed out that this type of ending is clearly descended from such operas as Handel's *Alcina*, Gluck's *Armide* and Cherubini's *Médée*, in which the chief character is a sorceress who flies away on the back of a dragon or makes some other form of sensational exit, often leaving the hero to enjoy prospective happiness in the arms of some less exciting lady. We may compare also Mozart's *Idomeneo*, where the exciting lady, Electra, disappears in a very bad temper, although not in a cloud of smoke; Idomeneo also retires by abdication, leaving the young couple, Idamante and Ilia, to represent the happy end. The exciting lady is a favourite character in Romantic Opera, and one never knows whether she will be a soprano or a contralto. German opera on the whole inclined to make her a contralto villainess, preferring virginal innocence as the attribute of the soprano; Italian opera often made the exciting lady a soprano, and enlisted the sympathies of the audience on her side, but it was difficult to make suitable matrimonial arrangements for her at the end, so that in the course of the century it was generally found more convenient to let her die.

Norma shows strong French influences; that of *La Vestale* is obvious, and there is the further influence of *Ossian,* or any other opera dealing with bards and Druids. The scene is supposed to be laid in ancient Wales, where Norma is a Druidess of the temple of Irminsul. Irminsul is described in the opera as a goddess; but it has been suggested that this is really the German word *Her-*

mannsäule, a column set up in memory of Arminius, often an object of worship in the Dark Ages. The opera takes place during the Roman occupation of Britain; but it would be indiscreet to inquire too closely into its chronology. Druids and warriors meet by moonlight at the sacred oak; Norma, at the bidding of her father the Chief Druid Oroveso, is to cut the sacred mistletoe. Pollio, the Roman Proconsul, enters with his friend Flavius, after the Druids have left the stage; he explains that although he has had a love affair with Norma, resulting in the birth of a family, he is now tired of her and starting another affair with Adalgisa, a younger priestess in the same temple. The Romans go away, and the Druids, etc. come back to perform a long and elaborate ceremony, during which Norma prophesies the destruction of Rome and cuts the sacred mistletoe. It is in this scene that she sings the famous invocation to the goddess, 'Casta Diva'. The Druids and warriors leave the stage to a rousing march, and there follows a scene between Pollio and Adalgisa, who is deeply in love with him, but hesitates to accept his suggestion that she should elope with him to Rome.

The scene changes to Norma's house. We see her with her children, who are a source of some embarrassment, all the more since she has heard that Pollio is recalled to Rome. She tells her servant to hide the children, as Adalgisa comes in. Adalgisa, quite unaware of Norma's past, confesses that she has fallen in love with a young man and is thinking of eloping with him. Norma understands the whole situation at once, having been through similar experiences. She is prepared to be thoroughly sympathetic; this makes an admirably expressive duet. Suddenly Pollio enters, and the stage direction sums up the situation in the fewest possible words: *Pollione è confuso, Adalgisa tremante, e Norma furente*. There is a long trio, in which Pollio gets the worst of it from both the ladies, until the chorus is heard behind summoning Norma once more to the temple. This brings Act I to an end.

Act II opens with the same scene at night: Norma, after a long and very interesting instrumental introduction, enters with a lamp, carrying a dagger, with the intention of murdering her sleeping infants. After a long scene of soliloquy, the children wake up and she changes her mind. She decides to commit suicide herself, but first sends for Adalgisa. She tells Adalgisa of her intention, and requests her to take the children to Rome and hand them over to their father. Adalgisa, very much surprised to hear of the existence of the children, decides to renounce Pollio and do her best to effect a reconciliation between him and Norma.

The scene changes to the sacred forest, where Oroveso has a long political conversation with his warriors. They must put up with the Romans for the time being, but they mean to get rid of them as soon as practicable. The men go away, leaving the stage free for Norma and her servant Clotilde, who informs her that Pollio is coming back and intends to carry off Adalgisa from the very altar of the goddess. Norma at this decides on vengeance. She summons the Druids and warriors; Clotilde explains that a Roman has seduced one of the temple virgins, and it is decreed that he must be sacrificed to the goddess. Norma has a last private interview with Pollio, in which she reduces him to complete defeat by threatening to kill her own children if he does not give up Adalgisa. The Druids and warriors come back, and Norma informs them that she herself is the guilty person. The chorus at first refuse to believe her, but when she confesses to her father Oroveso that she is a mother, it is too much for him, and the opera ends with her being led to execution. Moved by her heroism, Pollio joins her on the sacrificial pyre. What happens to Adalgisa we are not told; she has disappeared from the opera after her scene with Norma at the beginning of this act.

We see here the type of nineteenth-century Romantic Italian opera in which the story is a mere conventional background and everything turns on the exploitation of a single personality, possibly of two or three. As matters stand at the present day, *Norma* is generally put on for some very well-established prima donna, so well-established in fact that in two recent performances which I saw in different countries the Adalgisa was a better and younger singer. It is an opera for which great singing is indispensable, and for that reason it is now seldom performed; but it is astonishing how impressive the work can be. Modern critics make fun of it because of its orchestration, which is either thin or noisy, sometimes indeed both, and even those who are moved by the beauty and dramatic force of the solo numbers are generally reduced to laughter at the choruses and the military marches.

We have to remember that in Italy the Romantic Movement was mainly political. The Italians have never shown the slightest interest in any sort of movement for the reform of the theatre; artistic idealism of that kind is entirely foreign to their mentality. The theatre was a place of amusement, and in these years it became a place of communal aspiration. The censorship, which had been troublesome enough in Vienna, as we remember in the case of *Fidelio*, was far worse in the various states of the Italian peninsula. Madame Pasta, when she came with Bellini to London in 1833, told Lady Morgan that she had narrowly escaped being put in prison at Naples because she had sung the aria 'Cara patria' in Rossini's *Tancredi*; she was ordered to omit the word *libertà* from every rôle in which it occurred. The Italian public was ready to interpret every opera in a political sense, and in another ten or fifteen years' time it would hail Verdi as a secret acrostic for the name and title of Vittorio Emmanuele. We hardly realize, when we listen to the operas of Bellini now, that in his own day they were heralds of the Risorgimento. Norma's Druids stood for the Italians, and the hated Romans for the hated Austrians; the allegory was clear enough for the humblest workman in the gallery to understand. That is the reason why these operas are so full of military marches and patriotic choruses; they were tunes that could be taken up by the common people as symbols of liberation.

Bellini's music is so little known nowadays to the average lover of music that it may be difficult for him to understand what constitutes its individuality and genius. Ever since the music of Wagner was accepted by the general public, Rossini, Bellini and Donizetti have been lumped together as manufacturers of commercial trivialities. Modern times have seen a great revival of the early works of Verdi, and there has been a certain interest in the comic operas of Rossini and Donizetti, but only in their comic operas. I speak for the moment of the northern countries; in Italy, especially in provincial centres, the old favourites of a hundred years ago are still popular with audiences that have as yet hardly learned to approach Wagner. The influence of German music has always been towards instrumental music, and especially towards that of the orchestra; critics have almost lost interest in singing, and very few, even among the professional critics, are competent to form a judgment on the art, for they have allowed the operatic music of the great age of singing to fall into oblivion. Some of them have even acknowledged that for musicians of a hundred years ago there was an emotional appeal, made by singing alone, which is now lost and irrecoverable. It would be an excellent thing if such musicians were induced to put themselves through an intensive study of the operas of Bellini. I know the reply that many of them would make: 'Ah, but where can you hear Bellini sung nowadays?' You can hear Bellini, but I admit that the occasions are rare; the only thing to do is to sit down and read the scores, as one might read those of Monteverdi. It is 'old music', and the intensive study of it is a training for the imagination. Our modern imagination can be helped to understand it by the collateral study of the later instrumental music which was influenced by Bellini; this will interpret him for us almost better than the music of the early Verdi, which at times quite openly imitated him. To describe Bellini's music in words is impossible; the most one could do would be to print several pages of it with marginal comments, and that is impracticable. It will not do simply to hurry through a vocal score at the pianoforte; one has to weigh the emotional value of every note, and also of every word of the libretto, for Bellini is about the last of the Italian composers who took his libretto seriously, until the days of Boito and his collaboration with Verdi. What Pergolesi first initiated, that breaking up of pure Italian melody into something like natural conversation – in an aria, not in the recitative – was brought to its perfection by Bellini.

This art requires some analysis to make its purpose clear. I have already alluded once or twice to the pernicious methods employed by many Romantics outside Italy who thought that they could get rid of recitative altogether. When it was necessary, for the purposes of the drama, that certain things should be said which were entirely unsuitable for lyrical treatment, for pure singing, that is to say, they often made the orchestra go on playing in an unbroken melodious style, so as to keep up the purely musical interest, and made the characters sing their words to a monotone, or something like it. The words were in such cases often rhymed and in regular metrical rhythms. We find occasional cases of this even in Mozart, at any rate in the course of ensembles, but they are comparatively rare. They are much more common in the composers of the nineteenth century, especially in those who affect local colour and folk-music effects in their operas, such as Glinka, Smetana, Moniuszko and Hugo Wolf. The result is that the words are not heard clearly, and the episodes have neither musical interest nor dramatic effect. Bellini never does this. He uses recitative of the ordinary kind whenever it is appropriate; when he uses the conversational style in the course of an aria, it is for a special reason. Sometimes one person is singing an aria and another character makes short comments, probably 'aside', from time to time, as in the duet between Adalgisa and Norma; in other cases, such as the duet in Act II of *La Sonnambula* between Elvino and Amina, the character is too much overcome with emotion to sing. The orchestra plays the melody which Elvino is to sing later; it is the melody *she* would have sung, if she had had the strength, the melody that expresses her inward thought and feeling; all she can do is to utter a few broken phrases. But it should be noted that in Bellini these broken phrases are invariably melodious, and suited to the shape of the sentence. They are not monotoned in some stiff rhythmical pattern that follows the conventional instrumental rhythm; they are at the same moment both music and conversation, and it is in this that Bellini displays an almost unique genius for dramatic expression in music. His operas deal in the main not with pageantry or startling situations, but with human psychology, with the minute analysis of shades of feeling, and in this respect *La Sonnambula* offers an admirable example. Critics ignore this, because they are accustomed to regard themselves as connoisseurs of voices. Most of them are ignorant of Italian, and in far too much of a hurry to pay attention to Bellini's delicacies of expression; they are so in the habit of regarding all librettos as nonsense that it would never occur to them to study Romani's poetry. Bellini, even if he fails to give modern audiences much pleasure, is at any rate a composer who offers the researcher a stimulating exercise in emotional analysis.

12

CONCLUSION

We have traced the development of Romantic Opera from its beginnings, starting with the satirical comic operas of Naples in the early eighteenth century. It is not long before we see these comic operas sentimentalized; the process is very gradual, as comic opera becomes more and more popular, at Bologna, at Venice, and then at Paris. By the middle of the century comic opera seems almost to oust serious opera altogether. In Italy serious opera is continually produced, but only by composers who cannot claim now even so much as an antiquarian interest. In the last quarter of the century such serious opera as still exists is almost exclusively French; Mozart's two examples, *Idomeneo* and *La clemenza di Tito,* are the only exceptions of any real distinction. By this time comic opera has taken possession of the whole of Europe; it is acted in France, England, Scandinavia, Russia, as well as in Germany and Austria. It is of little matter whether it is performed in the original language or in that of the country; it is either French or Italian by origin, and native comic opera is negligible. This is as true of England as of Germany, for delightful as the little operas of Arne may be, they contributed nothing to European musical history.

It is the French Revolution which diverts the operatic current from comedy to romance. A new public for opera has arisen, and demands opera of a more exciting type. New mechanical devices are invented, and by the end of the century we see a style of opera which depends on scenery of an elaborate and sensational character. The plots appear to become suddenly Romantic in our modern sense of the word, but we find that nearly all of them are old stories which have furnished opera plots to the classical age of Scarlatti and Handel. The difference lies in their presentation, and in the music which clothes them.

The main difference between old Italian *opera seria* and French Romantic Opera of about 1800 lies in the employment of ensembles and choruses. The ensemble was an Italian invention; the use of the chorus on a large scale was French. Simultaneously with this dramatic development came in non-theatrical music the development of the modern – or, as we should generally call it, the classical – orchestra, the orchestra of Mozart. I call it the orchestra of Mozart in order that the reader may at once recall the sound of it to his imagination; but in reality it is the orchestra of Paris, and of the hundreds of forgotten symphonists whose works were being printed in Paris and played all over the musical world. The public began to take a new delight in the sound of combined voices, and whereas the old classical opera was a drama of solos, the new opera almost thrust the soloists into the background for the sake of protracted ensembles.

The development of the choral element was slow and variable, owing to the different conditions in different countries. France had always employed the chorus, notably in the operas of Rameau; we shall see that when composers of other nationalities begin to use it as an integral feature of opera, they start by associating it with the ballet. The result of this is that choral movements are nearly always in dance rhythms, as they were in the time of Monteverdi. During the first decades of the new century the chorus plays a more and more important part, and Romanticism of an obvious kind appears in the perpetual opportunities seized for the presentation of choruses of peasants, gipsies, hunters, sailors and warriors, to say nothing of priests and bards. All these groups implied music of an associative character which very soon became stereotyped and could be copied by anybody.

It was France too that supplied the descriptive element in music, all that we may call 'background music', 'music of nature', music suggesting such things as storms, the sea and waters generally, fire and associated ideas. All these things belong to the music of Lully in the seventeenth century, and were imitated in the English operas of Purcell; they are a characteristic feature of the French operas of Rameau, although they are absent as a rule from the Italian operas of that period and only to be found in the Italianized eclectics such as Handel and Steffani. It is from Rameau that they are inherited by Gluck. Historians are often inclined to suggest that instrumental music was mainly the work of the Germans. This is not consistent with the facts. It is true

CONCLUSION

that instrumental performance flourished in the German-
speaking countries, but the actual music was largely imported
from France in the seventeenth century, and in the eighteenth
the principal exponents of instrumental music were Slavs of
various kinds, Bohemians and Croatians.

Another important factor in the rise of Romantic Opera is the
disappearance of the *castrato* and the substitution of the tenor
as the voice for the hero. This is due mainly to the influence
of the French. The *castrato* was an almost exclusively Italian
phenomenon; it has been suggested that a certain number of
Spaniards submitted to the operation and there is definite evidence of a few Germans, but as far as can be ascertained there
were no French or English *castrati*. It is obvious that the chief
motive behind the practice in Italy, where thousands of boys were
treated in this way, must have been economic. Poverty may have
been no less acute in northern countries; but the chances of
developing a fine voice and one that could earn money were very
much smaller. The practice continued well on into the nineteenth
century; Velluti, the last of the famous operatic *castrati*, died in
1861. But the demand for *castrati* on the stage had been steadily
diminishing since about 1770, because the demand for *opera seria*
had fallen off. Casti's libretto about Kubla Khan throws an
interesting light on the subject; it says that the Italian who is
acting as the Khan's chief eunuch came from a church. Not from
a theatre; the church was evidently the last refuge of those whom
new fashions in opera had thrown out of honest employment.
It was the church which had introduced the practice originally,
long before opera came into existence, and it was the church
which continued to employ *castrati*, almost down to the present
century, long after the opera had discarded them.

The French had no *castrati*, but they assiduously cultivated a
peculiar type of tenor known as the *haut-contre*, for whom the
composers wrote the music in the alto clef. The hero in most of
the French operas from Rameau to Le Sueur is a *haut-contre*, and
the modern tenor would find the tessitura of his part uncomfor-
tably high. In the operas of Purcell the corresponding voice is
called the counter-tenor, with music written in the alto clef, and
it is always understood that this is the voice which we still employ
in our churches and cathedrals under the name of counter-tenor
or male alto, that is, a baritone who sings falsetto. To what extent

178

CONCLUSION

the French operatic singer sang falsetto I do not know; but all evidence points to its having been the general practice for all tenors to take their high notes in falsetto without scruple if they wished to do so. English and German tenors, and naturally Italian tenors as well, were in most cases trained in the eighteenth century by Italian *castrati*, or if not, by teachers who had devoted most of their lives to training *castrati*. The *castrato* was the model on which the entire school of singing was based, because no other existed. The common technical description *basso cantante*, as opposed to *basso buffo*, shows that, generally speaking, basses were not expected to sing, in the stricter sense of the word, at all.

It is necessary to go into this question in detail, because the history of Romantic Opera is closely bound up with that of the tenor voice. Modern practice distinguishes carefully between two types of tenor, called in Italy respectively *tenore di grazia* and *tenore di forza* – in Germany *lyrischer Tenor* and *Heldentenor*. The number of roles which require the real *Heldentenor* at the present day is very small, and they are hardly to be found outside the works of Wagner and Verdi. The *tenore di forza* seems in fact to have been brought into being gradually through the works of Verdi, and we may safely assume that for all operas composed before 1840, in whatever country, the type of tenor required is the lyrical, that is, for that period at any rate, a tenor utilizing his falsetto in high regions, and not attempting to produce the trumpeting noise of the forced-up baritone considered appro priate to the expression of exaggerated virility.

If we consider the principal tenor roles of the Romantic operas discussed in these lectures, we shall see that the main characteristic in every case is what we might describe as 'sensibility'. Not one of them is a consistently heroic character in the manner of Wagner's Siegfried or Verdi's Otello. I am using the word 'heroic' in its ordinary sense, and not in either the sculptural sense of 'somewhat larger than life' or the singing-teacher's sense of possessing abnormal power of tone. The tenor in these operas is invariably a young man of gentle and sensitive character, capable perhaps of heroism in an emergency such as a fire or a shipwreck, but certainly not making a consistent exhibition of exaggerated pugnacity. He is generally contrasted with the baritone or the bass in this respect, although there are cases in which another tenor, perhaps in tenor clef instead of alto, represents the unmistakable 'villain' of the story.[1] Hans von Bülow's well-known division of the musical sexes into 'men, women and tenors' could only have been made in a period when the *Helden-tenor* was practically unknown.

In this connexion it is interesting to observe the personalities of the men who made the Romantic Movement. Byron, Shelley and Keats all belonged more to the 'lyrical' than to the 'heroic' type, and the same may be said of Weber, Schubert, Bellini, Field, Chopin, Schumann and Mendelssohn.

It may be urged that Mozart created a new precedent in making baritones the principal characters of his operas, and this idea has often been rather irresponsibly brought forward by critics who happen to dislike tenors. But in Mozart's German operas (*Ent-führung* and *Zauberflöte*) the heroes are both tenors; the reason for the strange distribution in *Figaro* is probably the fact that this very unusual type of libretto made the normal arrangement impossible. Obviously Figaro himself, as the ordinary servant type, must be the *basso buffo*; we have seen that type in most of the French and Italian operas we have discussed. But can we regard the Count as the normal type of tenor hero? A French composer might conceivably have made him a tenor; it is possible that Mozart, remembering the tenor hero of *Die Entführung*, saw at once that the gentle and sentimental German tenor such as Adamberger would be hopelessly miscast as the Count. Probably Mozart knew from the first what singers he had at his disposal in the Italian company,[2] and settled the question simply on knowledge of their personalities; otherwise we might even have had Michael Kelly in the Count's part.

With *Don Giovanni* the case is even simpler; Don Giovanni is not technically the hero of that opera. He is more in the position of the Duke in *Camilla*; he suffers defeat at the end, not triumph, and is in fact the type which Romantic Opera eventually standardized as the 'villain' of melodrama. And, in any case, for Da Ponte's purposes Don Giovanni is the sort of part to be sung by the man who sang the Count in *Figaro*, for the first key to a right understanding of *Don Giovanni* is that it was modelled on the plan of the previous opera that had been so conspicuously successful.

I have discussed *Don Giovanni* here because it was necessary

---

[1] Othon in Méhul's *Ariodant* is an example of this.
[2] He certainly did know this.

CONCLUSION

to emphasize that it is not really a Romantic opera, in spite of the misinterpretation put upon it by E. T. A. Hoffmann. For this reason it has had no place in the general scheme of these lectures, and I mention it to-day simply in connexion with the question of the tenor hero and the vocal quality of the Romantic tenor. What I want to make clear is that the latter, in the first phase of Romantic Opera at any rate, must been much nearer to the *castrato* in style and method of production than to the *tenore di forza* of modern times.

Another interesting feature of the Romantic Opera is its attitude to religion. Religious ceremonies have been represented on the stage from the time of the seventeenth century, but with certain restrictions. In the Elizabethan drama they are generally presented as dumbshows, in which case they would as a rule have been accompanied by music. In English Restoration opera there are many examples of religious ceremonies, but they are all heathen, with the exception (if we may class it as opera) of the confirmation ceremony to Purcell's music in *Theodosius*, which is purely fantastic. In the Catholic countries it is evident that any representation of Christian ceremony on the stage was forbidden, and up to the middle of the eighteenth century (I have not verified the exact date) all librettos had to have on a preliminary page the author's printed statement that such words as *Dio, Nume, Fato*, etc., were to be understood in a poetic sense only, and that he himself professed the Catholic faith.[3] The French Revolution made such protestations unnecessary, even if custom had not let them lapse some time before.

With the general tendency of opera to be comic and sentimental rather than historical or mythological it became obvious that allusions to the divinities of antiquity soon became ridiculous; they survived at most as literary *clichés*.[4] But as sentimentalism merged into Romanticism and Romanticism into melodrama the religious emotion naturally acquired an increasing

---

[3] This practice appears to have been confined to Italy. In French opera Christian ceremonies were very rare, if not unknown, before the nineteenth century.

[4] The invocation of pagan and oriental deities, treated seriously, was very common throughout the period, from Gluck's *Alceste* and Mozart's *Die Zauberflöte* to Spohr's *Jessonda* and Bellini's *Norma*. There are prominent examples in Winter's *Das unterbrochene Opferfest*, Catel's *Sémiramis* and *Les Bayadères*, and Spontini's *La Vestale* and *Fernand Cortez*.

CONCLUSION

theatrical value, until prayer became a standardized effect; it was employed sometimes as a solo, sometimes chorally, and by the time that Auber's *Fra Diavolo* was put on the stage in 1830 prayer, both private and public, was considered a perfectly appropriate attraction in frankly comic opera. Its later developments are too well known to need description; Wagner and Meyerbeer utilized Christian devotions on the grand scale, and the idea was carried a step further by the Jewish ritual of Halévy's *La Juive* and the Anabaptist ceremonies of *Le Prophète*.

The religious effect had by about 1840 become a standardized *cliché*,[5] just like all the other standardized *clichés* on which Romantic music generally is based. It was a period of great religious intensity outside the theatre as well, especially in France and England; in Germany the so-called 'Nazarenes' were exploiting religion in painting, and Rückert and others in poetry. Italy seems to have produced no very conspicuous contribution to religion either in art or in life, but perhaps anything of that kind would have been superfluous in the permanent home of the Pope. It is evident from the Italian operas of the period that religion always provoked a successful response, for, as I mentioned in my last lecture, we find copious allusions to it, especially in association with the maternal domination of family life.

A more interesting subject than the subsequent development of opera is the influence of the Romantic Opera on the concert life of the nineteenth century. The whole of musical history is affected by the steady increase of middle-class prosperity and middle-class education. It was that social development which made possible the organization of public concerts on a large scale. At the present day music-lovers in America and England are so accustomed to take all this concert life for granted that we seldom give a thought to its origins and early developments. Before the French Revolution the whole of musical life was divided between the three main categories of church, chamber and theatre – I name them in chronological order. The mediaeval princes had maintained bodies of musicians which in every country were commonly called 'chapels' because their first function had been to provide music for the prince's devotions. But they also provided entertainment for his leisure, and this was the music of the *chamber*, a word which is associated with many other aspects of

[5] 'Organ in opera and style of Catholic organ-playing'. (E.J.D.)

CONCLUSION

court life and etiquette. The theatre was added to the establishment of the courts in the course of the seventeenth century, but it need not be pointed out that the employment of quasi-theatrical entertainers by princes can be traced several centuries further back. Public concerts are generally said to have been started in England in 1671; but all they amounted to was something like what we should call a small chamber-music club. It might be strictly a club, open only to regular subscribers, or it might be open like an ordinary concert to all comers on payment, but in any case its activities were on a very small scale, and throughout the eighteenth century concert life, though steadily developing in accordance with the increase in population and the improvements in comfort and in education, was a comparatively small affair. Two things must be borne in mind: first, that music, generally speaking, was simply an entertainment, and an entertainment mainly for the upper classes, and secondly, that there was no sharp distinction between what we now separate as chamber music and orchestral music. Musical life on the Continent was not very different from what it was in England, except that in France the Court played a more prominent part in social life, and in Germany and Italy there were a very large number of small courts, all anxious to make themselves as important as possible in the public eye. Orchestral concerts may be said to have begun in Paris with the Concert Spirituel, which, as its name implied, had certain religious traditions, in Leipzig with the Gewandhaus concerts arising out of the older University musical societies, and in London, rather later, with Salomon's concerts and the subsequent establishment of the Philharmonic Society.

All this concert life still bore to some extent the character of the subscription club. A different character and outlook was brought into music by the great choral festivals, in which England took the lead. The historical importance of the Handel Commemoration in 1784 is perhaps hardly realized. From that there started the great wave of choral music which was characteristic of the following century. Musicians of to-day find it difficult to understand how our forefathers could devote so much time and energy to the composition, the study and the performance of what Charles Lamb called 'the profanation of the cheerful playhouse'; but as historians we have to recognize that the oratorios of Spohr and Mendelssohn, together with their host of happily

183

forgotten imitators, were a phase of the Romantic Movement, and also that they were to a large extent derived from the Romantic Opera. And it was mainly this enthusiasm for choral festivals, in England as well as in Germany, which gradually brought about the semi-religious attitude towards music in general. The acceptance of music as a substitute for orthodox religion will be recognized by future historians of the art, I venture to predict, as a phenomenon of outstanding importance which has affected not only social life but also the technique and style of musical composition.

If music has been accepted as a substitute for religion, it is only in the northern countries of Europe and in North America that the phenomenon is conspicuous; it is associated mainly with the Protestant churches, and with those who have at least been brought up in those churches as children. This accounts for the fact that serious concert life is to be found only in these same countries; the cult of the symphony and of the symphony orchestra is very largely a cult of puritanism. It is the special cult of those puritans who hesitate to allow themselves the pleasure of seeing an opera, and in the course of time it has developed, even in Germany, where opera is still frequently and admirably performed, into a cult of aesthetic puritanism quite removed from any religious connexion.

It has been necessary to explain this ethical attitude to music in general as a preliminary to the consideration of the works which formed the repertory of public concerts. Setting aside the oratorios and cantatas, there remained concertos, symphonies and miscellaneous orchestral works on the purely instrumental side. On the vocal side there was nothing available that did not come from the theatre. Here it may be mentioned incidentally that a very large number of orchestral concerts were given in theatres, because there were not enough large concert-halls available until nearly the end of the nineteenth century, when the building of a large concert-hall could obviously become a practicable and profitable proposition. Of the instrumental forms, every one was ultimately derived from the theatre. The symphony, as we all know, was originally an operatic overture; the concerto was modelled on the operatic aria. Those were forms inherited from a past century; the new items were equally theatrical, for they were mostly ballet music or (in Wagnerian days) whole scenes from operas arranged for orchestra. The symphonic poem as created by Berlioz and Liszt might be something new as far as its outward form went, but its musical material inevitably had to be drawn from the theatre. Just as the mediaeval painters of religious subjects, such as Giotto, painted not what might have happened but what did actually happen when those subjects were presented in the mediaeval theatre, so the Romantic composers of the nineteenth century, when they wished to write descriptive music, utilized the *clichés* of the music which had accompanied the visible reproduction of those things in the opera. The scene-painter and the machinist provided a stage storm; the composer wrote rushing scales for the orchestra to accompany it. If Liszt or Berlioz wanted to describe a storm in the concert-room, they had only to reproduce the scale-passages, and the imagination of the audience automatically supplied the sort of storm that it had seen accompany these sounds in the theatre. The same thing is true for all the other operatic *clichés*; the appropriate music was subconsciously associated, not with the real things of life, but with the conventions of the stage.

It is characteristic of the Romantic symphony composers that they all turned to the theatre for inspiration. I do not wish to include Brahms here among the Romantics; his symphonies belong to a much later period. As far back as Haydn and Mozart we can see the influence of the opera on the musical material of the symphonies; it becomes more conspicuous in Beethoven, but when we come to the symphonies of Spohr, Schubert and Mendelssohn, the theatrical influence is far more striking. We feel at once, even without any attempt at historical analysis, without any preliminary study of musical style, that these younger composers have made a complete break with Mozart and a fairly complete break with Beethoven. What is it that is common to all three and explains their stylistic difference? It is the fact that all three naturally regard Cherubini and Spontini as the standard background of musical style. Cherubini is the one composer whom all the musicians of those days agreed in venerating; there is plenty of documentary evidence for it. It is not merely that their music reminds us of Cherubini's; we have the written records of conversations, letters and critical articles. And when young Mendelssohn walked away from the Berlin opera house with old Spontini and heard him say 'Mon jeune ami, il vous faut des idées

CONCLUSION

grandes comme cette coupole', pointing up at the dome of the Hedwigskirche – a dome which does not strike us as very large nowadays – where could young Mendelssohn look for grandiose ideas if not in the operas of his fatherly adviser?

Schubert's C major Symphony shows the influence of all sorts of theatrical music. The second subject builds up to its completion at the double bar just like an operatic finale, the technique of development, with the almost mechanical reiteration of small figures, is exactly that of Cherubini. The theme of the slow movement suggests a minor variation of 'Di tanti palpiti'; more obviously, it sounds like some sort of a ballet. The rushing triplet figures of the last movement at once remind us of Rossini. We think of alternate major and minor harmonies as a device invented by Schubert; it is clear that he got it from the *romances* of Méhul and other French composers. The symphonies of Mendelssohn derive most of their charm and their apparent originality from *clichés* of the ballet. The 'pilgrims' march' and the *saltarello* in the Italian symphony, the supposed 'reel' and the final 6/8 movement of the Scotch, are all derived from operatic sources. They are supposed to remind us of scenes in Italy or Scotland, but the scenery they call up is that of the theatre. The music for *A Midsummer Night's Dream* is itself theatre music, and perhaps the best incidental music that was ever written for any theatre; at the same time there can be no concealment of its indebtedness to the operas of Weber.

The name of Mendelssohn at once suggests the *Songs without Words* as perhaps the most typical works of his and of the later Romantic period. This later period is the age of conscious Romanticism, whereas the first period, that which has formed the main subject of these lectures, was to a large extent that of sub-conscious Romanticism. The second phase is remarkable for an enormous amount of pianoforte music, and for pianoforte music in irregular forms. We need not here go into the mechanical aspect of this, the new developments in the manufacture of pianofortes. The manufacturers provided what the artists required, just as the double-action harp was invented at the time when Ossianic Bards became a fashionable subject for operas.[6]

[6] Harp parts of increasing sophistication were common in French opera, chiefly in domestic scenes, before Ossianic subjects became fashionable. Sébastien Erard took out a patent for an improved harp in 1792 and perfected his double-action harp in 1810.

CONCLUSION

The pianoforte appears to be the characteristic instrument of the Romantic period. If I might dare to summarize the tendencies of the nineteenth century in a single word, the word I should suggest would be *aspiration*:

> The devotion to something afar
> From the sphere of our sorrow.

That word will cover the paintings of Watts, the poetry of Tennyson and Swinburne, the scientific research of Huxley, the idealism of Pusey and Bradlaugh, as well as the social and political movements of the age. I have named only Englishmen in the foregoing sentence, but I do not wish to imply that *aspiration* was limited to any one country. And if I were to select one piece of music as typical of that sense of aspiration, it should be the Prelude to *Lohengrin*. Recall that Prelude to your mind, and I think you will intuitively understand why I now invite you to consider, as a second summarizing word, the Spanish word *evocación*; I learned it from the music of Albeniz, but it will cover most of the music of Liszt, Chopin and Mendelssohn, especially their music for the pianoforte. The Romantic pianoforte is the instrument of *memory*. Reflect for a moment on all the familiar oddments of poetry – poetry of the first half of the Romantic century – in which the word *memory* occurs, and subconsciously you will recall, I feel sure, phrases, equally fragmentary and shadowy, from the *Songs without Words*, the *Nocturnes* or *Les Consolations*.

Musical puritans have often fulminated against the wickedness of 'transcriptions' for the pianoforte, and have spoken bitterly of 'hyphenated music': Bach–Tausig, Bach–Liszt and so forth. History obliges us to admit that the practice is as old as the keyboard itself. If we disapprove of Bach–Tausig, we ought to show the same disapproval of Vivaldi–Bach, or, to go back to the Elizabethans, of Morley's transcriptions of Dowland and many other things of the kind. Every keyboard instrument must be in a sense Romantic, because it enables one man to pretend to do the work of several. But he can only *pretend* to do it; the harpsichordist, and the modern pianist too, can strike the notes played by a consort of viols or by an orchestra, but he cannot sustain them. He cannot give them breath, and the most that they can do is to 'tremble away into silence'. Evocation, memory,

187

suggestion: did music-lovers in Shakespeare's day experience the same strange thrill from these things that we do from Chopin and Liszt? Ask Shakespeare; he is as sentimental about music as any poet of the nineteenth century.

Romantic music is an art of pretence, and we see it plainly in all this miscellaneous pianoforte music. It is all 'dressing-up' like the *Songs without Words*, like Liszt's symphonic poems and pianoforte concertos, like some of the variations of Tchaikovsky and others. The enlargement of vocabulary which the new century brought was simply its recollections of the opera. It fascinated the puritan type of music-lover, because it afforded him an opportunity of releasing his inhibitions in imagination and at the same time deluding himself with the idea that he was participating in an act of worship.

I cannot bring these lectures to an end without expressing my thanks, first to those who organized them and invited me to deliver them, secondly to all those who have taken part in the illustrations, and lastly to those who with such exemplary patience have sat and listened to me. You may well ask what was the use of talking for so many hours about operas which are now completely forgotten and never likely to be put on the stage again. There are some people who hold that the value of historical research lies in the advancement of knowledge – that is, in the accumulation on the shelves of your library of rows and rows of dissertations which can serve no purpose except to provide, after the lapse of some years, material for more dissertations. I sometimes suspect that all this research is of value only to the researcher himself. If you ask me what is the use of digging up all this old music, I reply that, whether we perform it or not, the work is, or should be, a training of the imagination. If it has any more durable value than that, it lies in the hope that we may store up some of that emotional experience in the museum of memory; and how long it is likely to last there you can imagine for yourselves. The function of lectures is not to convey information, which we can now obtain far better from books, but to stimulate interest in a subject; I should like to hope that I may have encouraged you to put your imaginations into training, to cultivate imaginative experience for the enrichment of memory and life, and at the same time, to develop a habit of perpetual scepticism and criticism as regards all so-called acknowledged masterpieces. If you have ever allowed yourselves to reverence the great masters, I hope you will abandon that attitude, which is merely a polite mask for lazy-mindedness. America has impressed upon me the duty of being always ready to discard my old typewriter of a few years ago and buy the newest model. It is a principle which we ought to apply not only to our mechanical conveniences but to our artistic experiences. Our minds are rendered sluggish by the constant habit of veneration; we must sharpen our critical faculties, so as to be able to discard past experience when it is no longer of real value to us, and then we shall have mental space as well as freedom of judgment to welcome and enjoy the art of to-day and to-morrow.

INDEX

acting, naturalistic, 152–3
Adelson e Salvini (Bellini), 163
Alfonso and Estrella (Schubert), 136–7
Algarotti, Count Francesco, 26, 28
Amor conjugale, L' (Mayr), 130
Anfossi, Pasquale, 132
arias
  of Bellini, 169–70, 174–5
  in binary form, 50
  of Cherubini, 62–3
  classification of, 17
  coda(s) added to, 53, 170
  conversational style in, 174–5
  interruption during, 72
  Italian rules for, 53–4
  in Lied style, 137, 140, 142
  as model for the concerto, 184
  'a quattro', 21, 53
  of Rossini, 117
  sonata form in, 5, 54
  see also coloratura, da capo aria
Ariodant (Méhul), 84–7, 159–60, 180n
Arne, T. A., 176
Auber, Daniel François Esprit, 75, 76
  Fra Diavolo, 103, 115, 119, 182
  Masaniello, 119
Axur (Salieri), 43, 44

Bach, J. S., 11–12, 105n, 114, 116, 125–6
ballad, in opera, 52, 151, 164
ballet, 34, 51
  association of chorus with, 50, 51, 76, 177
  in Télémaque, Le Sueur's directions for, 65
Barbaia, Domenico, 138
Barbiere di Siviglia, Il (Rossini), 114, 115n, 118
barcarolle, 72, 76, 115, 120, 164
baritone, 178, 179, 180
Barzun, Jacques, 95n
basso buffo, 18, 45, 56, 112, 163, 180
  patter-songs for, 22, 35

basso cantante, 179
Beaumarchais, 2, 38–9, 40, 42, 44
Beethoven, Ludwig van, 7, 12, 62, 125
  and Cherubini, 47, 49, 58, 63, 83, 92, 93, 132, 134
  Fidelio, 12, 58, 93, 113, 126–34; and Bouilly's original libretto, 59, 126–9, 131, 133–4; and Gaveaux's version, 129; Leonore No. 3 overture, 90, 133; versions: first (1805), 92, 128n, 131; second (1806), 90, 131; third (1814), 128–9, 130, 131–2; weakness of, 132–4
  and human feeling, 83, 93, 134
  and moral qualities, 83, 134
  and Mozart, 132
  and the polonaise, 105
  as a Romantic, 2, 10, 11, 134–5
  and Rossini, 114, 118
  and sentimental style, 113
  symphonies, 15, 62, 92, 125, 185
  as a theatre composer, 126, 134
  variations on themes by Paisiello, 35, 110
  vocal style, 23, 92
Bellini, Vincenzo, 7, 173–5, 180
  Adelson e Salvini, 163
  and the barcarolle style, 164
  and conversational style in arias, 174–5
  influences on, 165–6, 170
  and melody, 164–5, 169
  Norma, 42, 124, 166, 166n, 170–2, 181n; French influences on, 170; orchestration of, 172; plot, 170–2; and politics, 173
  Pirata, Il, 163
  political nature of his operas, 172–3
  Puritani, I, 166
  Sonnambula, La, 166–70, 175; chorus, 167, 168
  Straniera, La, 164, 166n

190

INDEX

INDEX

INDEX

INDEX

INDEX

INDEX